Schiffer Publishing ®

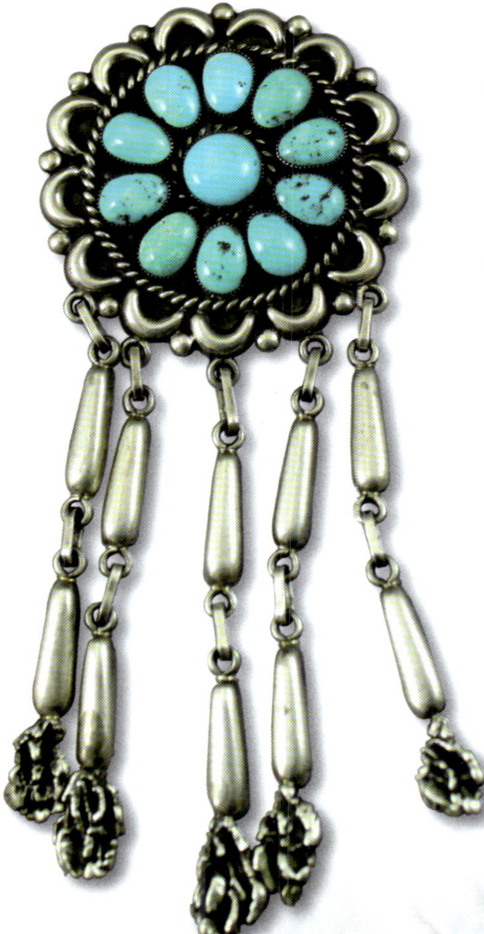

Non-Figural Designs in Zuni Jewelry

Toshio Sei

Schiffer Publishing Ltd
4880 Lower Valley Road • Atglen, PA 19310

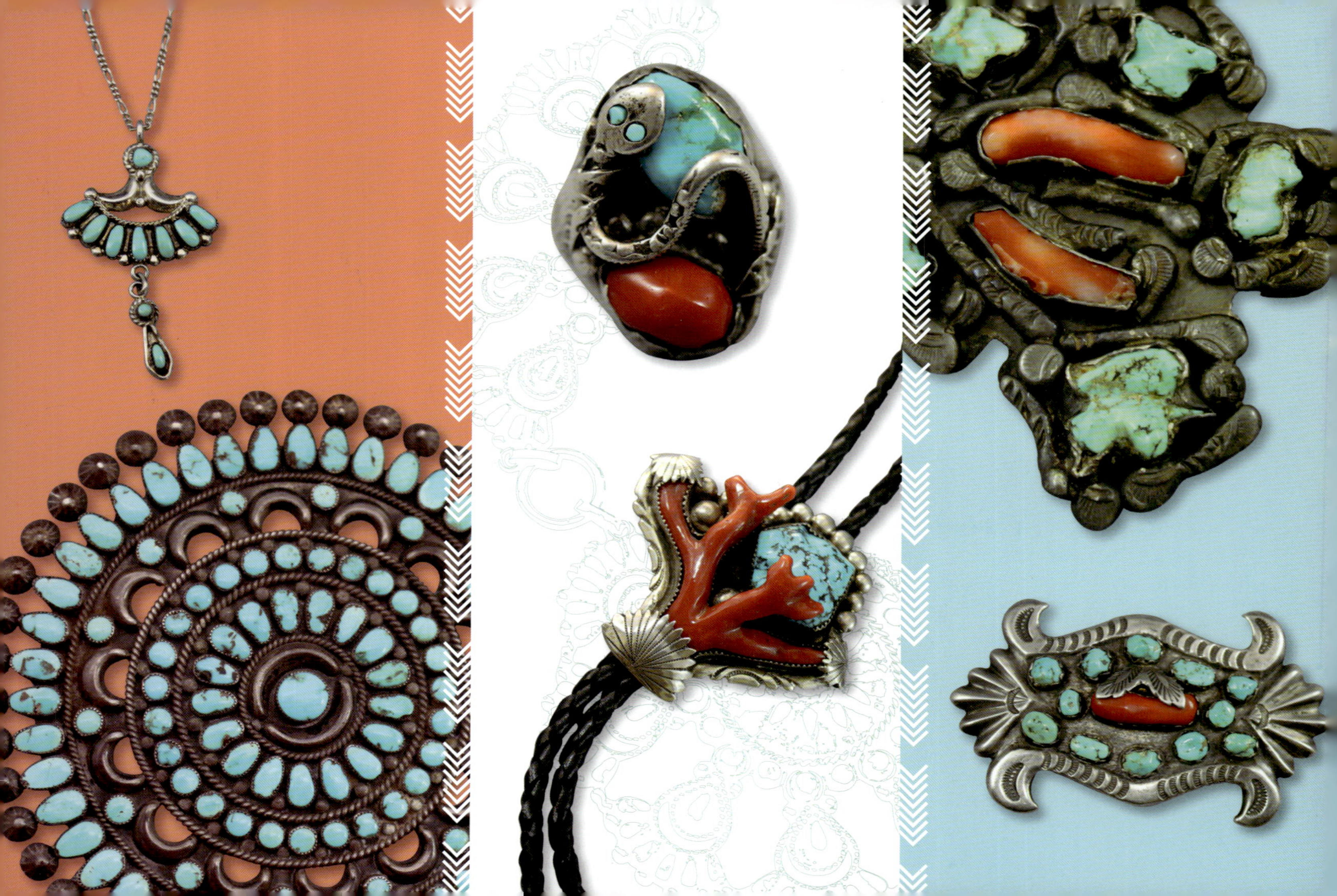

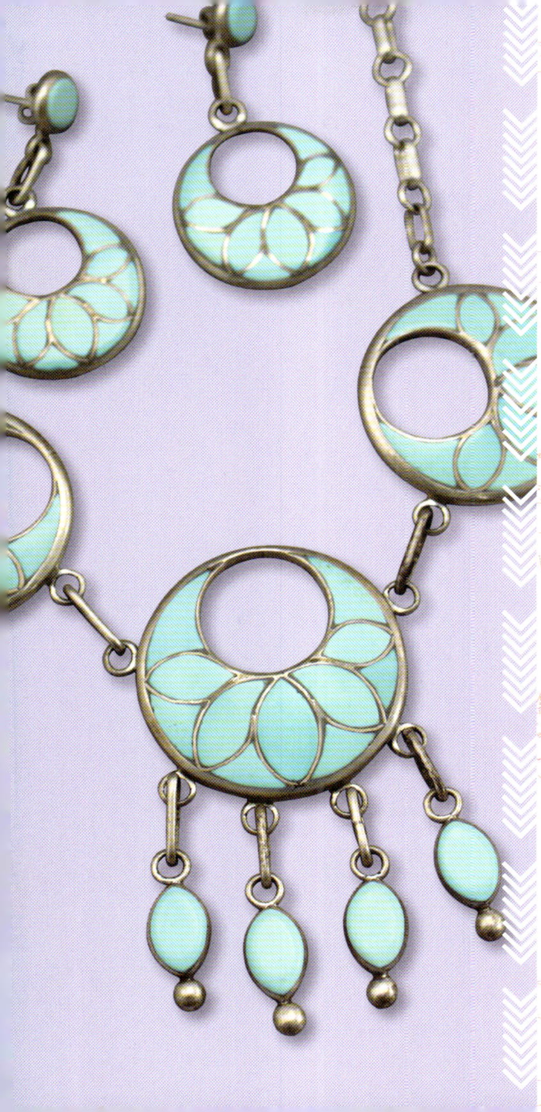
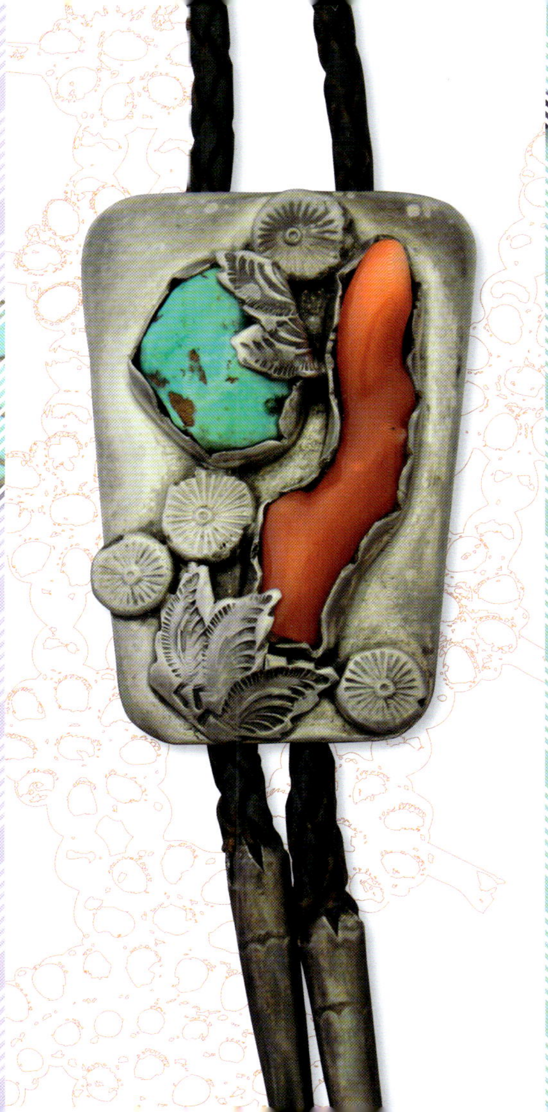
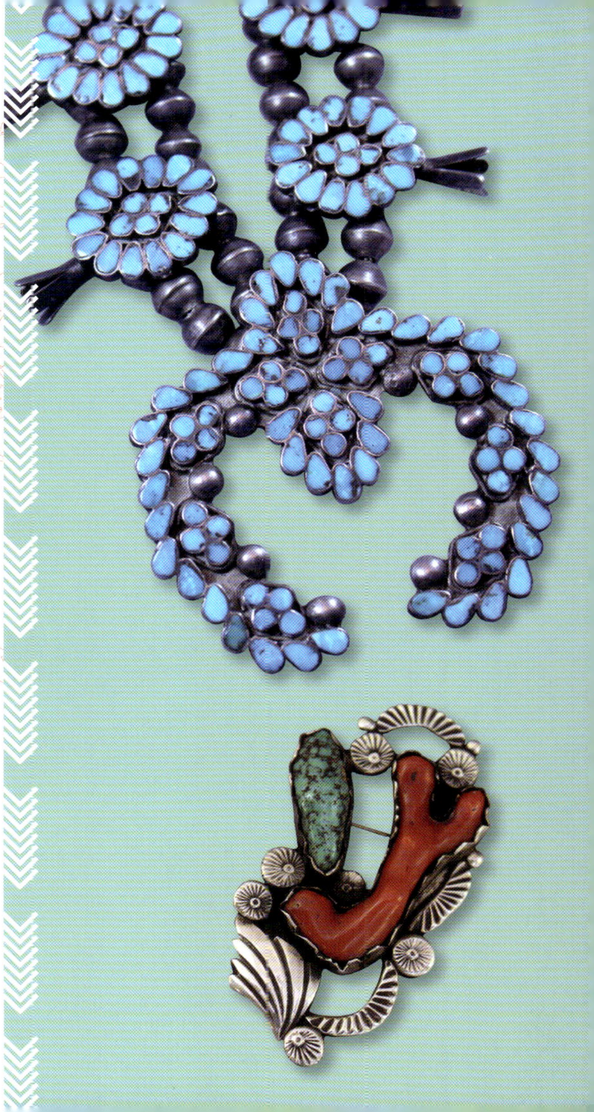

Other Schiffer Books by the Author:
Figural Designs in Zuni Jewelry
978-0-7643-4558-6, $24.99
Knifewing & Rainbow Man in Zuni Jewelry
978-0-7643-3548-8, $24.99
Hopi Bird & Rainbow Man
978-0-7634-3882-3, $24.99
Kachinas and Ceremonial Dancers in Zuni Jewelry
978-0-7643-4167-0, $24.99

Other Schiffer Books on Related Subjects:
Evolving Southwest Indian Jewelry, $59.95
978-0-7643-1723-1
Fred Harvey Jewelry: 1900–1955, $39.99
978-0-7643-4448-0
Southwest Silver Jewelry: The First Century, $49.99
978-0-7643-1244-1

Library of Congress Control Number:
2014950560

Designed by Molly Shields
Type set in Schneidler BT/NewBskvll BT

ISBN: 978-0-7643-4727-6
Printed in China

Published by Schiffer Publishing, Ltd.
4880 Lower Valley Road
Atglen, PA 19310
Phone: (610) 593-1777; Fax: (610) 593–2002
E-mail: Info@schifferbooks.com

CONTENTS

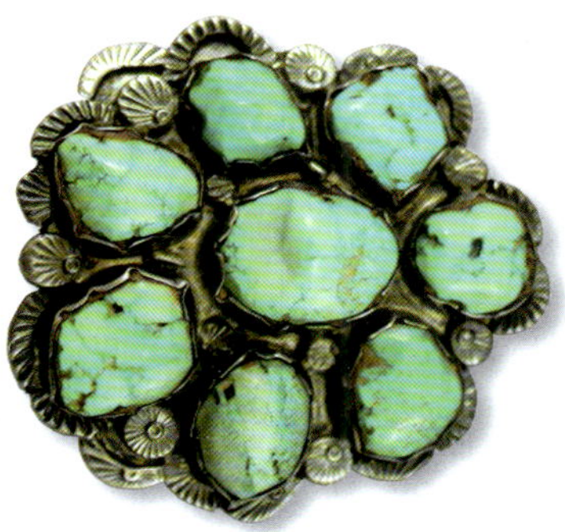

PREFACE

I have collected various things since I was a boy. First, in my elementary school and junior high school days, I collected Japanese postage stamps and old Japanese coins. In my graduate days, I suddenly fell love with traditional Japanese wooden dolls called Kokeshi and have amassed more than four thousand. They are extremely simple in form and appearance; they only have round heads and cylindrical bodies without arms and feet, and painted on their bodies are eyes, eyebrows, nose, mouth, hair and hair ornaments, and some traditional cloth patterns. I have learned through collecting Kokeshi dolls that the most important points are its form and facial expression. When I got a teaching job in a northern Japanese city called Tsugaru, I began to collect Tsugaru Picture Kites, which depict samurai and beautiful women. In my second teaching year, I began collecting Tsugaru lacquer ware, or Tsugaru-nuri. Then, I was fascinated by prints, such as lithographs, etchings, and oil paintings. Through these collecting days, I believe I have developed a solid understanding of what is good and what is not in arts and crafts.

I have been compiling Zuni art and craftwork since March 1993. Originally, I mainly collected small-stone Zuni carvings called fetishes and fetish necklaces, but soon switched to vintage Zuni jewelry. My main passion is for bolos made before the introduction of the Bennett type, factory-made bolo clasp in 1957. As almost all such bolos have no artist hallmark, when I got them, I could not ascertain for sure who had made them. In addition, there is little information available about these artists and their works from the 1930s to the 1960s. We only know the names of a handful of well-known artists, and collectors have attributed some of the most wonderful pieces to them, but not always correctly. For example, for a long time, Leo Poblano received credit for Knifewing and Rainbow Man pieces by Bowman Paywa, one of the greatest artists in Zuni Jewelry history.

My collecting policy is "Love comes first, and knowledge follows." When I acquire a piece of Zuni jewelry, I get it because I love it. Even if I do not know who made it, I will get it as long as it is lovable and appeals to me. Later, I bring these unknown pieces to Zuni Pueblo, New Mexico, and look for the original artists by: (1) asking my informants to attribute each of them to certain artists; and (2) visiting close relatives of the attributed artists and asking them whether they can confirm the attribution.

I believe all collections are the collector's representation of self. So naturally, my collection is the expression of myself as well. If we closely examine one's collection as a whole, we can understand that person well. In this sense, my books are similar to *Turquoise Jewelry* (Bennett, 1973) and *Masterworks and Eccentricities: The Druckman Collection: Navajo and Pueblo Jewelry and Metalwork 1880–1950* (Bauver, 2002). At the same time, my books strive to be informative. Therefore, I even introduce some of the pieces I do not love very much.

As to the estimated prices in the photo captions, they are my estimated gallery retail prices. Usually, the gallery price for new pieces is three or four times higher than the amount the artists receive; the latter is called the jobber price. The situation is similar for vintage pieces: if you sell your vintage jewelry at a gallery, it will pay half of the retail gallery price at best. If you want to buy such a piece, you have to pay three or four times what the gallery paid for it. Furthermore, the gallery retail price depends on the geographical locations of that gallery. In general, galleries in big cities, such as Santa Fe, Scottsdale, and New York demand higher prices, while galleries in wholesale-specialized cities, like Gallup, do not ask as much.

Some artists have complained to me that my pricing is too low. My pricing might not be high enough for some galleries either. I must apologize for this, for I would not like to interfere with the business of galleries or of current artists. On the contrary, some critics of my books have argued that my prices for most pieces tend to be set much higher than the amount I originally paid. Therefore, in their opinion, I am being unethical. My answer to this accusation is that my pricing follows average gallery retail prices, and we should agree that we generally only receive one third or fourth of the retail prices when I want to sell a piece. That's the business custom in the Native American arts and crafts world.

Lastly, my collector friends and I have maintained two Zuni jewelry groups on Facebook: "Historic Zuni Jewelry" and "Zuni Jewelry – Let the Buyer Beware." They provide various types of information on authentic vintage Zuni jewelry, which helps distinguish genuine pieces from their copies and forgeries. People are always welcome to join these groups and share in the enjoyment of collecting authentic Zuni jewelry.

ACKNOWLEDGMENTS

Special thanks should first go to the Sheche family: Thelma, my closest friend in Zuni Pueblo, her brother Curtis Kucate, her son Arden Kucate, and her daughter Lorandina Sheche. They have accepted me as a family guest for more than thirteen years and introduced me to other artists, such as Alice Quam, Rita Edaakie, Bessie Vacit, Sarah Leekya, and Juana Homer. These artists in turn introduced me to their relatives Raphael Homer Jr., Anna Rita Homer, Raylan Edaakie, and Bradley Edaakie, as well as their friends, including Lupe Iule Leekity. When I first began this project, Leonard Martza helped me identify some of the artists whose older pieces I owned. His elder sister, Genevieve Tucson, taught me who Harry Deutsawe was and what kind of pieces he made. This book owes a lot to these generous artist-informers.

My old friends and potters Milford and Randy Nahohai informed me where certain artists lived and drew me maps. Without the help of the Nahohais, I could not have visited and interviewed these artists. I always appreciated their hospitality and help.

After I published my first Zuni jewelry book, *Knifewing and Rainbow Man in Zuni Jewelry*, I became acquainted with Tom Kennedy, the director of the Zuni Tourism and Visitor Center. He helped me plan my collection show, book signing, and presentation for my first three books at the Visitor Center, where I met many wonderful Zuni people and artists, including Dan Simplicio Jr., Roger Tsabetsaye Sr., Marcus Peyketewa, and one of Arnold Cellicion's granddaughters.

I became friends with Ernie Bulow, contributor to *Gallup Journey* and *Indian*

Traders magazines, and we have conducted field research together on Zuni artists and jewelry. He introduced me to Arnold and Neva Cellicion's daughters. Ernie's wife, Michelle G. Peina, a Zuni jeweler herself, helped me identify earlier unsigned pieces her stepfather, Joe Zunie, great-grandfather Frank Dishta, and grandfather Virgil Dishta Sr., made.

Long-time Native American jewelry collector Gloria Dollar and I become friends via Facebook. She generously provided me with pictures of rare pieces Alice Quam made and one of the Weebothees' pieces.

My daughter Makiri, my son-in-law Chad, and my son Yuki have helped me compile this collection, and Yuki has also served as a primary proofreader. Lastly, without the generous support my wife, Noriko, has extended for my passion for collecting, this book would not have become a reality.

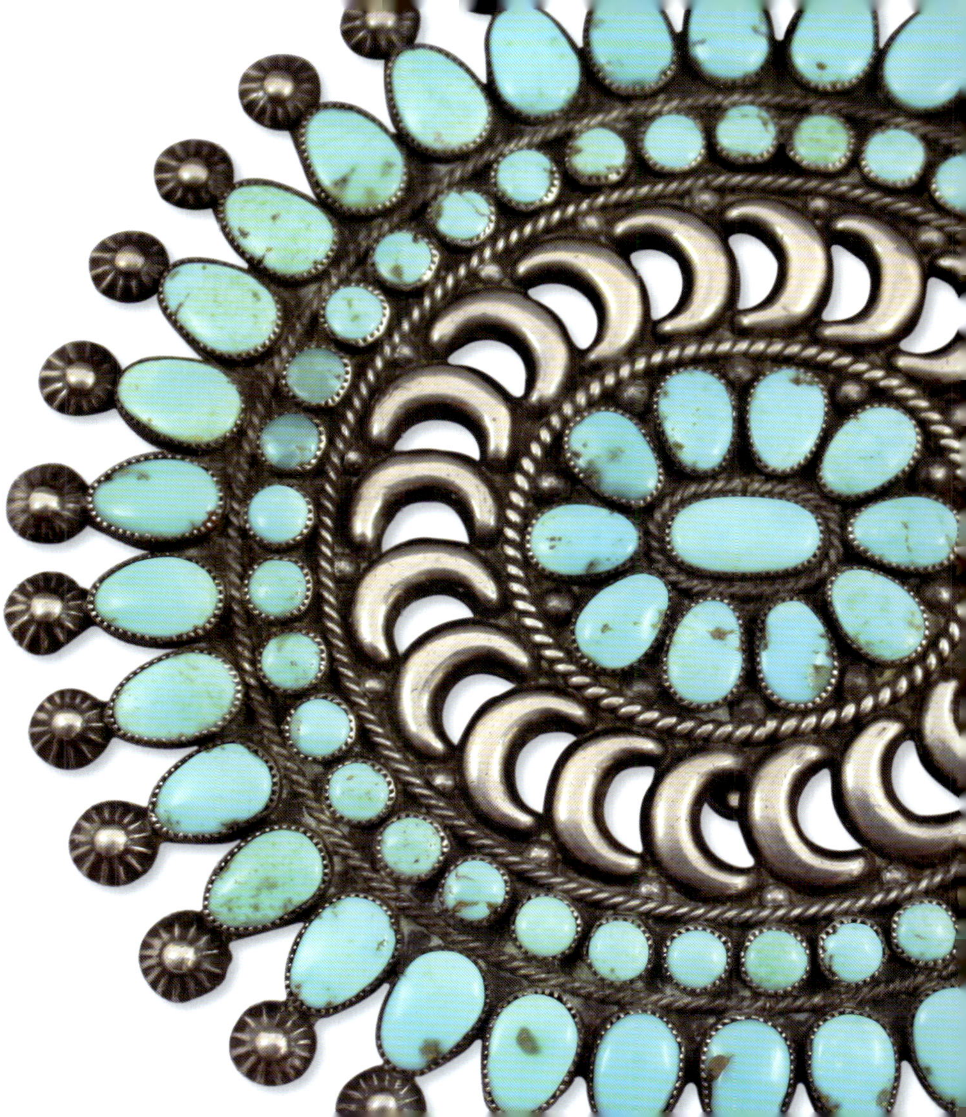

INTRODUCTION

I have published four Zuni jewelry books: *Knifewing and Rainbow Man in Zuni Jewelry*, *Hopi Bird and Sun Face in Zuni Jewelry*, *Kachinas and Ceremonial Dancers in Zuni Jewelry*, and *Figural Designs in Zuni Jewelry*. Consequently, I have already dealt with almost all figural designs in Zuni jewelry. In this book, I deal with all non-figural designs, or styles, such as nugget work, cluster work, needle point, channel inlay, and more.

Zuni silversmithing began around 1872, when the first Zuni silversmith, Laniyahdi, learned the art from the Navajo silversmith Atsidi Chon (Ugly Smith) (Ostler, et al., 1996, p. 57). Eventually, Laniyahdi taught the craft to his fellow Zunis. The early jewelry made by this small group of Zuni silversmiths is no different from that made by their Navajo teachers (ibid, p. 60).

The Zunis began setting stones in silver jewelry around 1890. According to Ostler et al:

> At first, there were only a few stones in rings and bracelets, but as the twentieth century advanced, more turquoise was available to the artists, and the traditional Zuni love of stones reasserted itself.
>
> These primitive silver and turquoise jewelry pieces are the forerunner to the more elaborate Zuni multi-stone works, such as cluster work and needle point, as well as a few stone works such as nugget work, although there might be no direct relationship between these and the earliest stone work. (Ostler, et al., 1996, p. 62)

As to the beginning of the cluster-work style, in *Indian Silver*, Vol. II, Dale Stuart King notes:

> [H. P.] Mera stated, "This exuberant style seems to have come into full flower during the early part of the 1930s…[with] no example of a record which can be safely dated much before that time" (1959, p. 43). He felt the style derived from the centuries-old habit of the Zunis to encrust their mosaics with small pieces of turquoise arranged in ornamental patterns.
>
> The classic bracelets he illustrated continued to be made in the following four decades, and the cluster, or "flower head," style invaded most of the other forms of Indian jewelry, particularly rings, earrings, necklaces, brooches, etc. (King, 1976, p. 50)

Thus, cluster work is one of the representative Zuni jewelry styles, along with mosaic inlay and mosaic overlay. Cluster work's influence not only penetrates all forms of Zuni jewelry, but also pieces by jewelers from other tribes, including Navajo. Navajo jewelers Victor Moses Begay and Larry Moses Begay made cluster-work jewelry in exactly the same style. Without a doubt, the single most famous Zuni cluster-work jeweler is Doris Ondelacy, formerly known only as Mrs. Warren Ondelacy.

Another famous Zuni jewelry style is needle point, in which both ends of turquoise cabochons are pointed like needles and set in individual silver bezels. This style was invented in Zuni in the 1930s at the latest. Influential collector C. G. Wallace contended that it originated when the Great Depression severely hit the Zuni (King, p. 55), and a famous jeweler in this style, Bryant Waatsa, recalled that he began to make jewelry in this style late in the decade (Bahti, 2007, p. 192). While these cabochons are usually arranged in the flower-head pattern, they are sometimes set in a row, in which case the style is known as row work. Rectangular, square, and even diamond-shaped turquoise cabochons are arranged in this row pattern.

Another important style in non-figural Zuni jewelry is petite point, in which one end of a turquoise cabochon is pointed and another is round. It is similar to the smaller version of cluster work, but is considered a different style because, in the case of petite point, one end of each cabochon is clearly pointed. These stones are arranged in the flower-head pattern.

The last multi-stone work category is snake eye, in which jewelers use small, round cabochons in flower-head or row patterns. These round snake-eye cabochons are also arranged in cluster-work jewelry.

There are other Zuni stone work jewelry styles, the most popular being nugget work, but this has no direct connection to earlier Zuni stone work samples from around the turn of the twentieth century. It was resurrected by Dan Simplicio. In *Indian Silver: Navajo and Pueblo Jewelers*, Margery Bedinger explains:

Dan Simplicio, a Zuni, claims to have originated this style in 1948 by setting finger rings, each with a large chunk of polished turquoise left in its original shape.

On either side of it, he soldered an irregular mass, or nugget, of silver, carefully formed to balance the stone. Varying heights of silver bezels and their differing outlines, plain, toothed or scalloped, play subtle parts in the design, as does the shape of prongs or their absence. The color and texture of silver, as always, gives pleasing contrast. Silver drops and wire in carefully planned lines and curves are tellingly employed. After it became available, coral in natural branches or small lumps was with silver alone, with turquoise, or with both, its color, shape and texture providing a multitude of effects. (Bedinger, 1973, p. 201)

While it might be true that, just after World War II, Dan Simplicio became the first to combine turquoise and coral nugget work with stamped silver drops and leaves, it's also possible that he created nugget work itself much earlier, in the 1930s. We can see an apparent influence of the art movement going on in France at the time on the former, while there is no such effect on the latter. There are several samples in the *C. G. Wallace Collection of American Indian Art* (Sotheby Parke Bernet, 1975).

In nugget work, the harmony of lapidary work and silver work is clear, while in other Zuni jewelry styles, silver work acts as the mere backing of the lapidary work. The thoughtful combination of these two elements is pleasing to the eye and may be the most important characteristic of nugget work.

In the case of channel inlay, the silver work is done first. It comprises many compartments and incorporates turquoise parts cut to fit these compartments. There is no difference between mosaic inlay and channel inlay as far as silver work is concerned. While, basically, one or more colors of stone or shell are set in one compartment—and several colors of stone or shell exist in general—in mosaic inlay, one color of stone, usually turquoise, is set in every channel in channel inlay.

As to the beginnings of channel inlay, Bedinger notes, "The technique called channel originated at Zuni just before WWII, and since 1940, has grown in popularity." (Bedinger, 1973, p. 196). In *Zuni: a Village of Silversmiths* the authors say that

> [a]nother innovation of the Kirks resulted in a special order of mosaic jewelry made for archeologist Frederick W. Hodge and inspired by the ancient mosaic work found at Hawikku. Teddy Weahkee (Meahkie) did the stone work for the piece but there is no description of what the pattern was. It occurred around 1935. (1996, p. 65)

According to the same text, C. G. Wallace ordered a necklace to be "made by Frank Vacit for his wife based on Hawikku pottery designs" (ibid, p. 95). This necklace is apparently made in the raised channel-inlay style. Although no information exists about its date of creation, it's possible that it could have been the late 1930s, when Vacit was in his early- to mid-twenties, since he was born in 1915.

Artist Juan de Dios, who died in 1944, made a lot of jewelry in cast and raised channel inlay, so this kind of raised channel work, theoretically, might already have been common in the 1930s or earlier. According to *Indian Silver,* Vol. II, it is possible that channel work existed as early as the early 1920s (King, 1976, p. 51). In his description, however, King does not specify whether it relates to channel work.

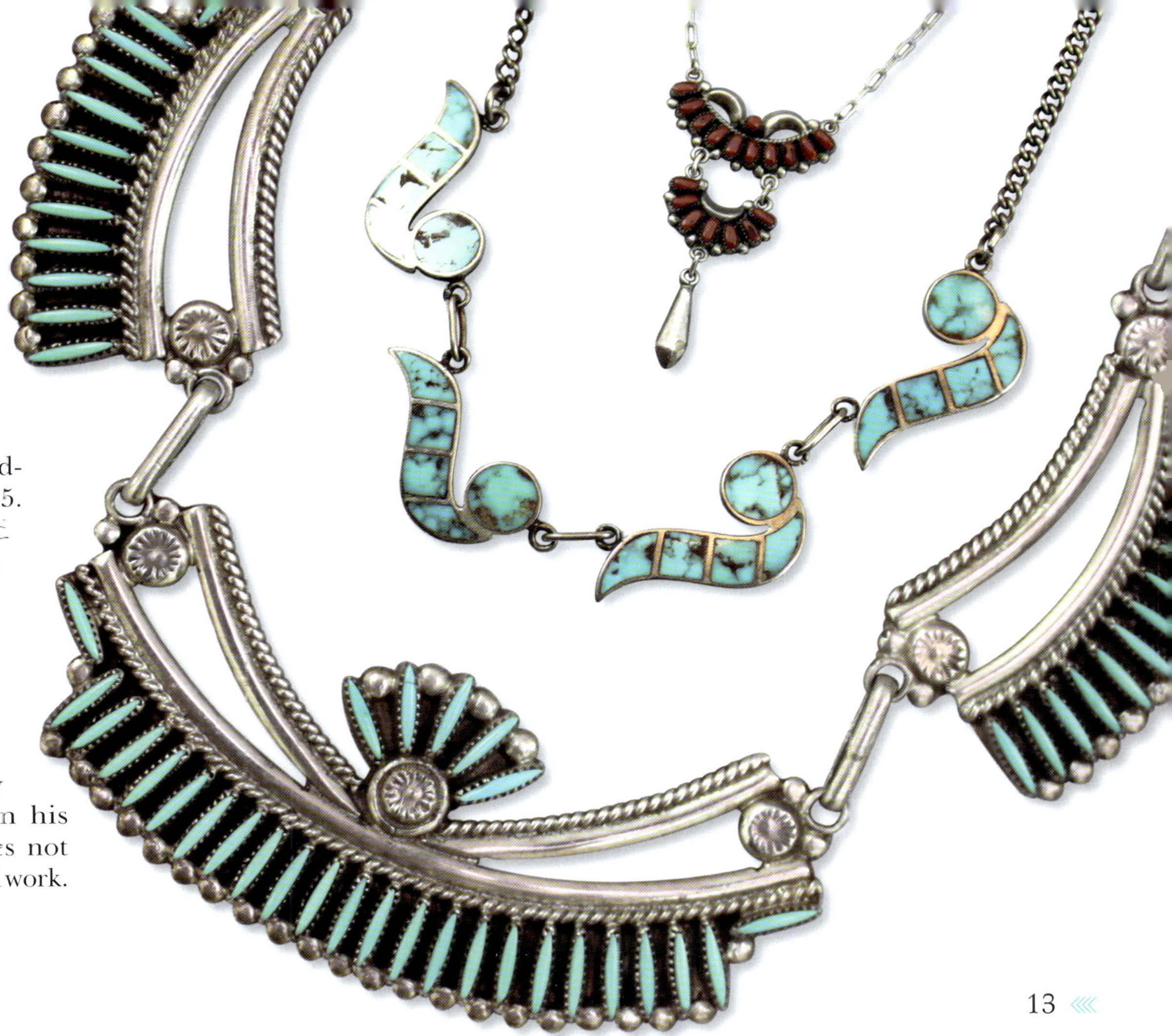

CHAPTER I

FEATURED ZUNI LAPIDARIES AND SILVERSMITHS

Eleanor Wallace Ahiyite

Eleanor Ahiyite had been active when I visited Zuni at the end of October 2012 and was still active in August 2013, when she was given the award for longest working silversmith. She is from the Wallace family and learned row work from her brother when she was about twenty-six years old. Now she is in her mid-nineties. She is featured in *Zuni: A Village of Silversmiths* (Ostler et al., 1996, p. 78.).

Della Appa

Della Appa (1889–1984) is known as the first female silversmith who had her own account at the C. G. Wallace trading post (as early as 1927). She worked mainly in beautiful nugget and cluster jewelry work (Slaney, 1998, p. 27).

A lot of her jewelry was in the *C. G. Wallace Collection of American Indian Art* as well as *Zuni Jewelry* (Bassman, 2006, p. 13). The latter attributed to her a Hopi maiden pin. I believe this attribution is correct because, although it is similar to the same design by Leo Poblano, his pieces have no pigment in their facial expressions, while the expression of Della's piece was applied with black pigment. She made a Pueblo man figure in traditional formal dress, and she might have made some turquoise channel works as well.

Edward & Madeline Beyuka

According to *Zuni: A Village of Silversmiths*:

> Although [Edward Beyuka (1921–2002)] had watched his parents making jewelry while he was growing up, he didn't make any himself until 1956. He practiced in the evening while his family was at the Night Dances. Then he taught his wife Madeline to work with him—she did the inlay and he did the silverwork. (Ostler et al, 1996, pp. 90–91)

After their divorce, Edward did both silver and lapidary work. I met him on December 24, 2001. Faye Quandelacy introduced me to one of her sons at his trailer house. He was doing inlay work for a Buffalo Dancer by his father. I said I would buy the piece when it was ready and I also asked if Edward could make a Little Fire God. While I relaxed in a room at the Inn at Halona, Edward visited me without notice and asked me to confirm that I wanted the two Kachina figures. I replied, "Yes, of course," and he made a silver backing for the Little Fire God and two pairs of silver drums for bolo tips.

I visited Madeline on December 28, 2009, and showed her my collection of pieces by her and her ex-husband. She showed me Edward's portrait, taken for the above-mentioned book, and told me where her sister Angela Cellicion lived. Simon Bica, a fetish carver, is Madeline's father. Madeline's sister Quanita Kallestewa is a potter.

Agnes & Hugh Bowekaty

Hugh Bowekaty (1927–) is the son-in-law of Walter Nakatewa and husband of Agnes Nakatewa. He has made jewelry since 1948, when he was twenty-one. He and Agnes have made Knifewing, Rainbow Man, and row-work jewelry in the needle-point style. Their designs and style are similar to those of Bryant and Esther Waatsa. Acording to Hugh, Douglas Lesansee also created needle point in the 1940s. Douglas, Hugh, and Bryant are in-laws through their wives.

Effie & Juan Calavaza

Juan Calavaza (1910–1970) learned silversmithing from his brother-in-law Dan Simplicio and taught the art to his wife, Effie. He hallmarked his pieces "Juan C." After he passed on, Effie hallmarked hers "Effie C." She shared this hallmark with her daughters.

Lela & Roger Cellicion

Roger Cellicion (1934–2007) is the youngest of the four Cellicion brothers. The other three are Oliver, Arnold, and Dexter. Based on Dexter and Roger's jewelry in Theda and Michael Bassman's book *Zuni Jewelry* (2006, p. 36), and Roger and his wife Lela's (1941–2009) Sun Face jewelry from my collection, I believe the couple proves they are one of the best husband-wife teams that ever worked in the mosaic overlay style. They should be regarded much more highly than they are.

Tony A. Chopito Sr.

Tony (1918–2001) is the brother of Mabel Lonjose and specializes in dot-and-dash jewelry in the row work style.

Bessie & Clark Couyancy

Clark Couyancy (1909–1998) worked as a silversmith from 1945 to 1990. While he worked on silver parts, his wife, Bessie, and her sister Emma Ketsinik set stones for him. Clark did not know what kind of turquoise they used, because his wife bought it for him (Ostler et al., 1996, pp. 76–77). Bessie Vacit told me that Bessie Couyancy collected small turquoise fragments, left over from Frank Vacit's mosaic work, from the Vacit's house, which is probably why Clark's turquoise cabochons are so tiny.

Leekya Deyuse

Leekya Deyuse (1889–1966) is the single most famous jeweler in the history of Zuni jewelry. He was "originally a maker of large tab, nugget, and disc bead necklaces in the old style" (Slaney, 1998, p. 27), and later became famous for his fetish carvings and fetish necklaces. As he was a turquoise worker, his lapidary works were mounted on silver backings by various silversmiths, including his son-in-law, Frank Vacit, and Dan Simplicio.

His son Robert Leekya has made wonderful nugget-work jewelry with his wife, Bernice Ondelacy Leekya. She is a daughter of Doris and Warren Ondelacy and sister of Alice Quam. "Old Man" Leekya's daughters Alice, Elizabeth, and Sarah all made mosaic inlay jewelry. Alice and Sarah made fetish carvings, and Elizabeth made fine bead work as well. Leekya Deyuse's wife, Juanita, also made beadwork and once created a gigantic horse for one of her grandchildren, who has since inherited it.

Frank & Pauline Dishta

Frank Dishta (1902–1954), creator of the Dishta channel-inlay style, worked for the C. G. Wallace Trading Post. In *Blue Gem, White Metal: Carvings and Jewelry from the C. G. Wallace Collection*, Deborah C. Slaney claims that Wallace encouraged him to make channel work for the trading post around 1939 or 1940. She notes:

> Dishta's channel designs are easy to recognize. His work was primarily geometric, with stones that were usually ground flush with the silver dividers. The stonework was often extremely minute, with circular stones as small as one millimeter in diameter arranged in geometric or flower-shaped cluster patterns. (Slaney, 1998, p.39)

Frank's great-granddaughter Michelle Peina told me he often used thin silver wire to encircle each cluster of channels that was set with tiny turquoise stones.

His wife Pauline made small earrings in a snowflake design in the Dishta channel-inlay style.

Virgil Dishta Sr.

Virgil Dishta Sr., the son of Frank Dishta, learned silversmithing in the 1930s and helped his parents make jewelry. He was making jewelry full-time by the 1940s, when he married Margaret. They have several children, including Virgil Dishta Jr., Duane Dishta, Vincent Dishta, and Joe Zunie's wife, Pauline Dishta. Virgil's hallmark, "V Dishta," was first used in the 1950s.

Jennie Eustace

Jennie is the daughter of Newman Eustace and sister of Ramona Eustace Lasiloo.

Annie Quam Gasper

Annie (1926–2001) was a daughter of Johnny Quam and sister of Ellen Quam Quandelacy. She invented the abstract hummingbird design and spider web design (Slaney, 1998, p. 40). In *American Indian Jewelry*, Vol. I, Gregory Schaaf says, "She [is] one of the great masters who will long be remembered and honored" (2003, pp. 159–160).

Raymond Gasper

Raymond is a brother of Pete Gasper and Susan Gasper Tsabetsaye. He has consistently worked in cluster-work jewelry, but his wife, Annie Quam, is famous for her channel inlay jewelry. He was once married to Bernice Ondelacy.

Joe & Lola Hechilay

Joe (1928–) and Lola (1934–) made channel inlay jewelry in the random pattern, similar to pieces created by Alice Leekya Homer. Their channel inlay is ground flush, however, while members of the extended Leekya family fashioned their pieces in the old raised channel-inlay style. Joe and Lola signed their jewelry with the hallmark "J. H. L. H. Zuni." They are included in *Zuni Jewelry* (Bassman, 1992, p. 19).

Alice Leekya Homer & Bernard Homer Sr.

According to his daughter Juana Homer, Bernard Homer (19[illegible]9–2007) is not a silversmith, but a lapidary. He used to work with his brother Lambert Homer at the C. G. Wallace Trading Post. Bernard and his wife, Alice Leekya Homer (1923–1988), made channel inlay jewelry in the random pattern. From the 1970s onward, she stamped her hallmark "ALH," which stood for the initials of her first name, maiden name, and acquired family name, on her random channel-inlay work, with turquoise. Alice, daughter of Leekya Deyuse, made all of the silver work and did lapidary work as well. She also made some mosaic works, including the figural designs Rainbow Man and Hopi Bird.

Lambert Homer Sr.

Lambert Homer Sr. (1917–1972) is undoubtedly one of the greatest mosaic overlay and channel inlay artists in Zuni jewelry history. His works have been continuously featured in many books, including the famous *C. G. Wallace Collection of American Indian Art* (1975). This catalog features numerous incredible works by Lambert Homer Sr., including a historic turquoise-inlaid concha belt made in collaboration with Roger Skeet—although they are all erroneously attributed to "Lambert Homer Jr." The story behind this mix-up remains a mystery, but in cases like these, it's usually safe to say the name Lambert Homer Jr. means Lamber Homer Sr. His wife, Juanita Lasarlley Homer, is the sister of Mary Lasarlley Kallestewa.

Anna Rita Huskie Homer & Lambert Homer Jr.

Lambert Homer, Jr. (1937–1988) and his wife, Anna Rita, are lapidaries. He was once a lapidary for the famous Hopi jeweler Preston Monongye. Their designs are Knifewing, Rainbow Man, Buffalo Dancer, and Apache Gahn Dancer and are inlaid in a mother-of-pearl background or on a naturally shaped shell. These unset, inlaid shell medallions are called inserts.

I visited Anna Rita Homer for the first time on September 19, 2010, and asked about their works. She showed me two small, unset Apache Gahn Dancer inserts, and I bought them. The Homers also sold their unset pieces to traders, who then let Navajo or Zuni silversmiths set them in silver. Consequently, many of these final pieces sometimes look Navajo.

Lambert died relatively young at age 51. We miss this great artist; if he had survived his heart attack, we would have been able to appreciate more from this couple's great collaborations. As he was the one who sawed out designs in a shell plate for his wife, she has not bothered with lapidary work since his death in 1988.

Alonzo & Helen Hustito

Alonzo Hustito (1903–1987) might very well be the creator of the first Rainbow Man design for sale in any style of Zuni jewelry and the first Knifewing for sale in the mosaic overlay and inlay styles.

He worked with his wife, Helen (1924–1996), a niece of Theodore Kucate's wife, Susie. He was twenty-one years older than she, and it appears that his jewelry designs changed significantly after marrying.

Horace Iule

Horace (1901–1978) was one of the older Zuni silversmiths whose name appears on a list compiled by John Adair in *The Navajo and Pueblo Silversmiths* (1944, 198–199). This list is an invaluable source of information concerning Zuni lapidary artists and silversmiths from the 1930s. The C. G. Wallace collection includes Horace as well.

His silverwork is mainly in the cast style set with turquoise. According to

Adair, Iule first learned blacksmithing at a school in Phoenix, Arizona, and silversmithing from his father, after graduating in 1924 (137–142). Adair interviewed him intensively, observed his whole silver work process, and described it in detail. Horace was the first silversmith to make a Knifewing figure in silver, in 1928 (1944, 139). However, he might be more famous for his cross-with-turquoise set, known as the "Iule Cross." He made other unique designs for pins and bolos as well.

I visited his daughter, Lupe Iule Leekity (1941–), for the first time on October 31, 2001. I showed her two types of Iule Crosses made by Horace. She told me there are indeed only two types of Iule Cross, but they may be made in different sizes. I also showed her a cast buckle with a turquoise and coral set that one of my informants attributed to Horace. She confirmed it was made by her father in the late 1940s or early 1950s. The back and front of this buckle were made as one piece, which is Horace's older cast work method. Later, he cast only the front piece and soldered it on to a silver plate. This buckle also has a handmade silver wire clasp instead of a factory-made swivel one.

Carrie Katsenih

Carrie started silversmithing when she was eighteen years old. She is famous for her needle point and her square stone row work. She is in *Zuni: The Art and the People*, Vol. III (Bell et al., 1977, p. 9).

Elsie & Fred Laconsello

Fred and Elsie sometimes provided Lambert Homer Jr. and Anna Rita Homer with silver work for their inserts. The Laconsellos signed their work "Fred and Elsie." Ruddell Laconsello is their son.

Julie Ondelacy Lahi

Julie is Fannie Weebothee Ondelacy and Andy Ondelacy's daughter and Doris and Warren Ondelacy's granddaughter. She made wonderful cluster-work jewelry as well as mosaic inlay jewelry and hallmarked her jewelry "Julie O Lahi."

Pesancio & Ramona Lasiloo

Pesancio (1932–1995) and his wife Ramona made jewelry in the petite-point style for a long time. Pesancio was the son of John and Mae Lasiloo.

Billy & Lucinda Laweka

Billy (1942–) and Lucinda (1942–2003) began making jewelry in 1968. Although she died in 2003, he continues to make wonderful cluster-work jewelry.

Francis Leekya

Francis (1928–2003) is a son of Leekya and Juanita Deyuse and brother of Robert Leekya, Roger Leekya, Alice Leekya Homer, Elizabeth Leekya Vacit, and Sarah Leekya. They are all silversmiths who specialize in the channel-inlay style. In *Hallmarks of the Southwest*, Barton Wright describes Francis's hallmark as a Zuni "tee" bird (probably Zuni thunderbird), which had been used since 1968 (1989, p.102).

Bernice Ondelacy Leekya & Robert Leekya

Robert Leekya is Leekya Deyuse's son, and Bernice Ondelacy Leekya is Doris and Warren Ondelacy's daughter. Robert and Bernice are famous for their nugget-work jewelry and have recently made cluster-work jewelry. They are included in *Zuni: A Village of Silversmiths* (Ostler et al, 1996, pp. 71–72).

Sarah Leekya

Leekya and Juanita Deyuse's daughter Sarah Leekya is a sister of Alice Leekya Homer, Elizabeth Vacit, Francis Leekya, Robert Leekya, and Roger Leekya. She is famous for her fetish carvings as well as her carved leaf necklace, but she used to be a silversmith and lapidary. She taught her niece Bessie Vacit the craft of silversmithing.

Matthew & Rosemary Lidase

Matthew and Rosemary Lidase are related to the extended Dishta family and make Dishta-style flush inlay jewelry. People sometimes wrongfully attribute their pieces to Frank Dishta or Virgil Dishta Sr.

Jake Livingston

Jake Livingston (1946–) is a son of Jake Haloo and brother of Dolly Banteah, Nancy Laconsello, Lorita Natachu, and Rolanda Haloo. He used to make traditional bird jewelry in the silver overlay–mosaic inlay style. These days he is a master artist in innovative, contemporary jewelry. He hallmarked his work "J-I Livingston."

Roy Nieto & Viola Calavaza Nieto

Viola adopted Dan Simplicio Sr.'s nugget-work style. She and her husband, Roy, made some beautiful nugget-work jewelry together. Viola comes from the Calavaza family.

Doris & Warren Ondelacy

Doris (1902–2000) and Warren (1895–1972) Ondelacy's cluster work is prominent in the famous C. G. Wallace collection. Doris is Theodore Kucate's younger sister, and therefore aunt of Thelma Sheche, the famous fetish carver. Doris and Warren had used the hallmark "D. & W." until he passed on; afterwards, she used her own hallmark, "D." Doris taught Thelma Sheche how to make a squash blossom necklace in the cluster-work style when Thelma wanted to make a gift for her mother.

Andrew (Andy) Ondelacy & Fannie Weebothee Ondelacy

Fannie Weebothee Ondelacy is a sister of Lee Weebothee and Leonard Weebothee. She married Andrew Ondelacy, son of Doris and Warren Ondelacy and brother of Alice Ondelacy Quam. Fannie's hallmarks are "FWO" or "F. W. Ondelacy." In *Hallmarks of the Southwest*, Barton Wright describes her husband as Warren, possibly because he believed her middle initial, W, stood for that name, but Warren is actually Andrew's father. In fact, it stands for her maiden name, Weebothee. She and Andrew made a lot of wonderful cluster-work jewelry, but because of his health problems, Andy did not make very many.

Bowman & Louise Paywa

Bowman Paywa (1913–2002) is very famous for his Knifewing and Rainbow Man figures, which people have often wrongfully attributed to Leo Poblano. Bowman also did incredible channel inlay and row-work jewelry. *Indian Silver* Vol. II features two of his bracelets in these styles (King, 1976, pp. 112–113). In the late 1960s or early '70s, he switched businesses from jewelry making to Zuni bread baking, and completely disappeared from the jewelry world. He came back just before he passed on and produced four sets of finished Knifewing and Rainbow Man figures, in addition to some unset silver backings.

Jim Paywa

Jim Paywa is Bowman Paywa's son. His rug pattern jewelry is in *Zuni Jewelry* (Bassman, 1992, p. 16). Presently, he works with his mother at her Zuni bread business.

Paul Peyketewa Sr.

Paul Peyketewa Sr. is a son of Peyketewa and the father of Paul Peyketewa Jr. He specializes in Kachina jewelry (Schaaf, 2013, p. 136).

Veronica Poblano

Veronica Poblano (1951–) is Leo Poblano and Ida Vacit Poblano's daughter. She was eight years old when her father died. She grew up near Madeline and Edward Beyuka, who helped her a great deal when she was learning silver and lapidary works. She once told Kari Chalker:

> When I was maybe thirteen years old, my neighbors Madeline and Edward Beyuka introduced me to silversmithing. I used to go visit and watch them work while they did their lapidary. They did a lot of mosaic inlay work, creating all kinds of Zuni dancers and Katsina figures. (Chalker (Ed.), 2004, p. 186)

In her mid-twenties, she was inducted into the Arizona Highways Hall of Fame under her married name, Veronica Nastacio (*Arizona Highways*, August 1974, p. 44). Her pieces from those days include Disney® characters, such as Mickey Mouse and Minnie Mouse. She carved those figures in a three-dimensional style. Her lapidary skills were far beyond the level of most in those days and continue to outshine her would-be lapidary peers today; although we may encounter some Disney characters made in mosaic work presently, they do not exceed Veronica's lapidary skill level in her prime.

After working as a beautician in California, she came home to Zuni Pueblo and worked as a creative jewelry designer and lapidary. She has been recognized as one of the representative artists in this area ever since.

Alice Ondelacy Quam & Duane Quam

Alice Ondelacy Quam (1929–2003) is Doris and Warren Ondelacy's daughter and Bernice Ondelacy Leekya and Andrew Ondelacy's sister. She married Duane (1919–2006) and made wonderful jewelry in the cluster-work style. I visited her in 2002 and purchased a bracelet directly from her. After Alice passed on, Duane made cluster-work jewelry with their old hallmark, "A. Q.," but he soon replaced it with his own, "D. Q."

Alvina Quam

Alvina Quam and Lorraine Waatsa's parents are Alice Ondelacy Quam and Duane Quam. In her younger days, Alvina made jewelry in the nugget-work style with the same stamp her mother used, "A. Q." Later, she used her own stamp, "Alvina Q."

Ellen Quam Quandelacy

Ellen (1924–2002) is Johnny Quam's daughter. Although she became famous for her horse fetishes, she and her sister Annie Quam Gasper both made wonderful channel inlay jewelry. Their works are very difficult to distinguish from each other.

Jennie Salvador & Lloyd Salvador Sr.

Jennie and Lloyd did row work with diamond-shaped stones and are famous for their channel inlay jewelry. They are in *Zuni Jewelry* (Bassman, 1992, p. 16; 39).

Alice Sanchez

Alice is the oldest sister of Horace Sanchez and Vincent Sanchez and made jewelry in the cluster-work style.

Eva Solomon Sanchez

Eva Solomon Sanchez, wife of Vincent Sanchez, made jewelry in cluster-work, petite-point, and needle-point styles.

Irma & Octavius Seowtewa

Octavius and his wife Irma invented their own style of needle-point jewelry. Octavius is the son of Alex and Odelle Seowtewa.

Dixon Shebola & Martha Hustito Shebola

Dixon (1937–1976), son of Josephine Nahohai, married Martha Hustito Shebola, daughter of Alonzo Hustito and sister of Linda Hustito Wheeler and Erma Hustito. The couple made wonderful mosaic jewelry and used to tour art shows, becoming popular and rising to success in the 1970s. During their business trips, my friend Milford Nahohai babysat for their children.

Their signature piece is a Plains Indian Warrior with a war bonnet in the mosaic inlay style, which is in the book *Skystone and Silver* (Rosnek and Stacey, 1976, pp. 102–103). This piece was copied, however, outside the United States—and so accurately, that we must be careful when we consider purchasing this kind of piece on the antique market. If a flower-like ornament on the Warrior's right hand is removable and usable as a tie tack, it should be an authentic Shebola piece. I have also noticed that he signed his signature as "Shebala," using an electric pen.

It should be noted that Dixon Shebola, Randolph Nahohai, Milford Nahohai, and Randy Nahohai are brothers.

Aaron & Thelma Sheche

Thelma Sheche (1928–), a daughter of Theodore and Susie Kucate, is famous for fetishes she made with her husband Aaron Sheche. Her jewelry-making origins can be traced back to when she watched her mother's brother Jerry Dixon working. In the late 1940s, under the tutelage of her father's sister Doris Ondelacy, she made her first squash blossom necklace in the cluster-work style and gave it to her mother. The metal beads of the necklace were originally nickel silver. Just before Susie died, she gave it back to her daughter. Later, the beads were replaced with real silver.

Thelma says she is the first artist to make jewelry in the long needle-point style. For a while after their marriage she and Aaron specialized in fetish carving and silver. In 1972, Thelma decided to concentrate solely on fetish carving, however, and gave her jewelry tools to her brother Curtis Kucate.

Dan Simplicio Sr.

Dan Simplicio (1917–1969) is credited as the creator of the nugget-work style, which makes use of natural shapes of turquoise nuggets and coral twigs alongside filed and stamped silver leaves and stamped silver drops.

He was married to Esther Romancito Simplicio (1925–1971) and sometimes collaborated with his wife's mother, Helen Shebola. His mother was the youngest sister of Juan de Dios. According to Dale Stuart King, "[i]t was Juan de Dios who helped to encourage Dan to become a good craftsman. He taught Dan to melt silver coins and to make leaves of different sizes. This was in the middle '20s" (*Indian Silver*, Vol. II, 1976, p. 60). The mid-1920s might be too early, however, as Dan was only eight or nine years old at that time.

After Dan established his nugget-work style, he taught silversmithing to his brothers Chauncy Simplicio and Mike Simplicio and his nephew Juan Calavaza, the husband of Effie Calavaza.

Although he was most well known for his nugget style jewelry, he did mosaic inlay work as well. His Knifewing brooch from the late 1920s or early '30s and Knifewing earrings from the 1930s or '40s appear in *Southwest Silver Jewelry* (Baxter, 2001, pp. 111 and 132, respectively). They are all in the Lynn D. Trusdell collection. It is extremely rare to see such an early Zuni piece attributed to a specific artist.

In an interview in *New Mexico Magazine*, Dan Simplicio Jr. recalled his late parents' silversmithing situation in the 1960s:

> He worked for a trading company in Gallup, and she stayed home.... He would do the silverwork and leave it behind, and go out to work the next day. She would set the stones and polish them as well, so by the time he got back, those would be finished and he could start on another set.
>
> The elder Simplicio worked with Navajo silversmiths in Gallup, a unique situation that led to an exchange of ideas and techniques. "They were bouncing ideas off each other, and I think they produced some of the greatest pieces of that time," Simplicio said, referring to the 1960s. "A whole different style came out of that, and they were some of the pioneers." ("The Allure of Turquoise", p. 35)

Chauncy Simplicio

Chauncy Simplicio is the younger brother of Dan Simplicio, who taught Chauncy and their brother Mike how to make jewelry. Their specialty is the horse head, which is similar to Dan's. It is in *Zuni: The Art and the People*, Vol. I (Bell, 1975. p. 60).

Mike Simplicio

Mike Simplicio made nugget style jewelry similar to his elder brother, Dan Simplicio Sr. His first wife was Rita and he is currently married to Carmelita. His son Michael Simplicio makes raised mosaic inlay jewelry with his wife, Sarah.

Marietta Soseeah

Marietta began silversmithing around 1948. Her favorite motif is Sun Face, in the mosaic inlay style, but according to *Zuni: The Art and the People*, Vol. 1, she designed others upon request (Bell, 1975, pp. 50–51). She is the sister of Morris "Red" Leekela, Howard Leekela, and Neva Cellicion.

Bernice & Roosevelt Tekala

Roosevelt and Bernice have made jewelry since the 1940s in the Dishta inlay style. They are in *Zuni: the Art and the People*, Vol. I (p. 72).

Edith Tsabetsaye

Edith is a daughter of Joe and Susan Tsabetsaye and was once married to Leonard Lonjose. In her younger days, she made cluster-work and mosaic inlay jewelry, but now she specializes in her own unique, three-dimensional needle-point jewelry. She is the single most famous contemporary Zuni needle-point jeweler and is included in *Zuni: A Village of Silversmiths* (Ostler et al., 1996, p. 83).

Roger Tsabetsaye Sr.

Roger is a brother of Edith and Raymond Tsabetsaye. He is an innovative, multi-talented jewelry and textile designer.

Joe & Susan Tsabetsaye

Joe and Susan are the parents of Edith and Roger. Susan is a sister of Raymond Gasper and Pete Gasper. Joe, Susan, Edith, Roger, and Raymond all made wonderful cluster-work jewelry very similar to Doris and Warren Ondelacy. The extended Gasper family is one of the most important families to have worked in the cluster style.

Myra & Lee Tucson

Myra Tucson was a highly acclaimed and accomplished jeweler. She was in her prime from the 1940s to the '60s, and represented Zuni artists in the exhibit "Southwest Indian Arts II," held at the California Palace of the Legion of Honor in San Francisco in 1965. According to Gregory Schaaf, among the other major artists present at that show was innovative Navajo jeweler Kenneth Begay (*American Indian Jewelry*, 2003, p. 314).

As my informants have attributed many pieces to her, she is recognized as one of the most important artists by many older artists today. Her ex-husband was Homer Vacit.

Joseph, Nellie & Irma Unkestine

Nellie, her husband, Joseph, and their daughter Irma all made jewelry in the row work style.

Bessie Vacit

Bessie Vacit (1943–) worked for Ernie Vanderwagen for three years, starting in 1970. These days she does inlay work for concha belts made by Navajo silversmiths. In 1973, her aunt, Sarah Leekya, taught her how to weld silver and told her to begin silversmithing. Bessie made silver and lapidary works mainly in the turquoise channel-inlay style, like Sarah and her other aunt Alice Leekya Homer. She calls it the "Random Pattern." Since 1975, she has been using the same "ear of corn" hallmark as her father, Frank Vacit. After major surgery in 2006, she stopped making jewelry and switched to bead work, like her mother, Elizabeth Leekya Vacit.

Elizabeth Leekya Vacit & Frank Vacit

Frank Vacit (1915–1999) is one of the most prolific artists featured in the C. G. Wallace Collection. He married Leekya Deyuse's daughter Elizabeth Leekya (1919–2005), who was a lapidary and bead work artist. His younger brother, Homer Vacit, is also a wonderful mosaic jewelry artist. Frank has a son, Gary Vacit, and three daughters, including Bessie and Jovanna. All his children are skilled lapidaries.

The book *American Indian Jewelry*, I, identifies Leo Poblano's last wife, Ida Vacit Poblano, as Frank Vacit's niece, while *Blue Gem, White Metal: Carvings and Jewelry from the C. G. Wallace Collection* describes her as his daughter (Schaaf, 2003, p. 257; Slaney, 1998, P. 42). According to Frank's daughter Bessie Vacit, Frank is not Ida's father.

Bessie also told me that Frank's friend in California presented him with a gigantic sea turtle shell in the 1950s, and her father used it as a background for mosaic figures instead of an overlaid silver one.

He stamped his jewelry with his "ear of corn" hallmark at the end of the 1940s, and from the mid-1970s on, he stamped "F. Vacit" and his ear of corn hallmark together.

Homer Vacit

Homer Vacit is the younger brother of Frank Vacit. His former wife Myra later married Lee Tucson. Homer's name did not come up in either my earlier field or literature research, but I showed a photocopy of an old Rainbow Man necklace from *Arizona Highways* (August 1952, p. 10) to an older informant, who told me Homer made it. That was the first time I heard his name. Since then, the name Homer Vacit has come up consistently in discussions with my informants. He was an excellent lapidary who could compete with any famous Zuni artist.

Jovanna Vacit

Jovanna Vacit is a daughter of Frank Vacit and Elizabeth Leekya Vacit and younger sister of Bessie Vacit. She made her jewelry in the 1980s and used the same "ear of corn" hallmark as her father.

Bryant Waatsa Sr.

In his younger days, Bryant Waatsa Sr. did cluster-work and row-work jewelry similar to his father's. He married Esther Nakatewa and created needle-point jewelry in the late 1930s (Bahti, 2007, pp.190–193).

Lorraine Quam Waatsa & Luwayne Waatsa

Lorraine is a daughter of Alice Ondelacy Quam and Duane Quam and granddaughter of Doris and Warren Ondelacy. Luwayne Waatsa is the son of Bryant Waatsa Sr. They are included in *Zuni: a Village of Silversmiths* (Ostler et al, 1966, 00.79-80).

Tom Weahkee

Tom is a brother of Teddy Weahkee, who was adopted. In *The Navajo and Pueblo Silversmiths,* John Adair describes Tom as one of the best turquoise workers in the pueblo (1944, p. 140). He is in *Zuni: The Art and the People*, Vol. I (Bell, 1975, p. 42).

Lee & Mary Weebothee

Lee Weebothee (1929–) is a brother of Leonard Weebothee and Fannie Weebothee Ondelacy. He and his wife, Mary Chico (1933–1995), created their own style of cluster-work jewelry together and were eventually inducted into the Arizona Highways Hall of Fame. Mary was an inlayer for her uncle, Joe Napoleon, in her younger days.

Leonard Weebothee & Lula Q. Weebothee

Leonard (1923–1992) is a brother of Lee Weebothee and Fannie Weebothee Ondelacy. Lula (1930–2007) was Leonard's wife. They made cluster-work jewelry similar to Lee and Mary Weebothee.

Jack Weekoty

Jack Weekoty was raised by his uncle and aunt, Horace and Lupe Iule. Horace taught Jack silversmithing. It is no wonder their jewelry designs are so similar. He is in *Zuni: the Art and the People*, Vol. I (Bell and Bell, 1975, p. 73).

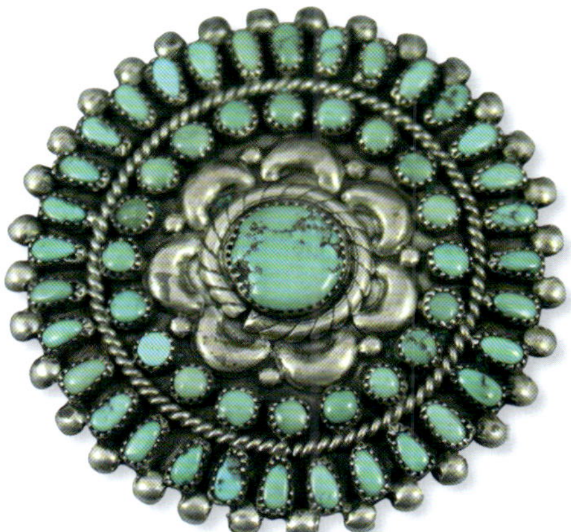

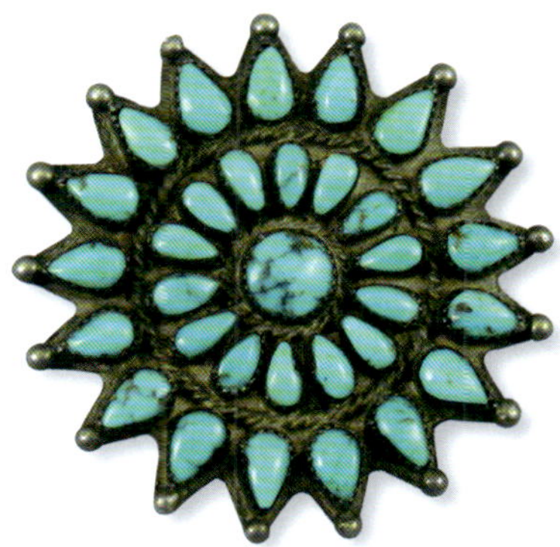

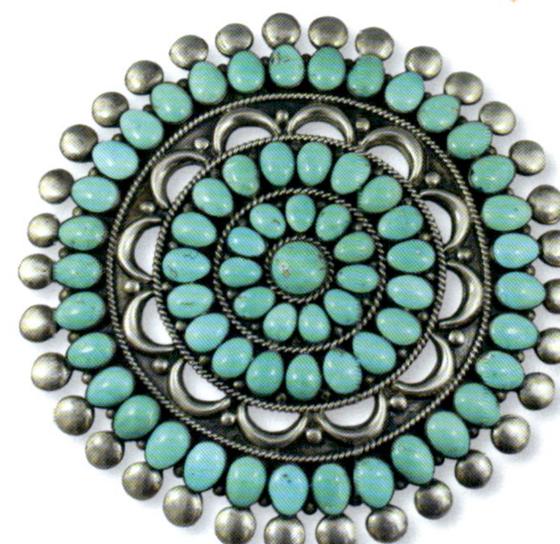

CHAPTER II

ZUNI LAPIDARY WORKS WITH FEW STONES

Although Zuni jewelry is famous for its lapidary work, including cluster work and needle point, that is set with many stones, some pieces, such as those made in the nugget-work style, are set with only a few stones. When Zuni lapidaries set turquoise cabochons on silver backings, they might have used a limited number of stones because of the scarcity of turquoise. According to Ostler, "[t]he Zunis did not set stones into silver jewelry until around 1890 (Adair, 1944, 128). At first, there were only a few small stones in rings and bracelets, but as the twentieth century advanced more turquoise was available to the artists and the traditional Zuni love of stones reasserted itself" (Ostler et al, 1996, p.62).

Thus, in the early twentieth century, many stone works, such as cluster and petite point, flourished in the Zuni jewelry community. Artists set many beautifully polished turquoise cabochons in a uniformly curved pattern. As described earlier, from the late 1930s to the 1940s, Dan Simplicio, who created nugget work, set only a few naturally shaped turquoise and coral cabochons adorned with stamped silver leaves and silver drops. Soon, Dan's brother Mike Simplicio, his brother-in-law Juan Calavaza, Chester Mahooty, and Leekya Deyuse's son Robert Leekya followed.

While they all used naturally shaped cabochons, some innovative artists, including Lee and Mary Weebothee, Andrew Ondelacy, and Julie Ondelacy Lahi, used pear-shaped cabochons for their jewelry. These Zuni jewelry styles are made for retail purposes.

A different Zuni jewelry style is created instead for ceremonial purposes. The Zunis love gigantic pieces for use as pins fastened along the side of traditional black dresses called manta. These huge cabochons can be as large as five inches. While there are huge cluster pins out there, large, single-turquoise, nugget-work pins also exist. I have seen such pins with lapidary work done by Thelma Sheche and silver work by her brother, Curtis Kucate. Duane Quam's Comache Dance tomahawk is another good example of this kind of jewelry (Ostler et al, 1996, p.70).

Nugget-work jewelry

When I got my first turquoise and coral nugget-work bolo, which an auctioneer attributed to Dan Simplicio, I had to confirm the attribution, because it is always very difficult to say for sure whether a certain nugget-work piece is Dan Simplicio's or his younger brother Mike's. I asked Carmelita Simplicio if it was her husband Mike Simplicio's. She confirmed it was his and told me she had the exact same die for a smaller leaf.

Two sets of stamped silver leaves and stamped silver drops adorn each naturally shaped cabochon of the bolo to the right. Each stamped silver drop has a dimple in its center. In addition, the longest vein of the stamped leaf touches the outer side. If one of these embellishments is in a nugget-work piece, it is probably Dan's. Dan Jr. confirmed that those characteristics, seen in this bolo, are consistent with his father's work.

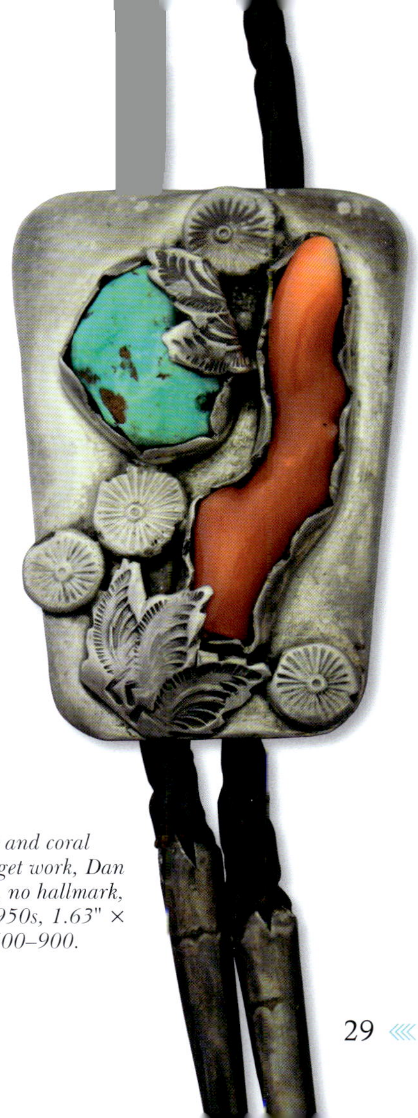

Turquoise and coral bolo, nugget work, Dan Simplicio, no hallmark, 1940s–1950s, 1.63" × 2.35", $600–900.

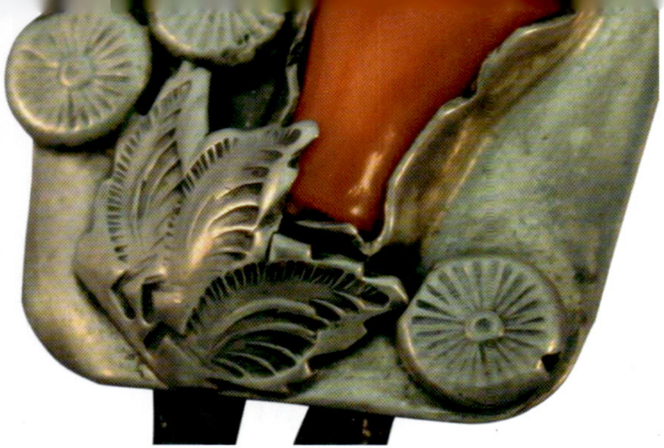

Close-up of stamped silver drops and leaves.

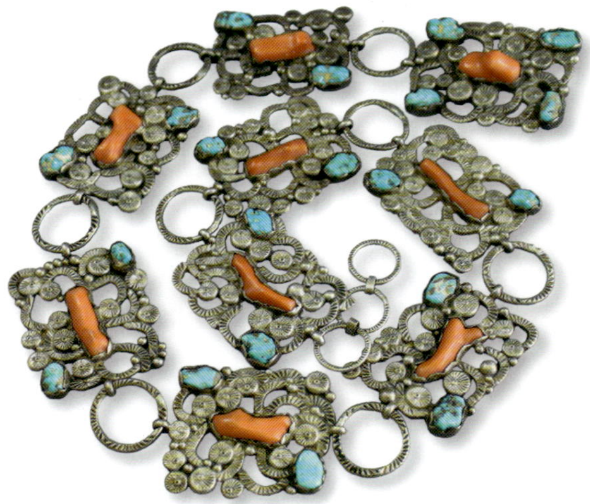

Turquoise and coral link belt, nugget work, Dan Simplicio, no hallmark, 1940s–1950s, 28.8" long, $6,000–9,000.

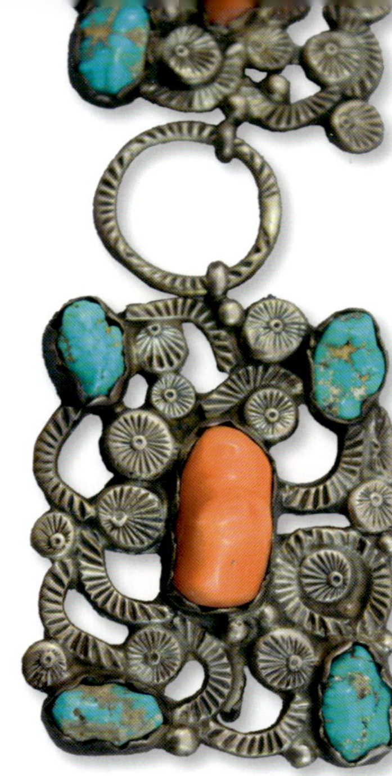

Close-up of the link belt buckle.

However, judging by the close-up photo above, when we compare it to a Navajo bracelet made by Charles Begay in 1932 in *The C. G. Wallace Collection of American Indian Art*, we can conclude that the stamped silver drops in these two pieces are nearly identical (Sotheby Parke Barnet Inc., 1975, p. 114, #667).

This ladies belt is one of Dan Simplicio Sr.'s signature pieces. It consists of eight conchas, one buckle, and his characteristic stamped silver drops, stamped silver wires, and naturally shaped turquoise and coral cabochons.

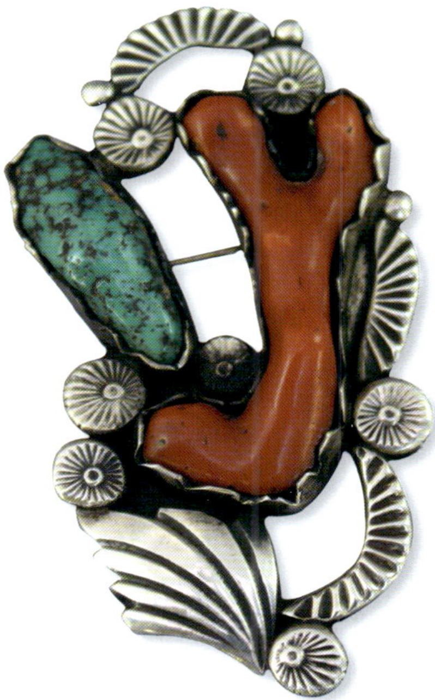

Turquoise and coral pin, nugget work, Dan Simplicio, no hallmark, 1940s–1950s, 1.55" × 2.84", $700–1,050.

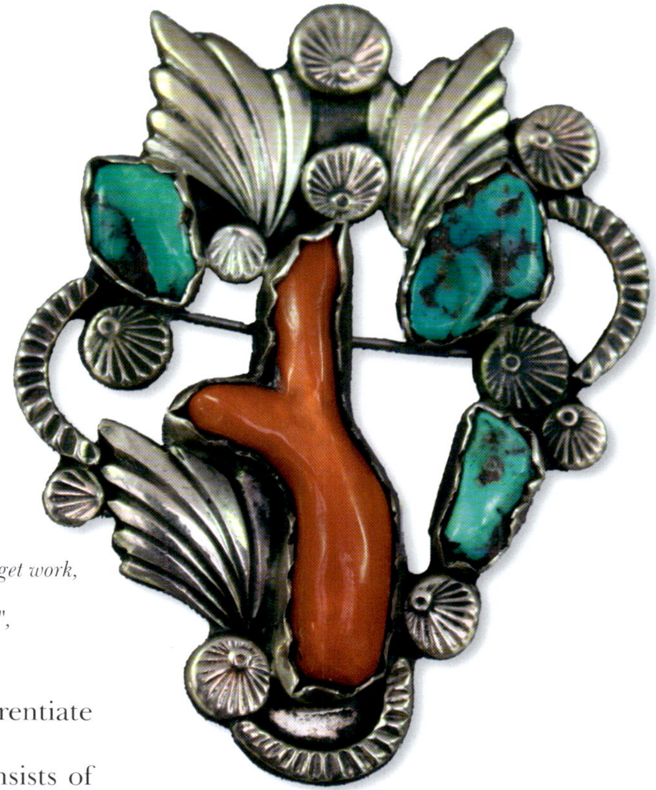

Turquoise and coral pin, nugget work, Dan Simplicio, no hallmark, 1940s–1950s, 1.55" × 2.84", $700–1,050.

The pin above consists of stamped silver drops, stamped silver wires, and turquoise and coral cabochons, in addition to the stamped silver leaves seen at the beginning of this section. This stamped silver leaf is very similar to the one used by his brother Mike, so we cannot use this criterion in order to differentiate Dan's pieces from others.

The wider pin at right consists of the identical stamped silver drops, stamped silver wires, a stamped silver leaf, and turquoise and coral cabochons.

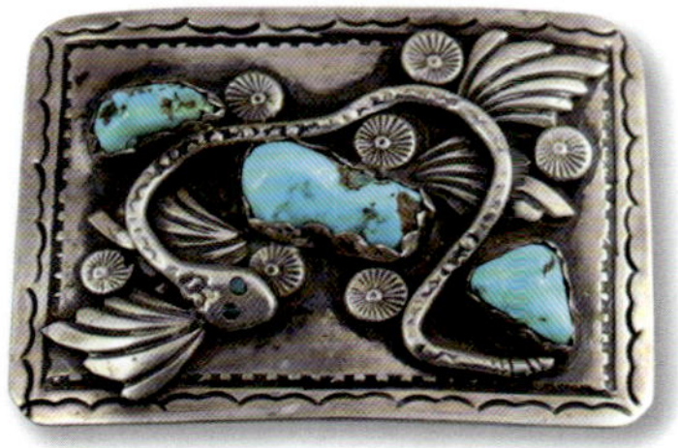

Turquoise buckle, nugget work, Dan Simplicio, no hallmark, late 1940s to early 1950s, 2.43" × 3.42", $1,000–1,500.

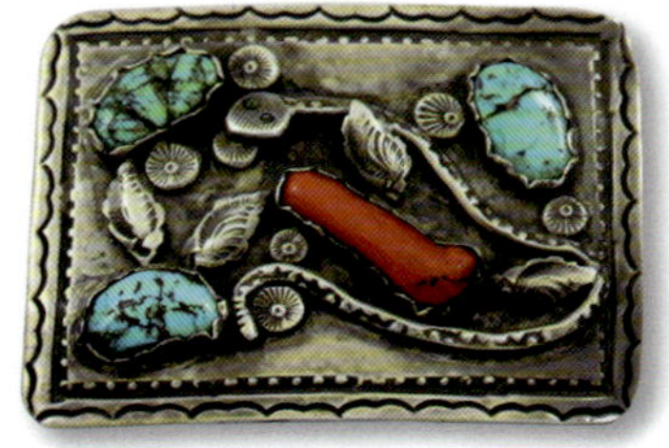

Turquoise and coral buckle, nugget work, Dan Simplicio, no hallmark, 1950s–1960s, 2.51" × 3.43", $1,000–1,500.

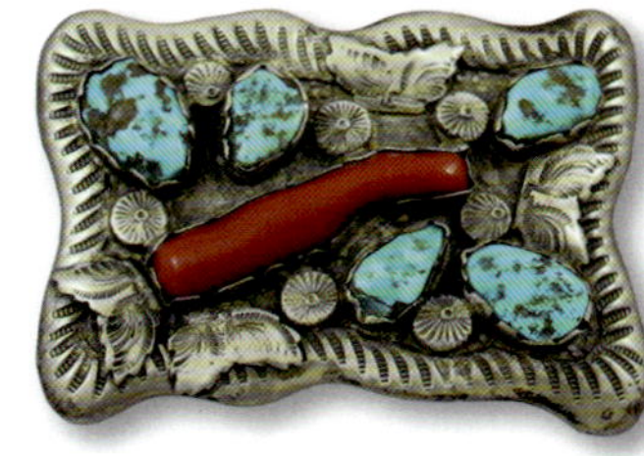

Turquoise and coral buckle, cast and nugget work, Dan Simplicio, no hallmark, 1950s, 2.39" × 3.24", $1,000–1,500.

Based on the handmade silver wire clasp on the buckle above, which receives a leather belt, it's safe to say Dan Simplicio Sr. is the artist. It features three turquoise cabochons, seven stamped silver drops (uniquely Dan's), four stamped silver leaves (commonly observed in the works of other relatives, such as Mike Simplicio), and a cast and stamped silver snake. Its four sides are stamped, but the background encircled by those stamped sides remains unstamped. This unstamped area is considered characteristic of Dan's pieces.

The age of the middle buckle is an estimate based on the use of a factory-made clasp that receives a leather belt. It consists of three turquoise cabochons, one coral twig, six stamped silver drops and four stamped silver leaves (uniquely his), and a cast and stamped silver snake. Its four sides are stamped with two kinds of the same stamps observed in the previous buckle. Those stamped sides encircle the unstamped background.

The last buckle consists of five turquoise cabochons, seven stamped silver drops, and four sets of double stamped silver leaves, which are characteristic of Dan's pieces. Its silver backing is made entirely in the casting method. At 116 grams, it is quite heavy compared with the 88-gram turquoise and coral buckle previously described.

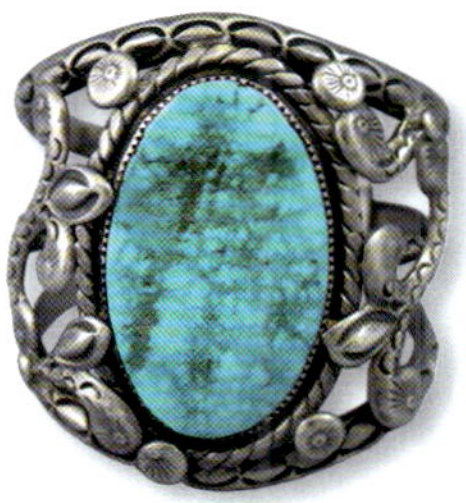

Turquoise bracelet, nugget work, silver work by Dan Simplicio and lapidary work probably by his wife's mother, Helen, no hallmark, 1940s–1950s, 1.45" × 2.24" central medallion, $1,000–1,500.

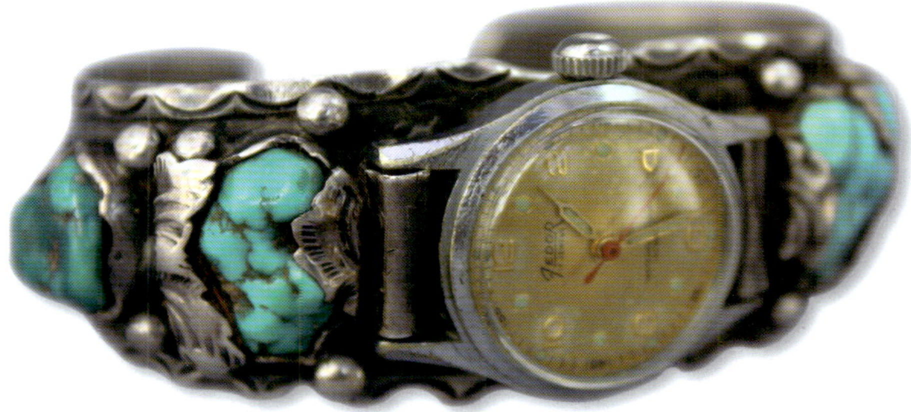

Turquoise watch bracelet, nugget work, Dan Simplicio, his signature star hallmark, late 1960s, 1.60" high, $300–450.

The stamped silver drops in the bracelet above are a clue that Dan Simplicio Sr. did the silver work. It has one oval turquoise cabochon and several stamped silver parts all over the cuff. A saw-toothed bezel fastens the turquoise, though Dan Sr. rarely used the saw-tooth pattern in his post–World War II pieces. Dan Jr. told me his mother-in-law, Helen Shebola, might have done the lapidary work.

The watch bracelet above has four raised, wavy edges. Its stamped inside background is rare for his pieces, although his brother Mike used it customarily. The presence of two sets each of single- and double-stamped leaves is characteristic of Dan's pieces.

Turquoise bolo, nugget work, Dan Simplicio, no hallmark, 1940s–1950s, 1.45" × 2.12", $500–750.

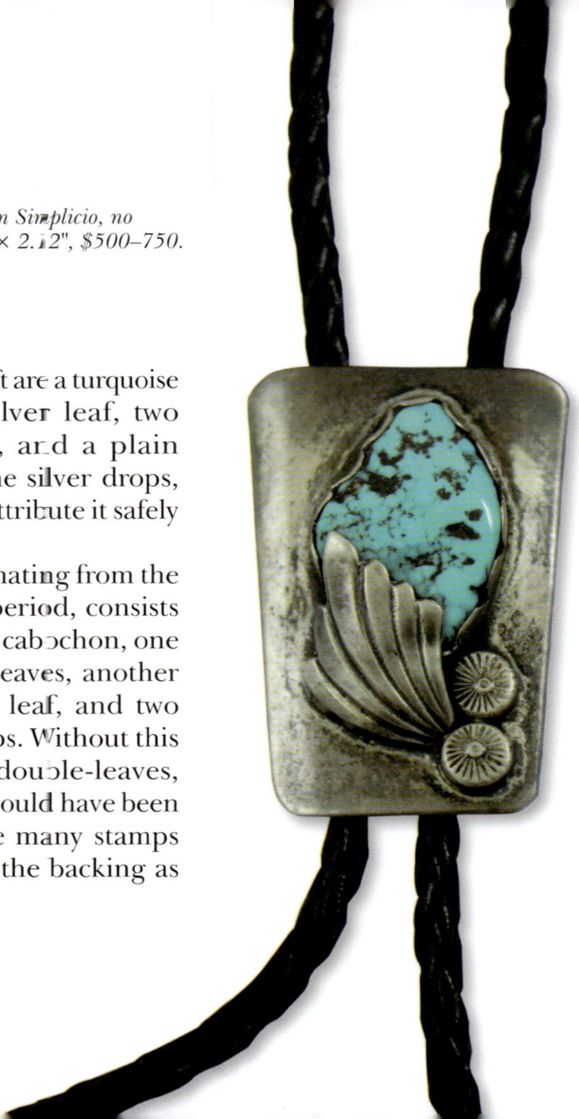

Comprising the bolo at left are a turquoise cabochon, stamped silver leaf, two stamped silver drops, and a plain background. Without the silver drops, we would not be able to attribute it safely to Dan.

The next bolo, originating from the around the same time period, consists of one chunky turquoise cabochon, one set of stamped double-leaves, another type of stamped silver leaf, and two smaller, plain silver drops. Without this set of stamped silver double-leaves, attributing it to Dan Sr. would have been very difficult. There are many stamps alongside both sides of the backing as well.

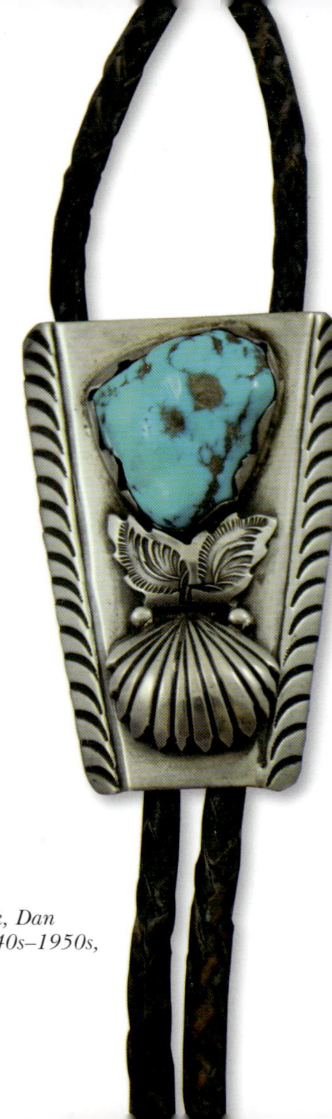

Turquoise bolo, nugget work, Dan Simplicio, no hallmark, 1940s–1950s, 1.51" × 2.28", $500–750.

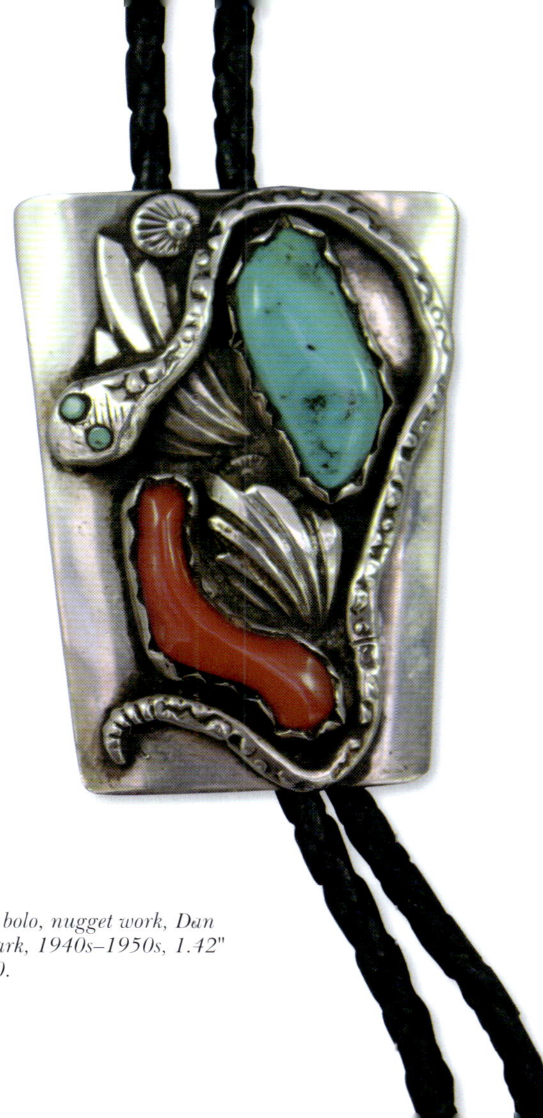

Turquoise and coral bolo, nugget work, Dan Simplicio, no hallmark, 1950s–1960s, 1.65" × 2.25", $600–900.

In addition to a turquoise cabochon and oxblood coral twig, the bolo at far left consists of two of Dan Sr.'s unique stamped silver drops, one common silver leaf, and a cast and stamped silver snake. The snake eyes look like diamond cabochons, and its silver backing is left plain.

The second, similarly designed, bolo also has a cabochon, twig, two silver drops, a snake, and a plain back, but two silver leaves instead of one. Two small, turquoise snake-eye cabochons fittingly mark the eyes of the snake.

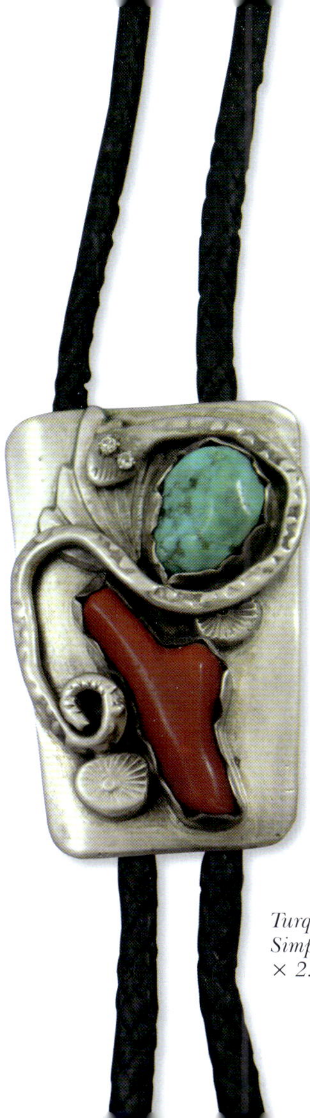

Turquoise and coral bolo, nugget work, Dan Simplicio, no hallmark, 1940s–1950s, 1.42" × 2.21", $600–900.

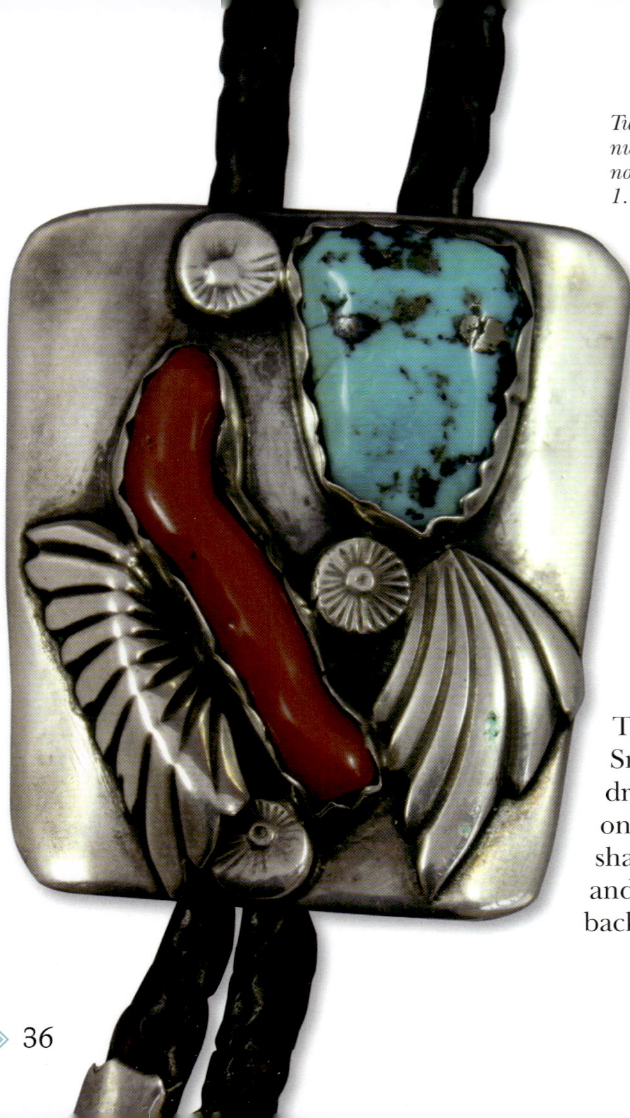

Turquoise and coral bolo, nugget work, Dan Simplicio, no hallmark, 1950s–1960s, 1.71" × 1.97", $500–750.

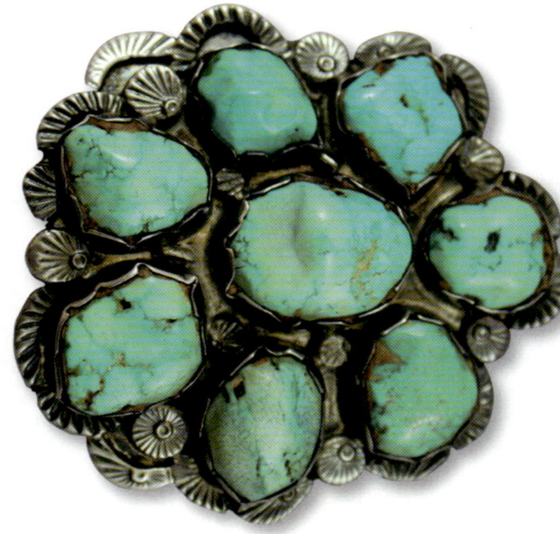

Turquoise bolo, nugget work, Dan Simplicio, no hallmark, 1940s–1950s, 2.29" × 2.42", $800–1,200.

This bolo consists of three of Dan Sr.'s characteristic stamped silver drops, two common silver leaves—one of which is folded in a roof shape—and a turquoise cabochon and oxblood coral twig. Its silver backing is left plain.

One turquoise cabochon is set in the center of bolo above, creating a flower-head–like shape, with seven surrounding turquoise cabochons. This might be a combination of cluster work and nugget work. Stamped silver drops and twigs surround the turquoise cabochons.

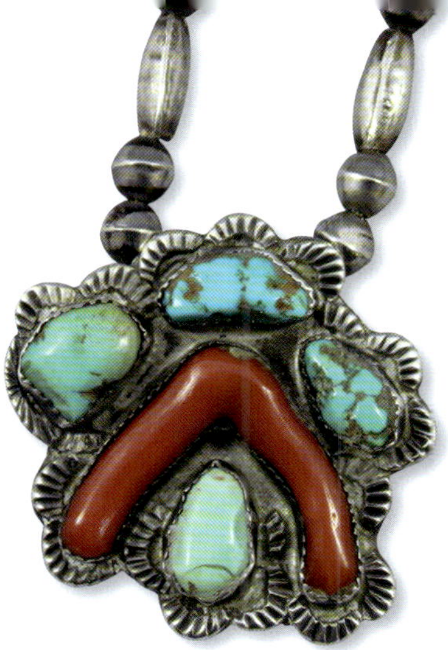

Turquoise and coral pendant, nugget work, Dan Simplicio, no hallmark, early 1950s, 1.74" × 1.78", $600–900.

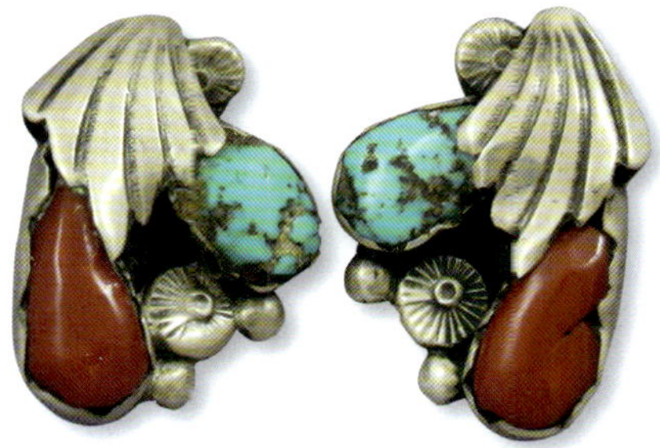

Turquoise and coral earrings, nugget work, Dan Simplicio and Esther Romancito Simplicio, no hallmark, 1940s–1950s, 0.62" × 1.28", $200–300.

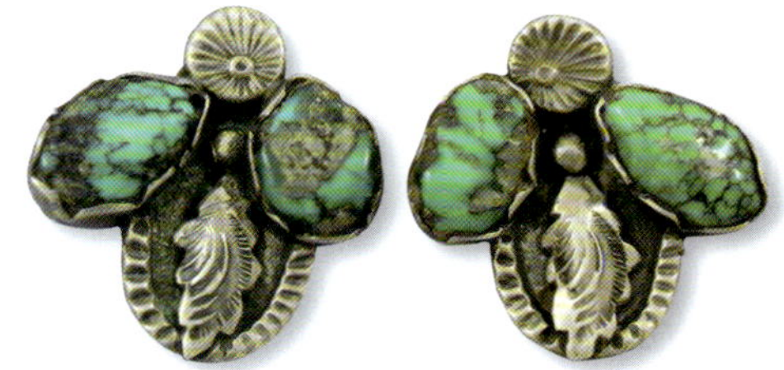

Turquoise earrings, nugget work, Dan Simplicio and Esther Romancito Simplicio, no hallmark, 1940s–1950s, 1.14" × 1.21", $200–300.

Although the nugget-work turquoise and coral pendant above does not have any characteristic stamped silver drops or leaves, the stamped, half-circle silver twigs and the overall arrangement of parts suggest that it is Dan Sr.'s work.

Dan and his wife, Esther Romancito Simplicio, made the turquoise and coral earrings above. In addition to a turquoise and oxblood–red coral cabochon, they also feature two stamped silver drops, two plain silver drops, and one common silver leaf.

The couple made these turquoise earrings in the same style. They consist of one stamped silver drop and leaf (both of which are characteristic of Dan), a half-oblong silver twig, and two green turquoise cabochons.

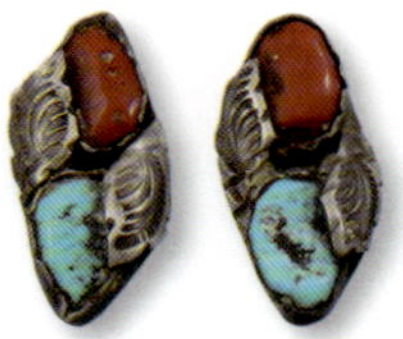

Turquoise and coral cuff links, nugget work, Dan Simplicio and Esther Romancito Simplicio, no hallmark, 1940s–1950s, 0.80" × 1.07", $200–300.

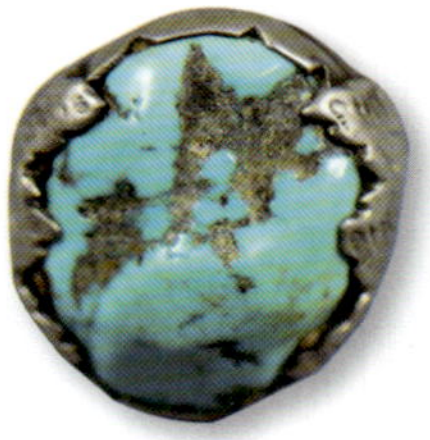

Turquoise ring, nugget work, Dan Simplicio and Esther Romancito Simplicio, no hallmark, 1940s–1950s, 0.99" × 1.16", $160–240.

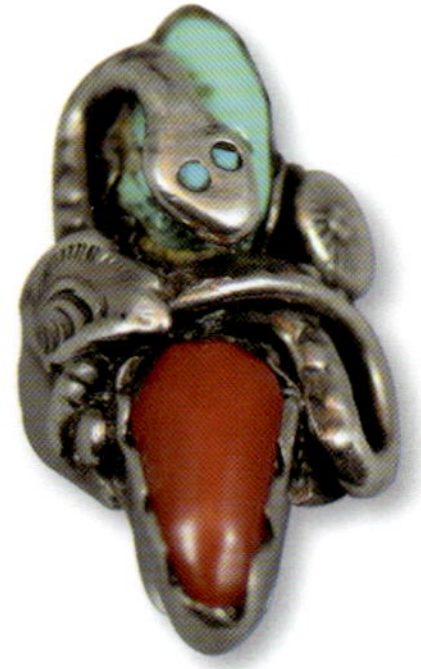

Turquoise and coral ring, nugget work, Dan Simplicio and Esther Romancito Simplicio, no hallmark, 1940s–1950s, 0.75" × 1.57", $160–240.

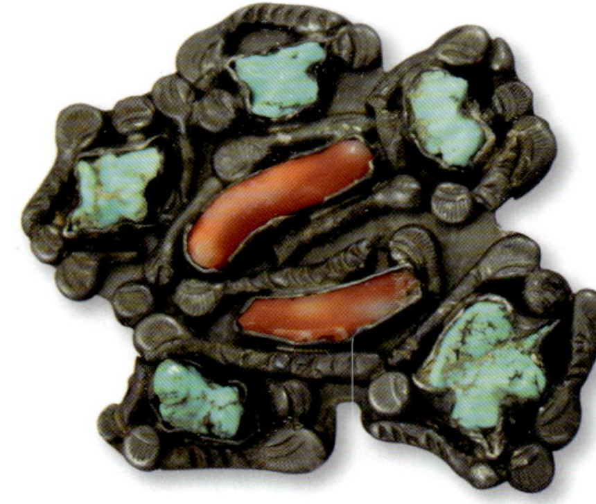

Turquoise and coral bolo, nugget work, Dan Simplicio, no hallmark, late 1940s, 1.79" × 1.97", $500–750.

Dan and Esther made the cuff links in the top left corner, which consist of two stamped silver leaves, one pair of turquoise cabochons, and another pair of coral cabochons.

The ring beneath the cuff links contains a chunky turquoise cabochon, and each side has a triple-stamped silver leaf, a major characteristic of Dan Sr.'s silver work.

Around the same time, the married couple made the turquoise and coral ring above. It consists of a combination of the stamped silver drop and leaf, a cast and stamped silver snake, a small, plain silver drop, a turquoise cabochon, and a coral cabochon.

Above is a bolo that consists of several cast and stamped silver parts, two coral twigs, and five naturally shaped turquoise cabochons. The crowding in this piece could signify it as an earlier work.

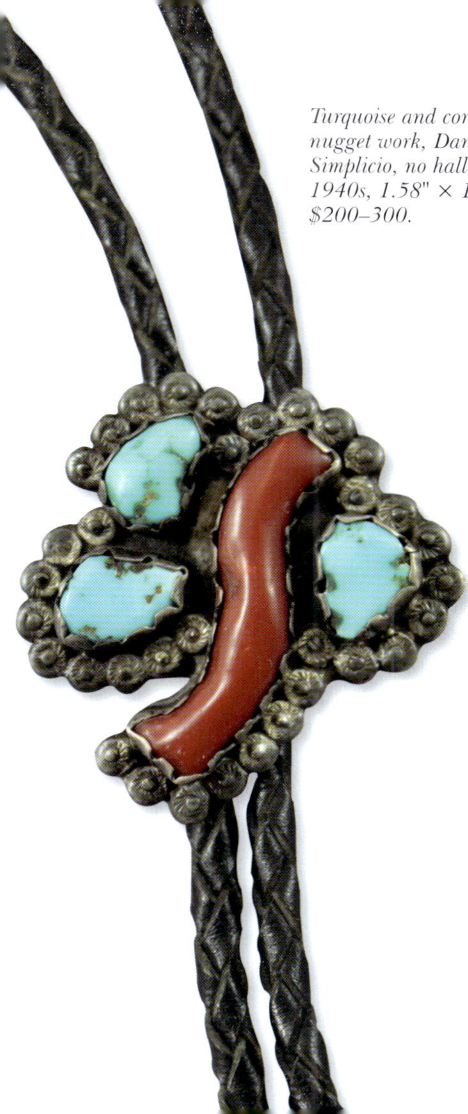

Turquoise and coral bolo, nugget work, Dan Simplicio, no hallmark, 1940s, 1.58" × 1.67", $200–300.

Several years ago, one of my Zuni informants attributed this Morenci turquoise and oxblood red coral bolo on the left to Dan Sr. I questioned it because this piece looks so different from his standard samples. I brought the bolo to Zuni in March 2013 and showed it to the same informant again and also to Dan Simplicio Jr., who confirmed it was his father's. We can see his crowded silver work here as well.

Dan Sr.'s brother Mike probably made this turquoise and coral bolo to the right. It consists of six stamped silver drops, which differ from Dan's, and one stamped silver leaf similar to Dan's, in addition to three turquoise cabochons and one coral twig. These turquoise cabochons are cut and polished more beautifully than his brother's pieces, but the backing is left plain, just like most of Dan Sr.'s pieces.

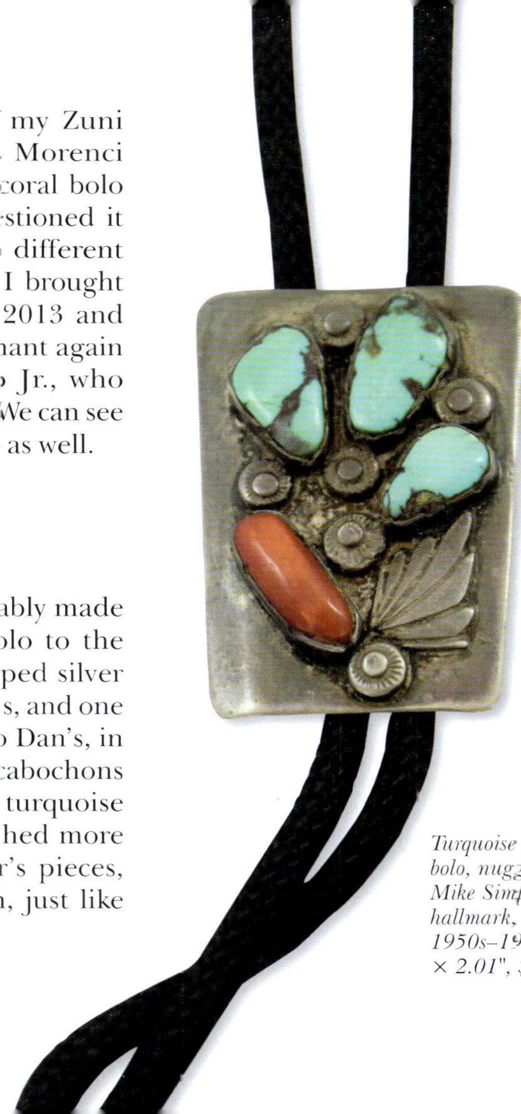

Turquoise and coral bolo, nugget work, Mike Simplicio(?), no hallmark, 1950s–1960s, 1.46" × 2.01", $240–350.

The seller of this bolo attributed it to Dan Simplicio Sr., but I visited Mike's widow, Carmelita Simplicio, who confirmed it was in fact her late husband's. She still had the leaf die. As shown in the close-up picture to the right, the veins do not touch the edge The piece consists of three stamped silver leaves and seven plain silver drops, in addition to two turquoise cabochons and one coral twig. All four sides are stamped.

Turquoise and coral bolo, nugget work, Mike Simplicio, no hallmark, 1940s–1950s, 1.57" × 2.03", $240–350.

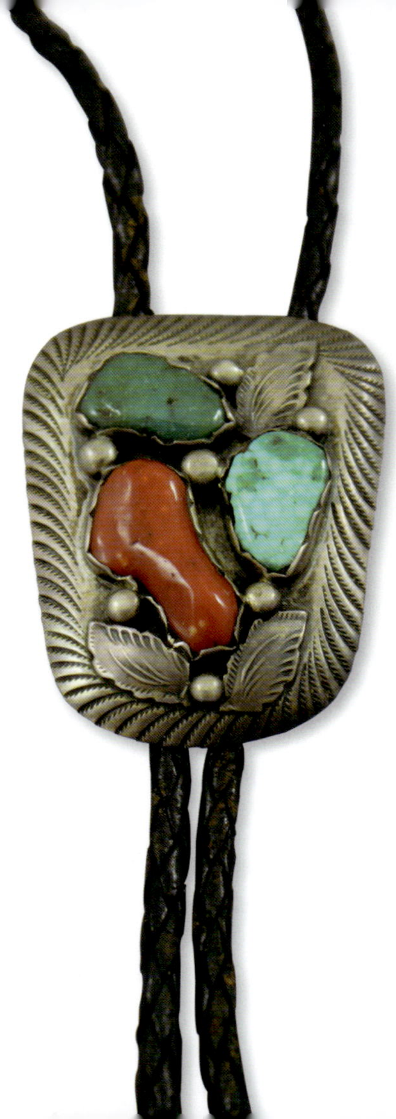

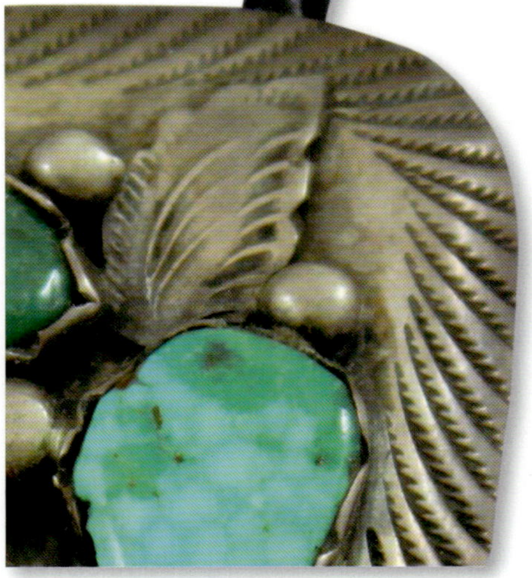

Close-up of the stamped silver leaf of the bolo.

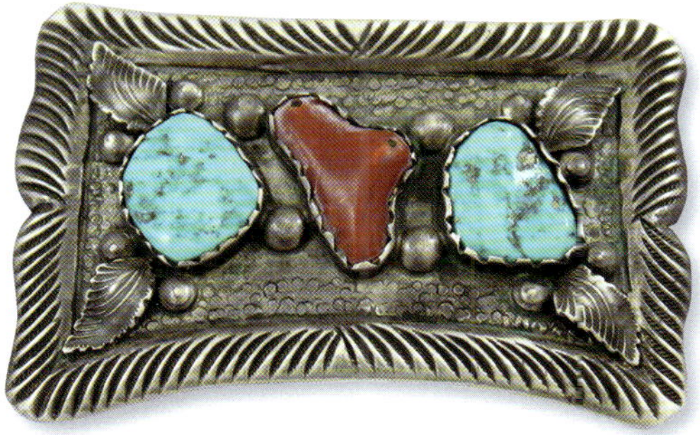

Turquoise and coral buckle, nugget work, Mike Simplicio, ~ over M, 1950s–1960s, 3.20" × 2.12", $300–450.

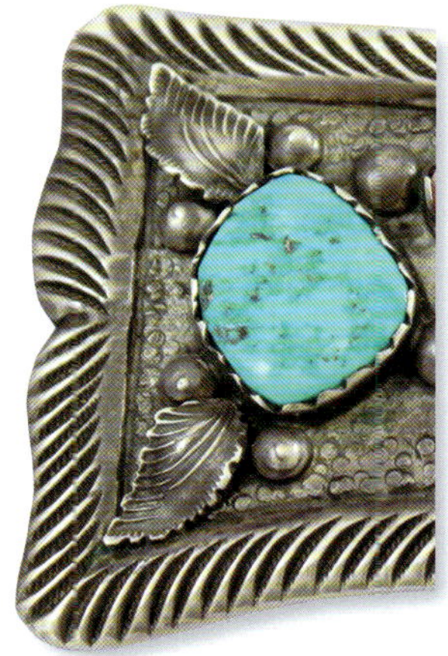

Close-up of the stamped silver leaf of the buckle.

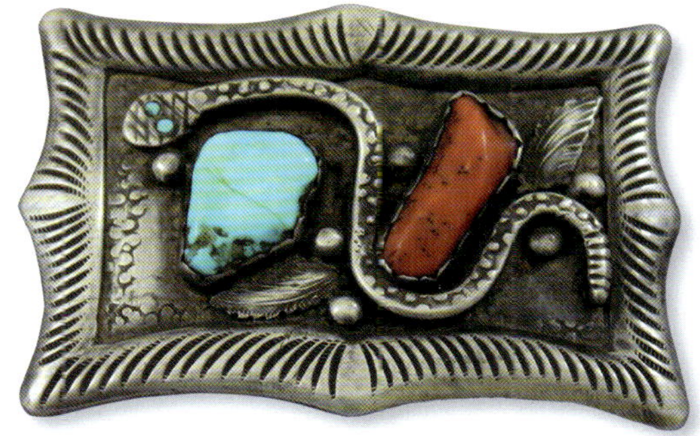

Turquoise and coral buckle, nugget work, Mike Simplicio, no hallmark, 1950s–1960s, 3.09" × 2.01", $300–450.

Mike Simplicio's cast turquoise and coral buckle consists of four stamped silver leaves and eleven plain silver drops, in addition to two turquoise cabochons and one red coral twig. As the close-up shows, the longest leaf vein does not touch its edge, while the middle vein does, which makes it different from both Mike's earliest work and Dan's work. All four sides are heavily stamped with the same crescent-shaped stamp, and the inside area is stamped as well. It has his hallmark, "~" over an "M."

The buckle above consists of two stamped silver leaves and six plain silver drops, in addition to one turquoise cabochon and one red coral twig. All three veins of the leaf touch its edge. That makes this Mike's third distinct leaf stamp. As for the silver backing, its raised edges are cast, and another backing was welded later. All four edges are stamped with the same crescent-shaped stamp, and the inner area was stamped as well.

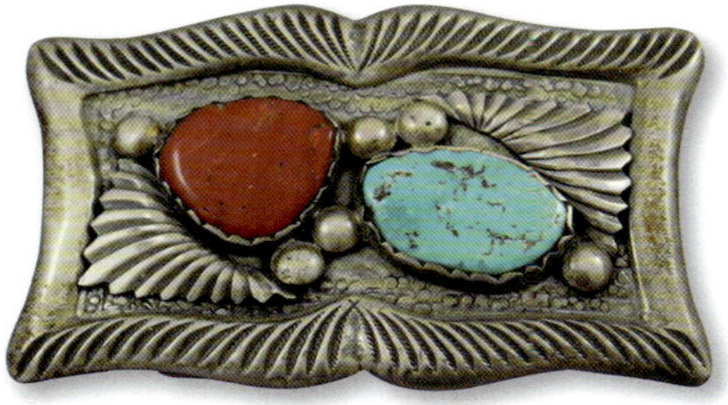

Turquoise and coral buckle, nugget work, Mike Simplicio, M. Simplicio, 1950s–1960s, 3.14" × 1.89", $300–450.

The buckle in the top left has the hallmark "M. Simplicio" and consists of two stamped silver leaves, six plain silver drops, and one turquoise and one red coral cabochon. Like the buckle described on the previous page, the raised edges are cast first, and a silver plate is welded under it as a backing. Its horizontal edges are stamped, while the other edges have been left plain. Like the other two buckles, its inner area is stamped.

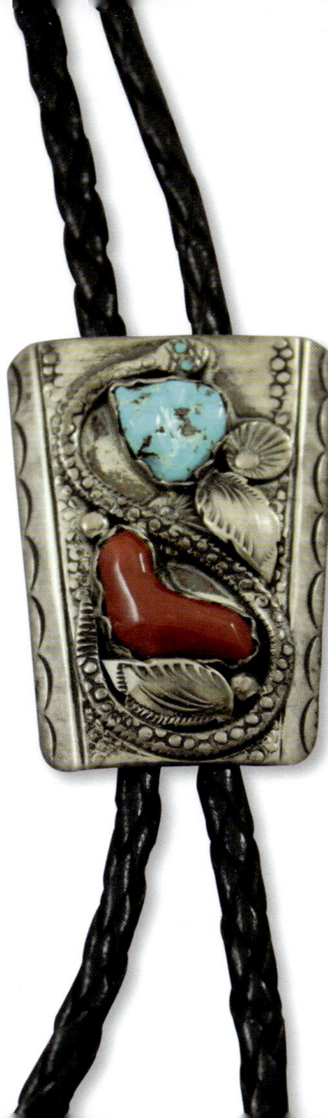

Turquoise and coral bolo, nugget work, Mike Simplicio, no hallmark, 1950s–1960s, 1.46" × 2.00", $240–360.

At left is a bolo by Mike, which consists of a cast and stamped silver snake, two stamped silver leaves, two stamped silver drops, and one plain silver drop. One turquoise cabochon and one red coral twig inhabit the top and bottom of the piece. These stamped silver leaves are comparable to those in his second bolo (p. 40). Both edges are stamped with a plain, crescent shape, and the inner background is also stamped.

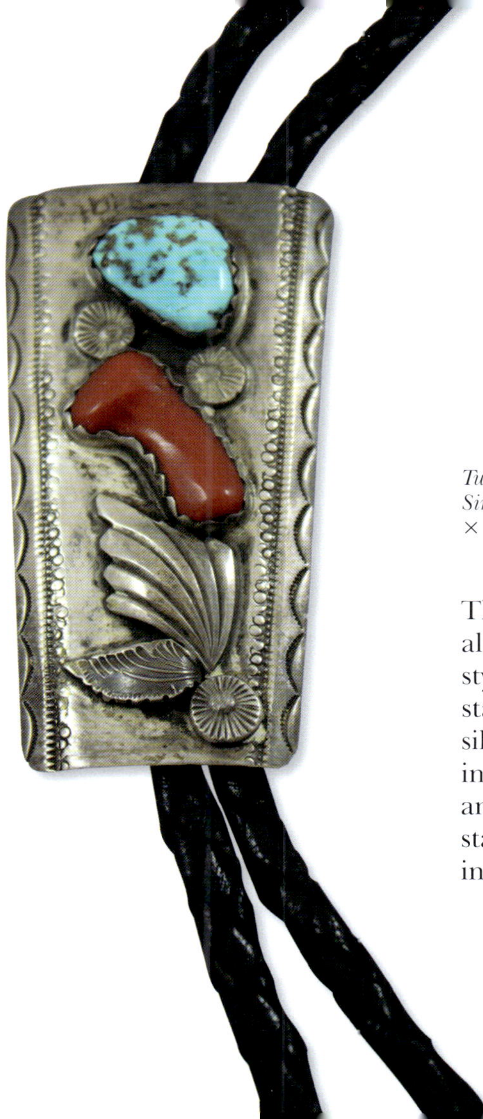

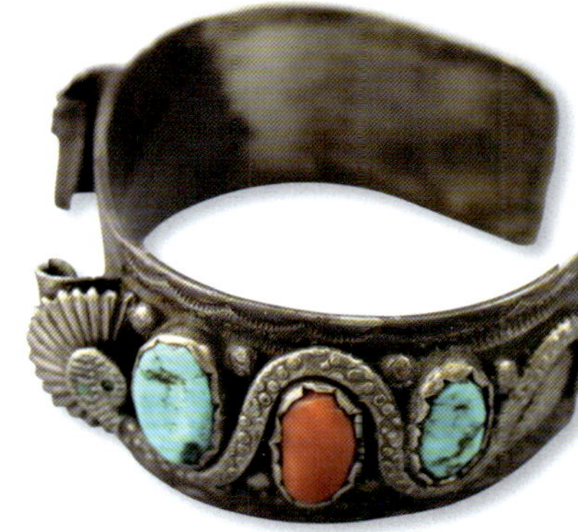

Turquoise and coral bolo, nugget work, Mike Simplicio, M. Simplicio, 1950s–1960s, 1.48" × 2.76", $240–360.

Turquoise and coral watch bracelet, nugget work, Mike Simplicio, M. Simplicio, 1950s–1960s, 1.10" high, $240–360.

The turquoise and coral bolo to the left, also made by Mike in the nugget-work style, consists of two of his second-type stamped silver leaves, three stamped silver drops, and one stamped silver leaf, in addition to one turquoise cabochon and one red coral twig. Both sides are stamped with the crescent die, and the inner area along the edges is stamped.

Mike's watch bracelet is hallmarked "M. Simplicio." It consists of one cast and stamped silver snake, one silver leaf with his second-type stamp, seven smaller plain silver drops, and three cabochons—two turquoise and one coral—on both sides of the cuff. Its outer edges are stamped with his crescent-shaped die.

The turquoise and coral bolo at right consists of two turquoise cabochons and one coral twig fixed with a cast and stamped silver snake, without any bezel. This method is very rare. Its silver backing is left plain.

On the far right, the turquoise cabochon is fastened on the silver base with a bezel, but the coral twig is fastened on the base with a cast and stamped snake and a triple-stamped silver leaf, without any bezel. The stamped silver leaf is somewhat similar to Mike's first example, but it is clearly not identical. Its silver backing is left unstamped.

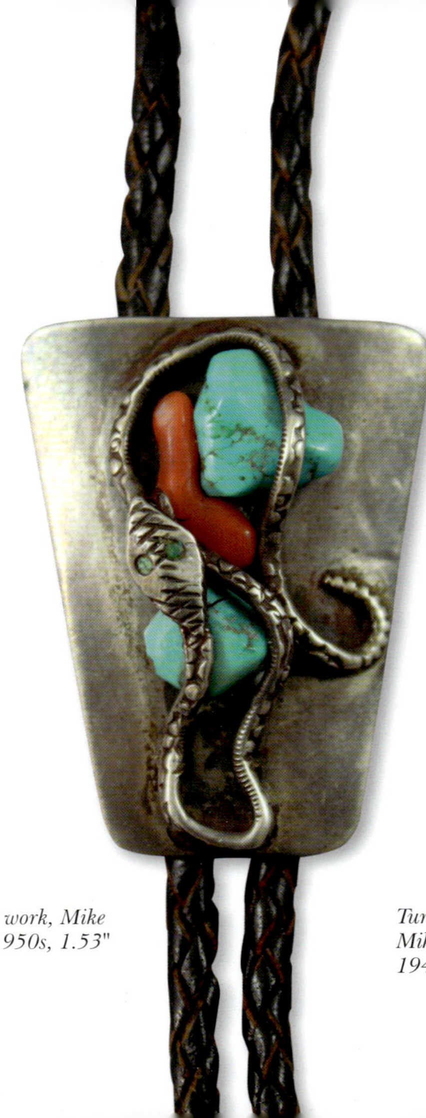

Turquoise and coral bolo, nugget work, Mike Simplicio, no hallmark, 1940s–1950s, 1.53" × 2.04", $240–360.

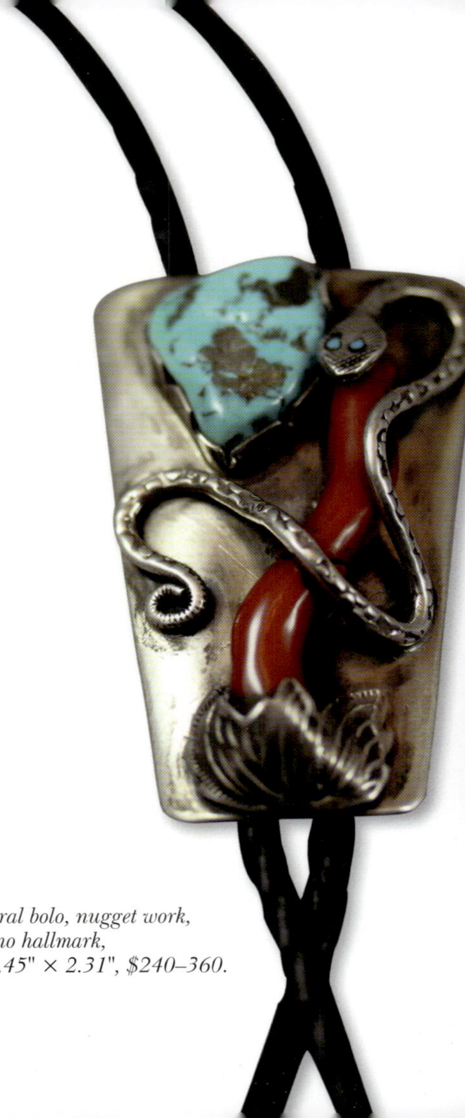

Turquoise and coral bolo, nugget work, Mike Simplicio, no hallmark, 1940s–1950s, 1.45" × 2.31", $240–360.

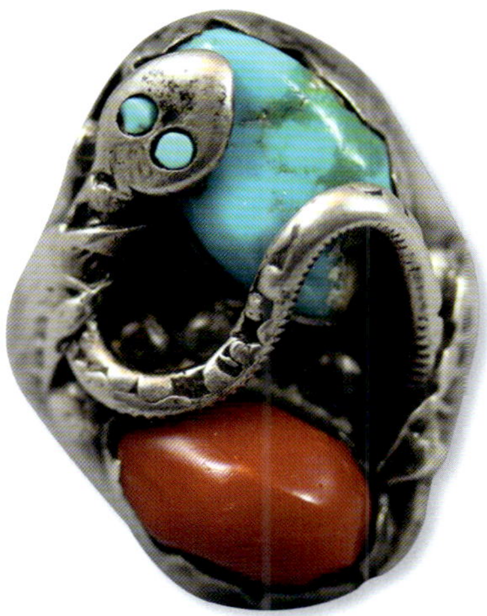

Turquoise and coral ring, nugget work, Mike Simplicio, no hallmark, 1950s–1960s, 0.91" × 0.12", $100–150.

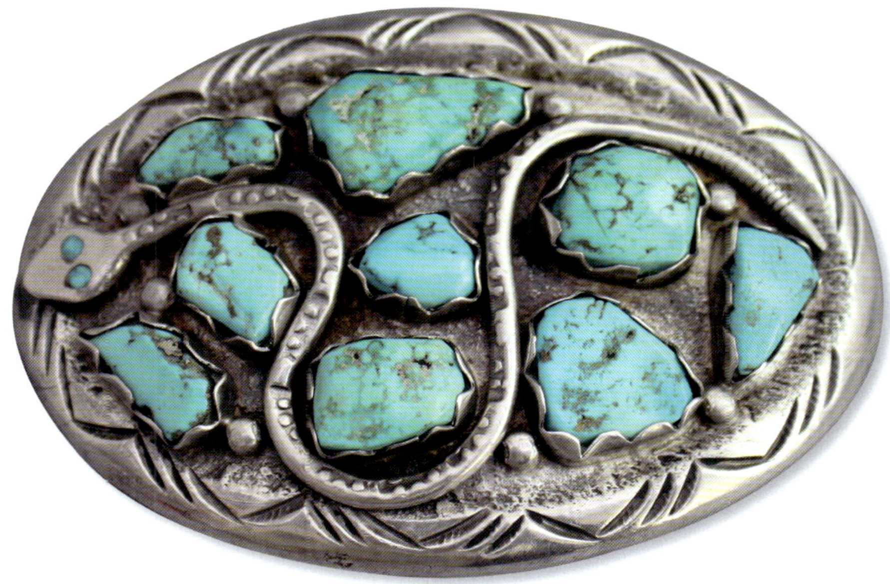

The ring above matches the preceding bolo. It consists of a cast and stamped silver snake, two small stamped leaves, and four small, unstamped silver drops, in addition to one turquoise and one coral cabochon fastened onto the silver base with bezels.

Juan Calavaza's turquoise buckle, above, consists of a cast and stamped silver snake, along with nine turquoise nuggets. Its oval edge is uniquely stamped, but the inner area is left unstamped.

Turquoise buckle, nugget work, Juan Calavaza, Juan C., 1960s–1970s, 3.25" × 2.25", $300–450.

Turquoise and coral bolo, nugget work, Viola and Roy Nieto, no hallmark, 1960s, 2.04" × 3.03", $300–450.*

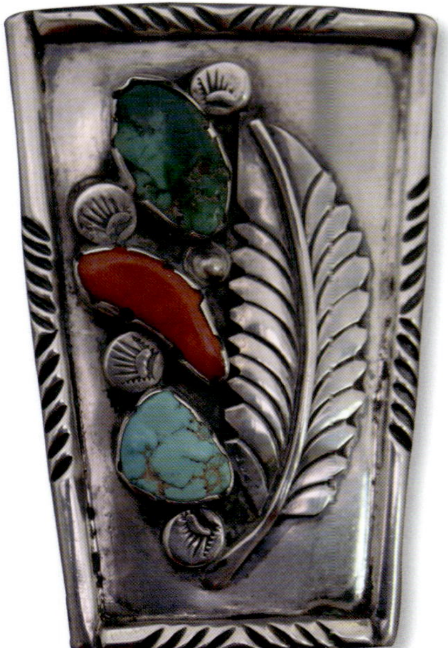

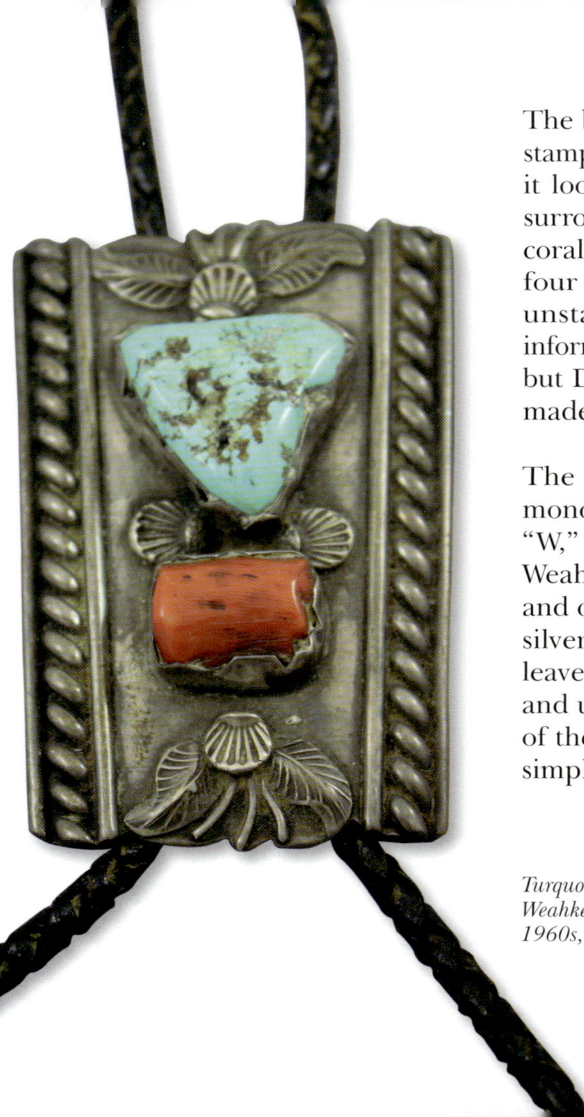

The bolo at the far left has four partly stamped edges—an approach that makes it look like a Zuni silver work—which surround two turquoise cabochons, one coral twig, a large stamped silver leaf, four stamped silver drops, and one unstamped silver drop. One of my informants attributes it to Teddy Edaakie, but Dan Simplicio Jr. confirmed it was made by Viola and Roy Nieto.

The next bolo is hallmarked with a monogram that combines "T," "F," and "W," indicating it was made by Tom Weahkee. It consists of one turquoise and one coral cabochon, four stamped silver drops, and four stamped silver leaves. Three silver wires are set over and under the silver drops. Both sides of the bolo slide are adorned with two simple silver wires and one twisted.

Turquoise and coral bolo, nugget work, Tom Weahkee, monogram consisting of T, F, and W, 1960s, 1.93" × 2.92", $500–750.

Chester Mahooty made both gorgets on this page for the American Indian Dance Theatre. I purchased them together as a package. The top sample has a pin with three turquoise nuggets in its center, two spiny oyster shells adorned with a turtle fetish, turquoise nuggets, and five strands of turquoise beads. They are fastened on black felt cloth, with magic tape attached to the ends of the cord for wearing, but as this gorget has neither stains nor cosmetics residue, it is probably unused.

The bottom one consists of one large turquoise nugget pin, two simple spiny oyster shells, and five strands of green turquoise beads. As neither magic tape nor hooks are applied for wearing, this gorget was not meant to be worn.

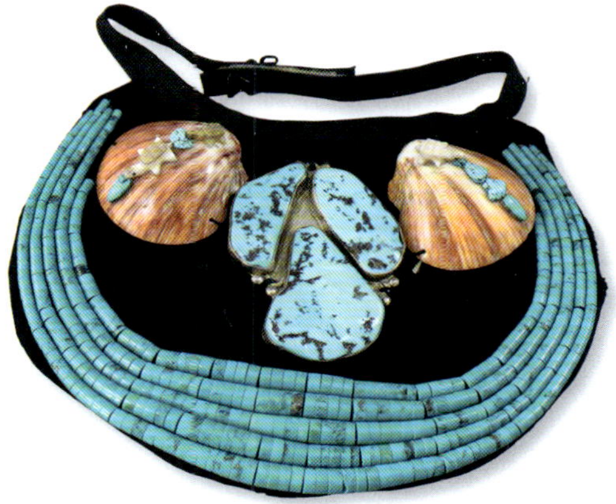

Turquoise and spiny oyster shell gorget for dancing, nugget work, Chester Mahooty, no hallmark, 1980s, central medallion 2.45" × 3.36", $600–900.

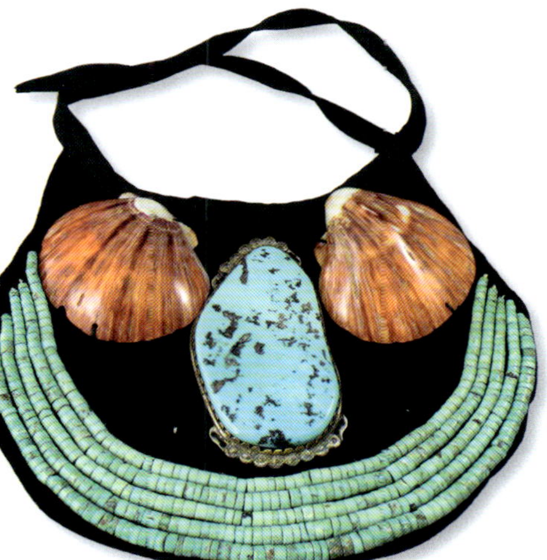

Turquoise and spiny oyster shell gorget for dancing, nugget work, Chester Mahooty, no hallmark, 1980s, central medallion 1.91" × 3.67", $600–900.

Robert and Bernice Ondelacy Leekya made these turquoise bolos. The first consists of four small, plain silver drops and three turquoise cabochons. Both sides are heavily stamped, and the artists added twisted silver wires.

Both sides of the second piece, framed with a twisted silver wire, are partly stamped. Three turquoise cabochons are fastened on the domed, silver, oval backing with bezels and larger, Dan Simplicio–style stamped leaves.

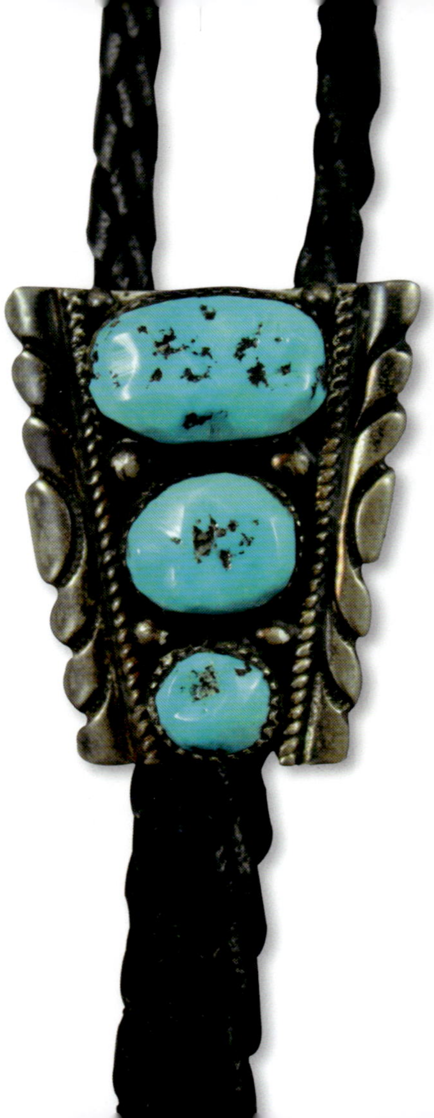

Turquoise bolo, nugget work, Robert and Bernice Leekya, monogram consisting of R, B, and L, 1980s–1990s, 1.24" × 1.26", $160–240.

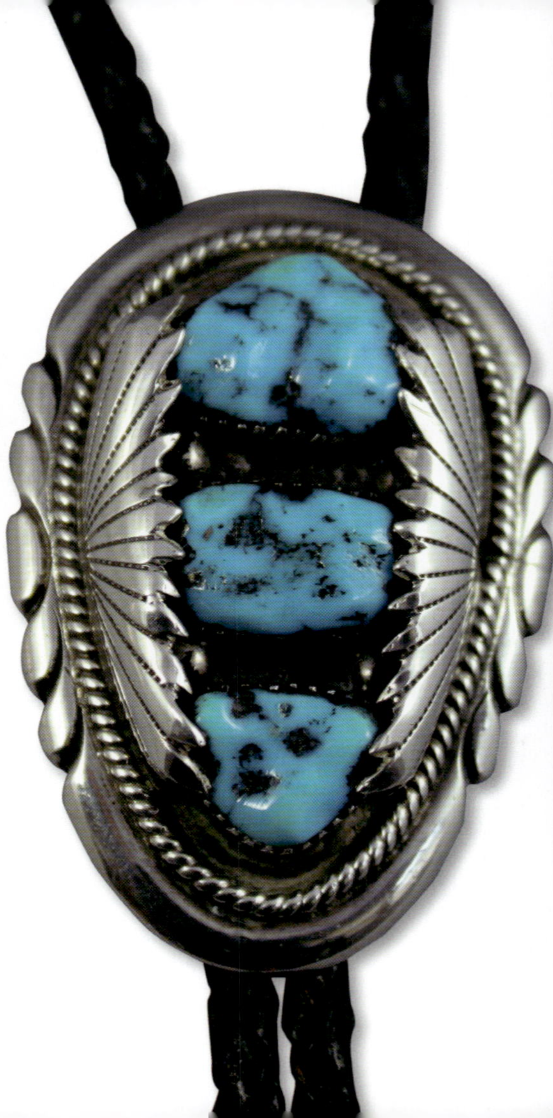

Turquoise bolo, nugget work, Robert and Bernice Leekya, monogram consisting of R, B and L, 1980s, 1.45" × 2.16", $200–300.

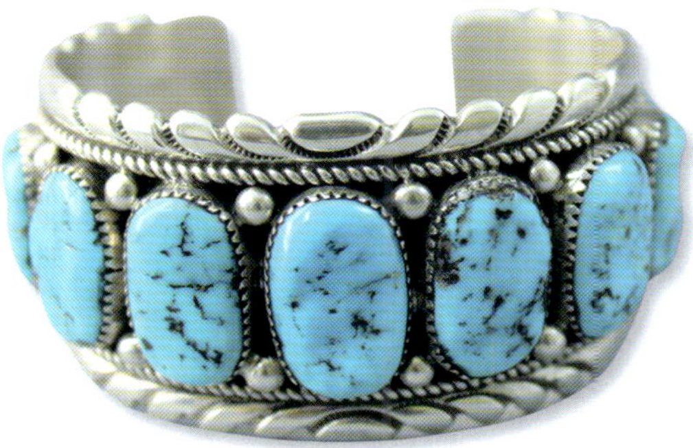

Turquoise bracelet, nugget work, Robert and Bernice Leekya, monogram consisting of R, B, and L, 1980s–1990s, 1.42" high, $500–750.

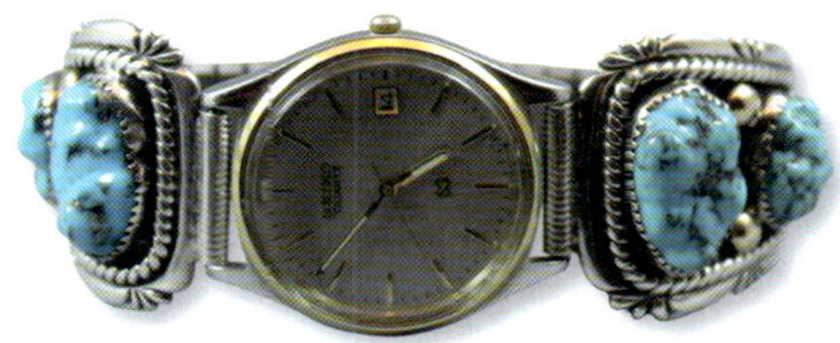

Turquoise watch bracelet, nugget work, Robert and Bernice Leekya, monogram consisting of R, B, and L, 1980s–1990s, 1.33" high, $400–600.

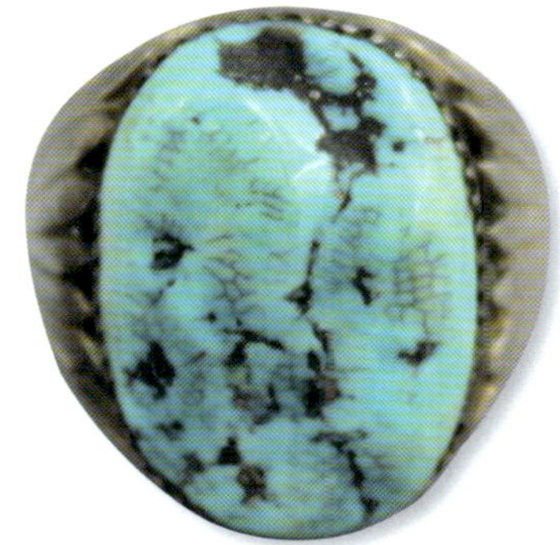

Turquoise ring, nugget work, Robert and Bernice Leekya, monogram consisting of R, B, and L, 1980s–1990s, 0.74" × 2.16", $100–150.

Robert and Bernice Ondelacy Leekya made all the pieces on this and the following page. The turquoise bracelet above consists of eleven turquoise cabochons, twenty plain silver drops, two twisted silver wires, and two stamped silver leaves in both ends.

The watch bracelet in the middle, made in the same style as the previous bracelet, consists of two turquoise cabochons on each side, two plain silver drops, one twisted silver wire, and stamped silver leaves in each tip.

The simple turquoise ring above contains a turquoise cabochon set with a silver bezel, and two stamped silver leaves on both sides.

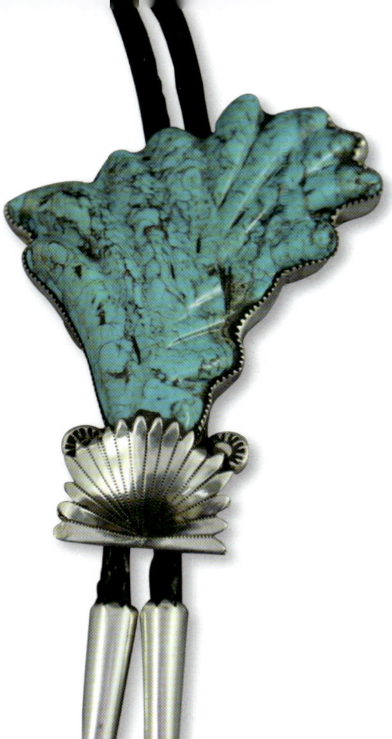

Carved Morenci turquoise bolo, nugget work, Robert and Bernice Leekya, monogram consisting of R, B, and L, 2000s, 2.82" × 3.85", $1,000–1,500.

Turquoise and coral bolo, nugget work, Robert and Bernice Leekya, monogram consisting of R, B, and L, 2000s, 2.77" × 2.40", $1,000–1,500.

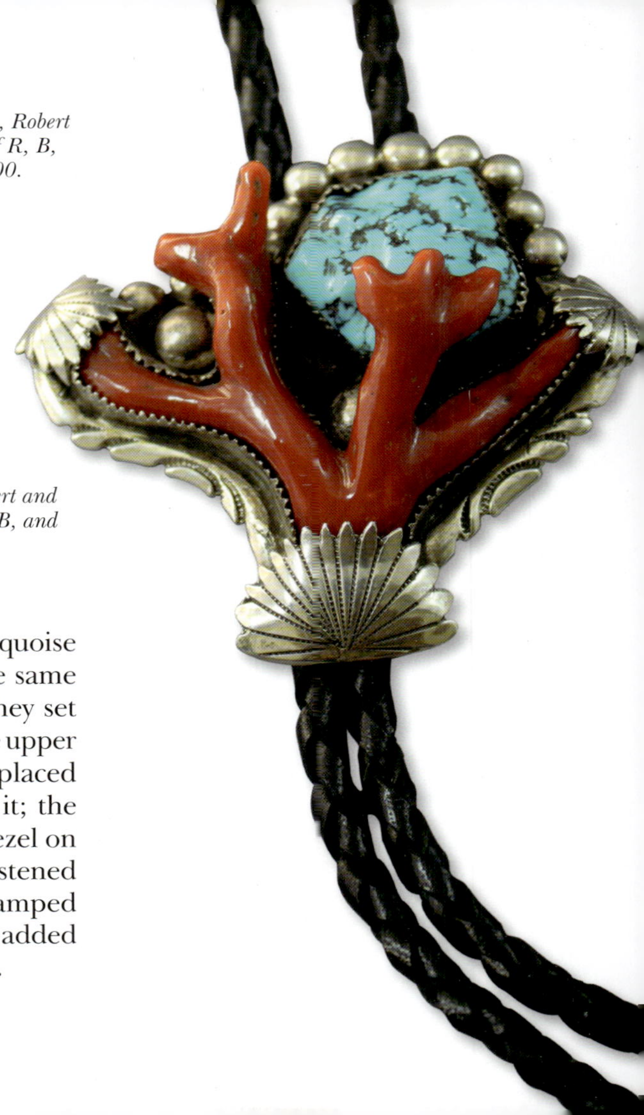

The silver-backed piece above contains a large, naturally shaped turquoise nugget carved in the famous Leekya–leaf style, two stamped silver drops, and a stamped silver leaf made in the Dan Simplicio style.

Robert and Bernice made the turquoise and coral bolo to the right in the same style as the previous example. They set a chunky turquoise cabochon in the upper part of the silver backing, and placed natural red coral branches over it; the former is fastened with a silver bezel on the backing, and the latter are fastened with the same, as well as three stamped silver leaves. For adornment, they added fourteen unstamped silver drops.

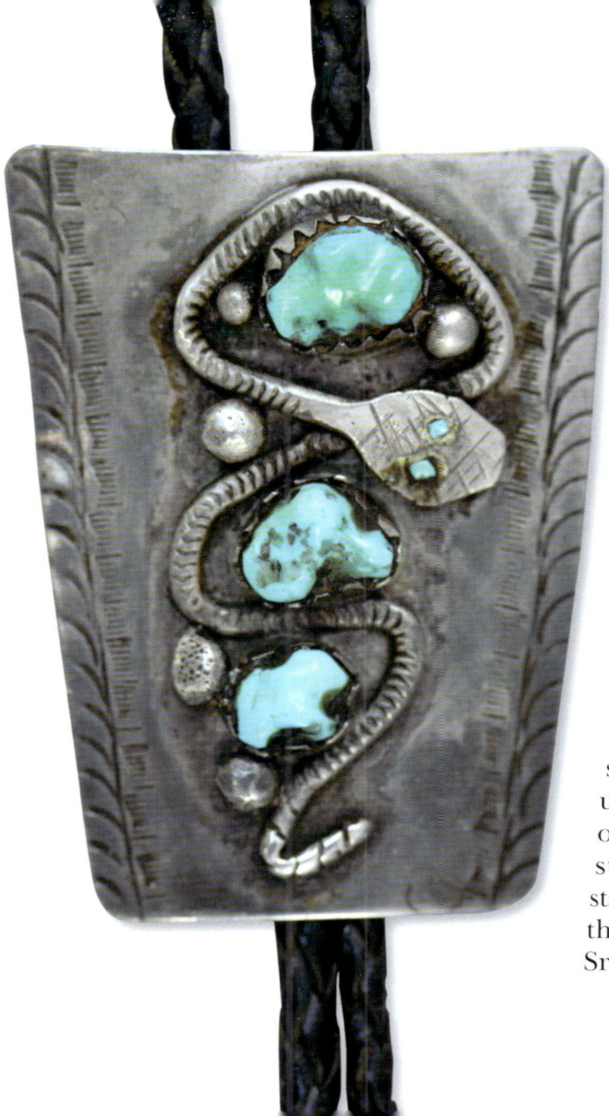

Turquoise bolo, nugget work, Dixon Shebola, no hallmark, 1950s–1960s, 1.90" × 2.48", $300–450

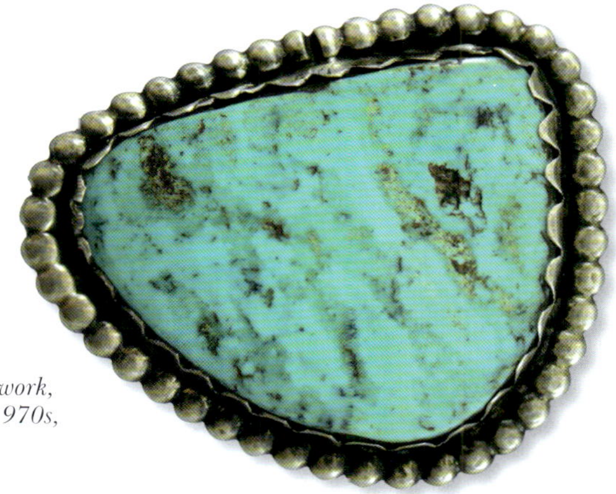

Turquoise scarf slide(?), nugget work, Edward Beyuka, EAB, 1960s–1970s, 1.62" × 1.88", $200–300.

One of Dixon Shebola's brothers confirmed that the turquoise bolo to the left was his. It consists of three turquoise cabochons, one stamped silver snake, and five unstamped silver drops. Both sides of the silver backing are crudely stamped. The snake's body is stamped in a simple fashion, proving that this piece is not Dan Simplicio Sr.'s or his brother Mike's.

The piece above is probably a scarf slide. Small silver drops encircle the oblong turquoise cabochon, which is set with a silver bezel on the backing. This simple design is rarely seen in Edward Beyuka's other pieces.

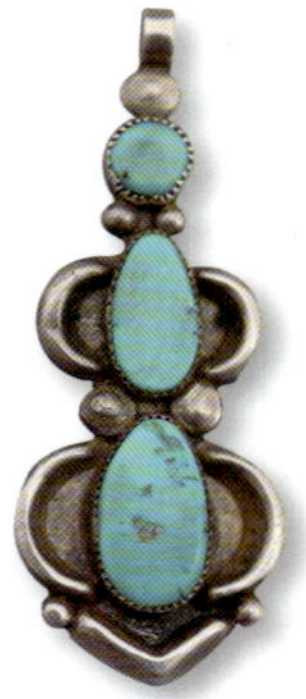

Turquoise pendant, three-stone work, Andy Ondelacy, no hallmark, 1950s–1960s, 0.89" × 2.30", $100–150.

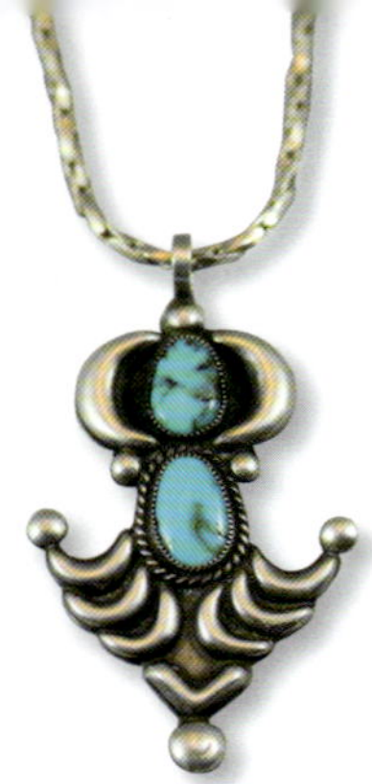

Kingman turquoise pendant, two-stone work, Andy and Fannie Ondelacy, no hallmark, 1950s–1960s, 1.07" × 1.86", $100–150.

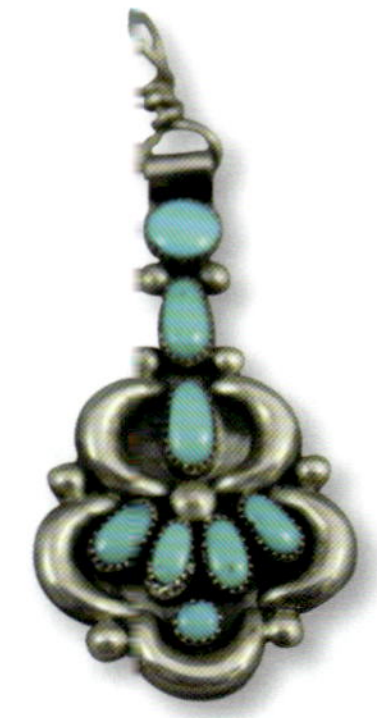

Turquoise pendant, eight-stone work, Julie Ondelacy Lahi, Julie O Lahi, 1970s–1980s, 1.08" × 2.03", $100–150.

This turquoise pendant consists of one snake-eye and two pear-shaped turquoise cabochons, as well as two large and two small embossed crescents, one embossed silver chevron, and seven plain silver drops. I bought it from a close relative of the artist, Andy Ondelacy. This may be the original piece in a group that includes the following two pieces, even though the cabochons in this piece are flatter than the others.

Andy and Fannie Weebothee Ondelacy made this pendant together. It consists of six small and two large embossed crescents, one embossed silver chevron, six plain, unstamped silver drops, and two pear-shaped, high-quality Kingman turquoise cabochons.

The couple's daughter, Julie Ondelacy Lahi, made the piece above in the eight-stone work style. It is similar to, yet distinct from, her parents' pendants. This example consists of six long, pear-shaped and two snake-eye turquoise cabochons, five embossed silver crescents, and nine unstamped silver drops. It is very interesting to see how the parents' original design gets inherited and developed by the next generation.

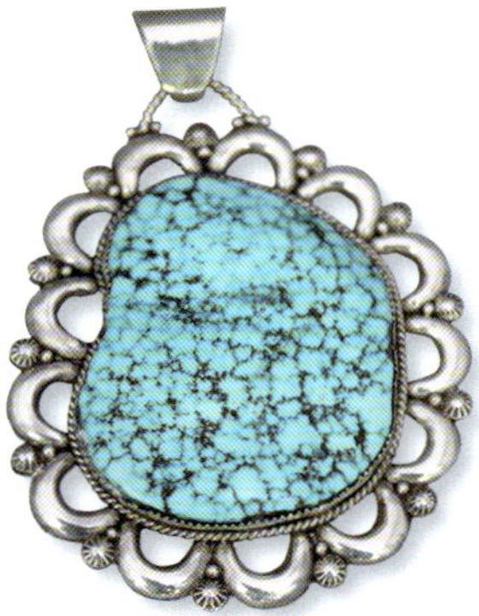

Morenci turquoise pendant, nugget work, Lorraine Waatsa, LW, 2012, 2.89" × 3.71", $800–1,200.

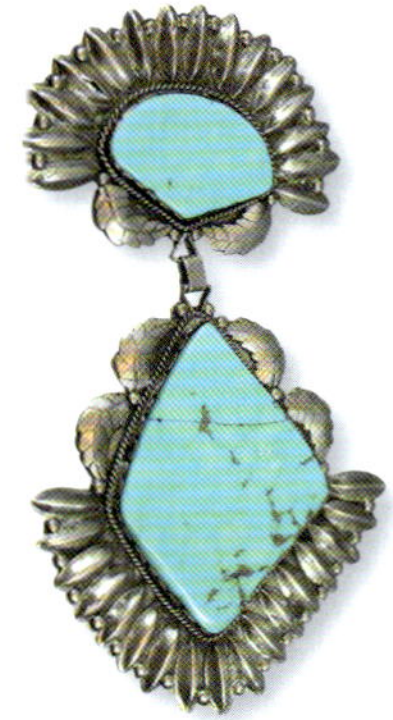

Turquoise pin/pendant, nugget work, Roger and Lela Cellicion, Roger and Lela Cellicion, 1970s–1980s, 4.54" × 8.00", $800–1,200.

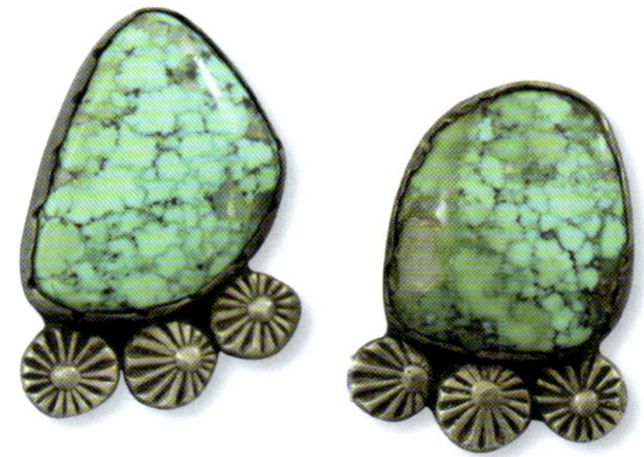

Turquoise earrings, nugget work, artist unknown, CWE, 1960s–1970s, 0.79" × 1.17", $200–300.

Lorraine Waatsa's father, Duane Quam, bought the turquoise for first piece above, which she realized just before I visited her in July 2012. The cabochon itself measures 1.98 inches wide and 2.37 inches long. She offered to set it on silver and sell it to me, and I promptly replied, "Of course."

Roger and Lela Cellicion made the second turquoise pendant, or manta pin. On the back of the top part is a pin and a loop for a chain. The reverse of the lower part has three loops for sewing on a manta. The cabochons are enormous: the upper stone is 2.07 inches wide and 1.29 inches long, and the lower one is 2.62 inches wide and 3.41 inches long.

The lapidary who made the pair of turquoise earrings above is unknown. I do not recognize the hallmark "CWE." Each earring consists of one spider web turquoise cabochon with crystal inclusions and three stamped silver drops. One of my Zuni informants attributed it to Leekya Deyuse, but I have not been able to confirm it.

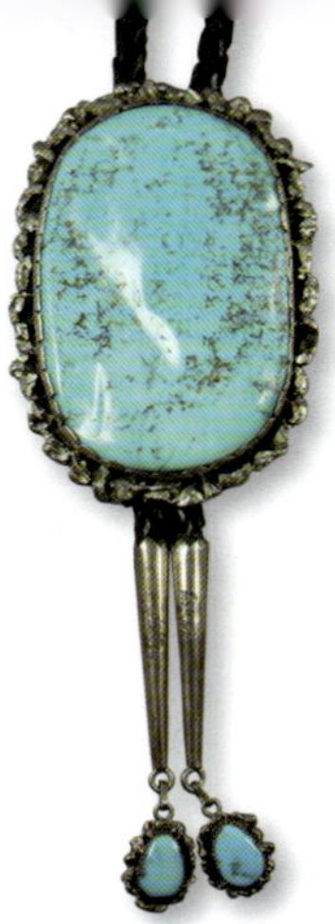

Morenci turquoise bolo, nugget work, Lee and Mary Weebothee, Lee & Mary, 1970s–1980s, 2.24" × 3.33", $1,400–2,100.

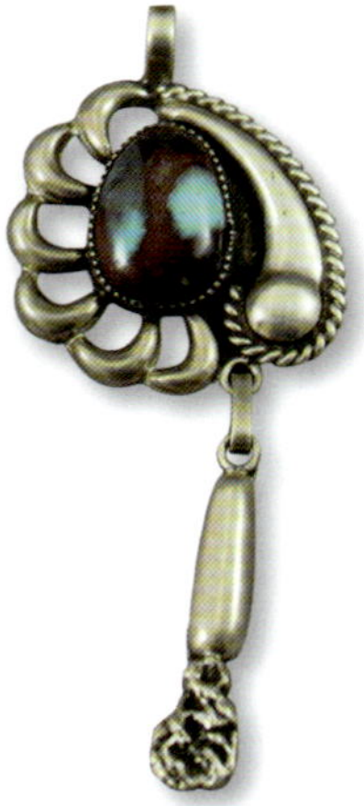

Smokey Bisbee turquoise pendant, nugget work, Lee and Mary Weebothee, Lee & Mary, 1970s–1980s, 1.12" × 2.74", $400–600.

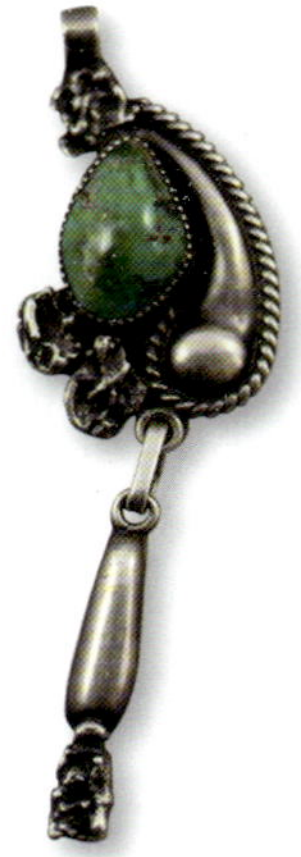

Blue Gem turquoise pendant, nugget work, Lee and Mary Weebothee, Lee & Mary, 1970s–1980s, 0.84" × 2.82", $300–450.

Lee Weebothee's characteristic silver work encircles a huge natural, oval, Morenci turquoise cabochon set in the center of the silver backing in the bolo above. It has matching tips.

This innovatively designed Smokey Bisbee pendant's cabochon is set in the center and encircled by six embossed silver crescents on its left. One comet-shaped, embossed silver part is outlined with a twisted wire on its right side. Set off-center to the right, on the bottom, is one dangling silver attachment, which is frequently seen in the Weebothee's pins/pendants.

Above is a similar Blue Gem turquoise pendant. The only difference is the use of three irregular silver parts—characteristic of Lee's silver work—replacing six embossed silver crescents.

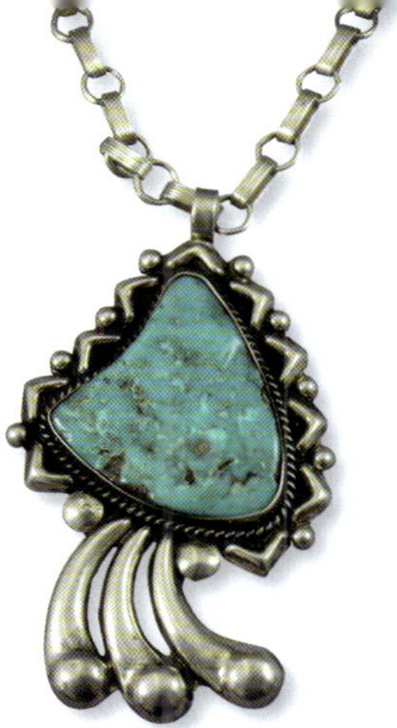

Kingman turquoise pendant, nugget work, Lee and Mary Weebothee, Lee & Mary, 1970s–1980s, 1.64" × 2.77", $400–690.

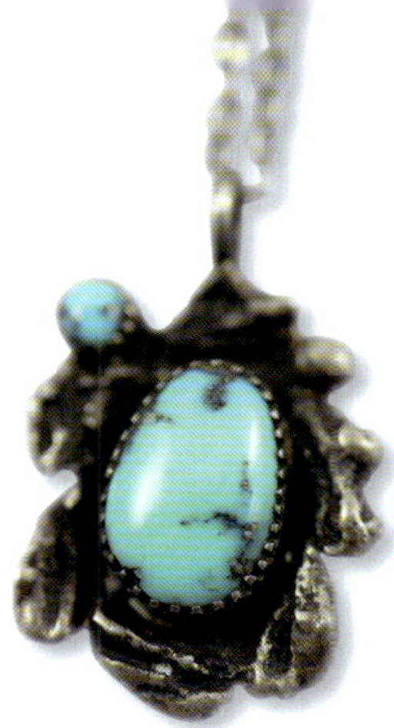

Kingman turquoise pendant, nugget work, Lee and Mary Weebothee, Lee & Mary, 1970s–1980s, 0.58" × 0.91", $100–150.

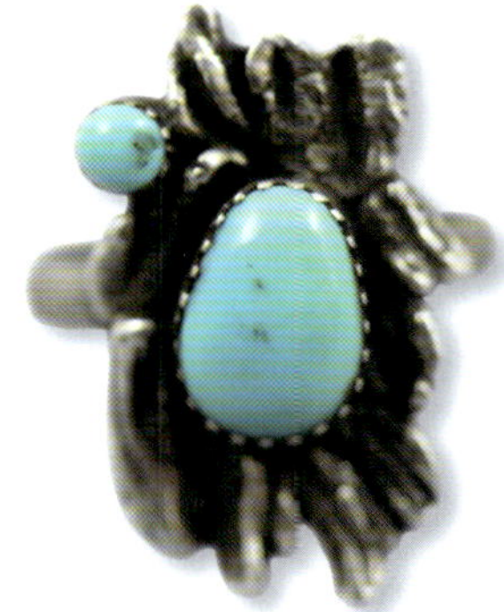

Sleeping Beauty turquoise ring, nugget work, Lee and Mary Weebothee, Lee & Mary, 1970s–1980s, 0.55" × 0.86", $100–150.

The Weebothee pendant above consists of a green turquoise cabochon, eleven embossed, silver chevrons, three comet-shaped silver parts, and two large and ten small unstamped silver drops.

Lee and Mary set a large, pear-shaped, Kingman turquoise cabochon in the center of the second, unique pendant. They set a small, snake-eye, turquoise cabochon in the upper left corner, and Lee's characteristic silver adornments surround the centerpiece.

The conceptual design of the ring, above, is the same as the pendant to its left, although the silver backing is different. Made in the two-stone work style, they look like matching pieces.

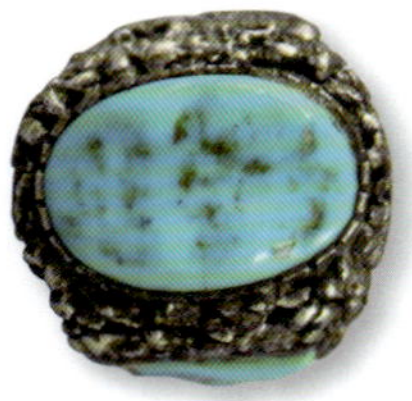

Sleeping Beauty turquoise ring, nugget work, Lee and Mary Weebothee, Lee & Mary, 1970s–1980s, 0.88" × 0.95", $200–300.

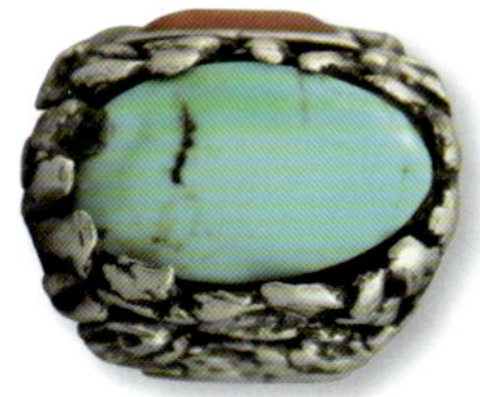

Turquoise and coral ring, nugget work, Lee and Mary Weebothee, Lee & Mary, 1970s–1980s, 0.88" × 0.95", $200–300.

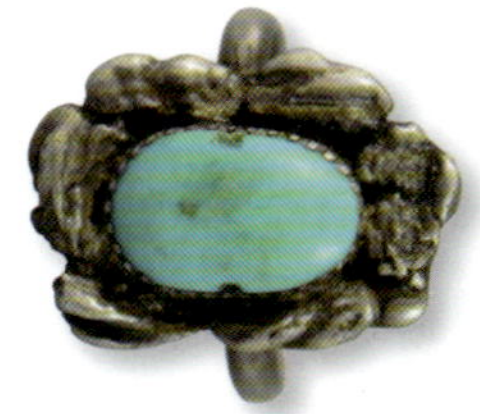

Sleeping Beauty turquoise ring, nugget work, Lee and Mary Weebothee, Lee & Mary, 1970s–1980s, 0.55" × 0.86", $100–150.

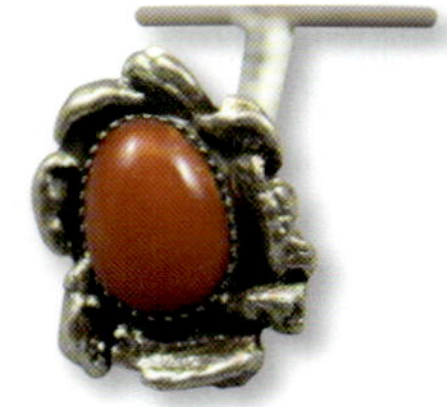

Coral tie tack, nugget work, Lee and Mary Weebothee, Lee & Mary, 1970s–1980s, 0.55" × 0.71", $100–150.

The Weebothees made all four pieces on this page. The first, unique, ring consists of one oval, turquoise cabochon in front, surrounded by Lee's characteristic silver adornment, and a trapezoidal turquoise cabochon on one side.

The concept does not change in the second example. We see an oval turquoise cabochon surrounded by silver work, with coral pieces inlaid in the trapezoidal frame and on one side.

Following is a ring made in the one-stone work style. It looks like an ordinary Weebothee piece because it lacks a turquoise, snake-eye cabochon.

The last piece is a one-stone coral tie tack. The Weebothees set a pear-shaped coral cabochon in the center and surrounded it with silver. The design may seem common but, nonetheless, it is undeniably beautiful.

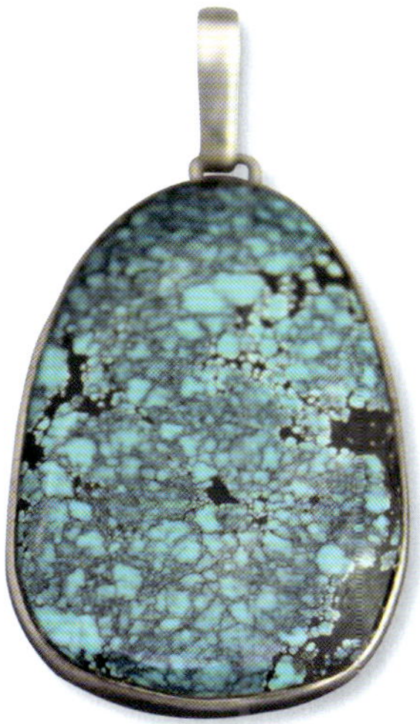

Turquoise pendant, nugget work, Roger Tsabetsaye Sr., R. Tsabetsaye with his Knifewing shield, 1980s–1990s, 1.18" × 1.90", $300–450.

The simple, yet elegant, pendant above contains a natural, Chinese spider web, turquoise cabochon.

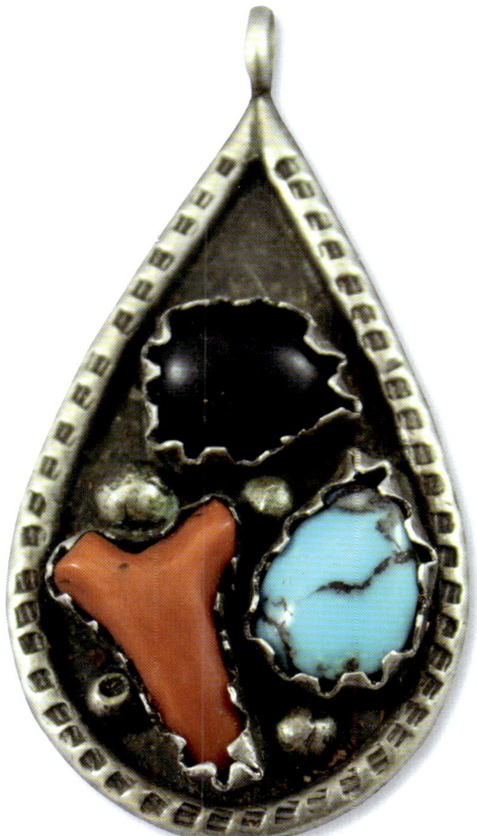

Turquoise and coral pendant, nugget work, artist unidentified, E. Tsabetsaye, 1970s–1990s, 1.13" × 2.15", $100–150.

The pendant to the left consists of turquoise, coral, and jet colored cabochons and four unstamped silver drops set on a silver, teardrop backing with a raised, stamped edge. One of my informants told me it might be Edward Tsabetsaye's work, and it is indeed signed "E. Tsabetsaye," but Roger Tsabetsaye Sr. said he was unaware of anyone named Edward in his family. It was similar, Roger believed, to a design by Griffin and Evangeline Tsabetsaye, but they signed their work "Vangie Tsabetsaye," "GV," or "GTV."

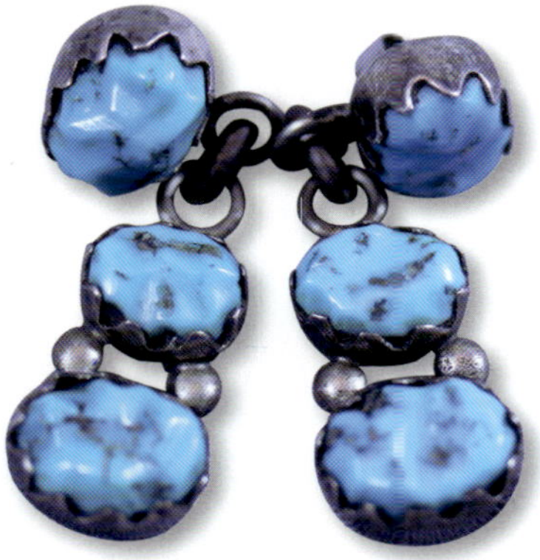

Turquoise earrings, nugget work, Alvina Quam, A. Q., 1970s–1980s, 0.43" × 1.59", $100–150.

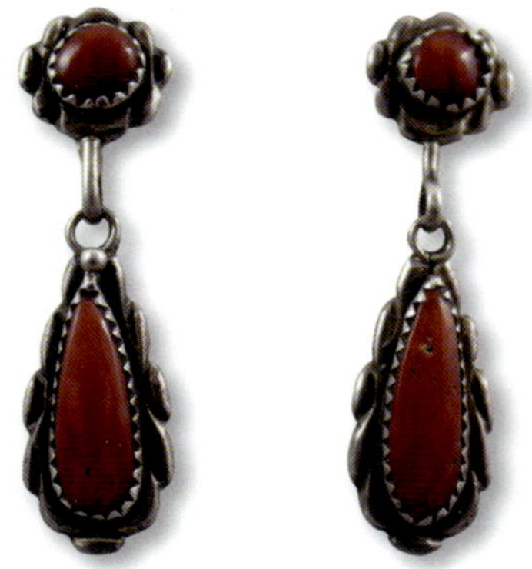

Coral earrings, nugget work, Alvina Quam, Alvina Q., 1980s–1990s, 0.43" × 1.53", $100–150.

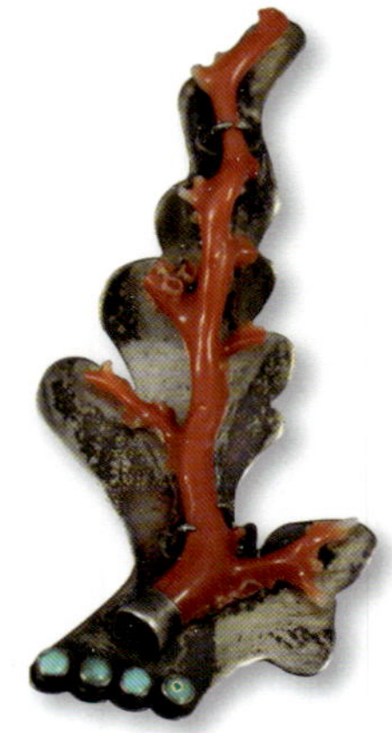

Turquoise and coral pin, nugget work, Paul Peyketewa Sr.(?), no hallmark, late 1950s, 1.63" × 3.46", $500–750.

The turquoise earrings above have the same "A. Q." hallmark Alvina Quam's mother, Alice, used. Each earring has three deep blue turquoise cabochons with two unstamped silver drops.

Alvina gave the coral earrings, above, to her aunt Thelma Sheche, and Thelma then presented them to my wife as a souvenir.

A large, natural coral branch is set in the center of this piece above, a coral and turquoise pin, and four turquoise, snake-eye cabochons are set underneath. My main Zuni informant attributed it to Paul Peyketewa Sr. I believe he's correct, but one Zuni artist I know says it's Smokey Gchachu's work.

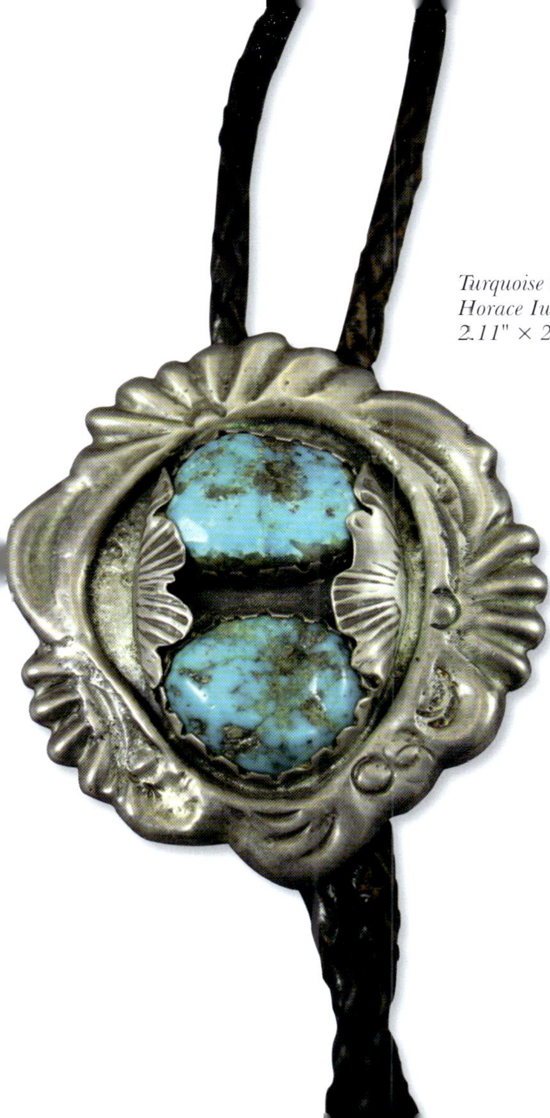

Turquoise bolo, cast and nugget work, Horace Iule, H. Iule, 1950s–1960s, 2.11" × 2.24", $300–450.

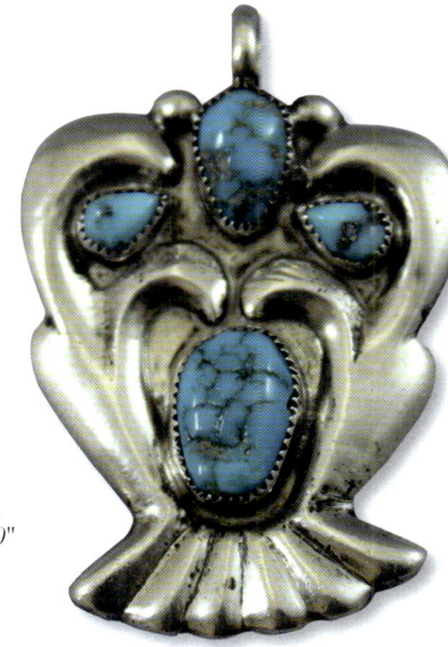

Turquoise pendant, cast and nugget work, Horace Iule, H. Iule, 1960s–1970s, 1.30" × 1.90", $200–300.

The bolo to the left consists of two green turquoise cabochons set in a cast silver frame with saw-tooth bezels, which looks like a stamped flower head cut in half. Two stamped silver leaves curve in and partly cover the stones.

A uniquely designed cast silver backing adorns the pendant above, which consists of four deep blue turquoise cabochons and two unstamped silver drops.

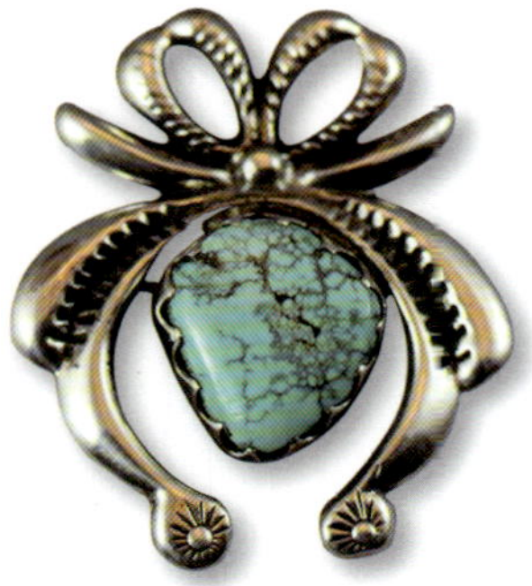

Turquoise pin/pendant, cast and nugget work, Horace Iule, H. Iule, 1960s–1970s, 1.83" × 2.17", $300–450.

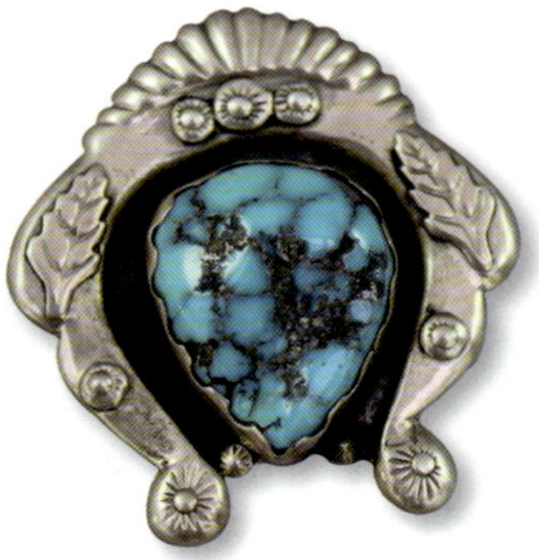

Turquoise pin probably converted from bolo, cast and nugget work, Horace Iule, H. Iule, 1960s–1970s, 1.88" × 2.01", $300–450.

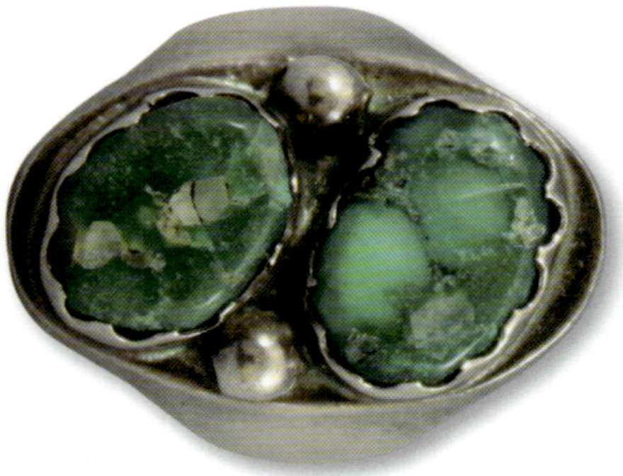

Turquoise ring, cast and nugget work, Horace Iule, H. Iule, 1960s–1970s, 0.67" × 1.07", $100–150.

This turquoise pin/pendant's silver backing, which looks a combination of a naja and a ribbon, is cast and stamped first, and the reverse of the turquoise is welded to it. A turquoise cabochon is then set.

Horace first cast and stamped the naja-shaped silver part of the Kingman turquoise pin above. Then, he welded a silver platelet over its center, set a chunky deep blue turquoise cabochon with a saw-tooth bezel, and added five small, stamped silver drops and two silver leaves on the naja. Finally, he put two much smaller stamped silver drops just below the turquoise cabochon.

This simply designed turquoise ring consists of two deep blue-green turquoise cabochons and two unstamped silver drops.

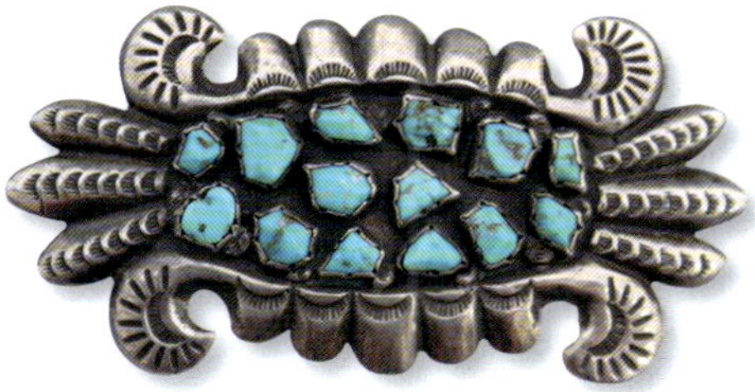

Blue Gem turquoise buckle, cast and nugget work, Horace Iule, no hallmark, around 1950, 1.76" × 3.49", $1,000–1,500.

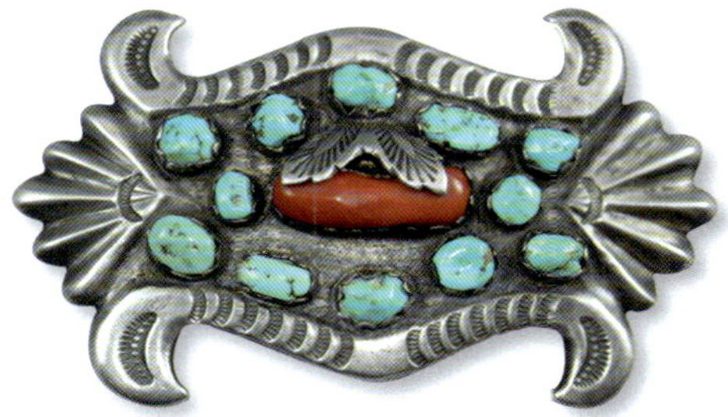

Turquoise and coral buckle, cast and nugget work, Horace Iule, no hallmark, around 1950, 2.18" × 3.73", $1,200–1,800.

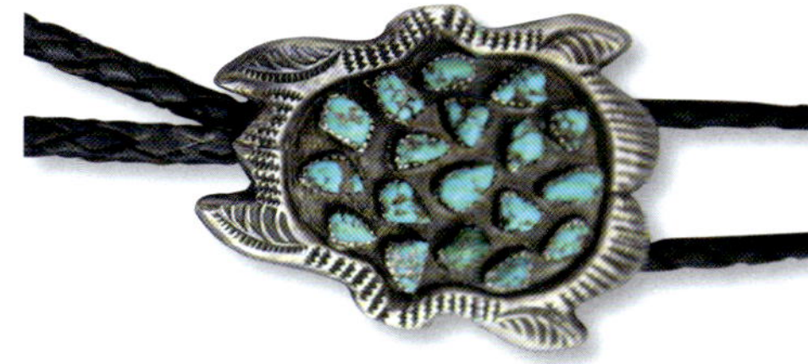

Blue Gem turquoise bolo, cast and nugget work, Horace Iule, no hallmark, mid-1950s, 1.92" × 2.55", $300–450.

The silver backing on the buckle above, including its center, is cast and stamped. Fourteen small Blue Gem turquoise cabochons are set with twelve stamped silver drops between them. This buckle was not attributed to any artist by its seller, but I noticed the stone setting was similar to George and Lupe Leekity's works. Lupe, Horace Iule's daughter, confirmed her father made it around 1950.

Horace also made the red coral buckle above, center. The complete silver backing, including its center, is first cast and stamped. A coral twig is then set in the center using a silver bezel, and then it is covered partly with a double-stamped silver leaf adornment. Afterwards, twelve small Blue Gem turquoise cabochons are set around the coral twig. Again, Lupe confirmed it was Horace's work and that he probably made it in 1950. The approximate ages of this and the previous piece are based on the handmade silver wire clasps on their backs.

Horace stamped the silver frame on the third bolo with two types of die casts, and welded on a silver plate from the back. He then welded eighteen silver bezels all over the center, and set turquoise cabochons. This kind of setting is similar to the two buckles. At first, I was not certain whether it was his or his son-in-law George's, but Lupe confirmed it was her father's.

CHAPTER III

WORKS WITH MANY STONES

1. Cluster-work style

The Zuni lapidary cluster-work style is characterized by pear-shaped turquoise or coral cabochons set in the flower-head pattern. The most famous and prolific lapidary is Doris Ondelacy, who worked with her husband, Warren Ondelacy. For this chapter, however, I will start with the work of the great Leekya Deyuse, since I had a unique opportunity to take photos of his bracelet with his direct descendants' permission.

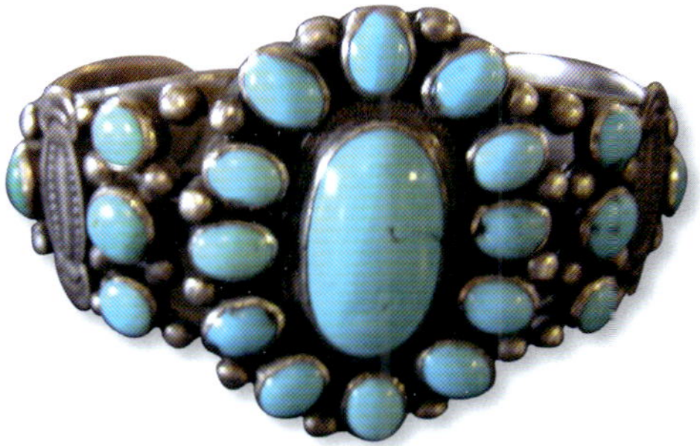

Turquoise bracelet, Cluster work, Leekya Deyuse, no hallmark, 1940s, 2.18" × 3.73", $12,000–18,000. Courtesy of the extended Leekya family.

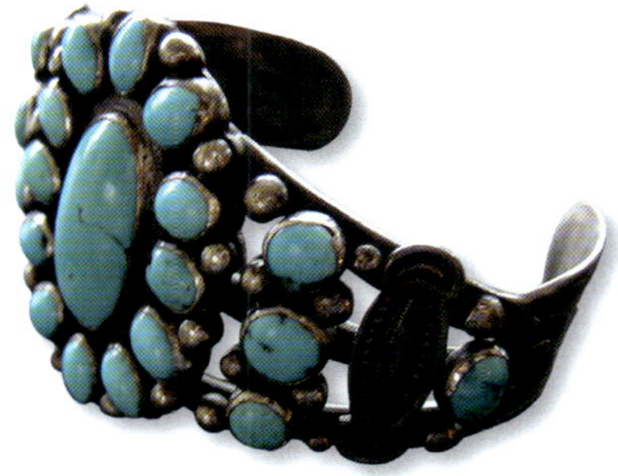

Side view of the Leekya bracelet.

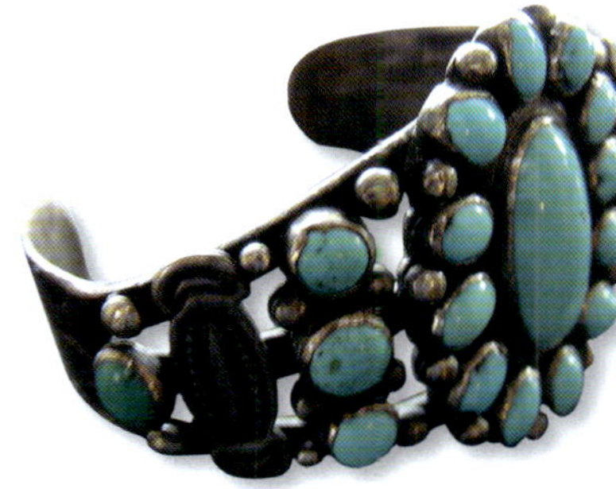

Side view of the Leekya bracelet.

Leekya Deyuse's daughter once owned this bracelet, but gave it to her daughter, who later gave it to her own niece. The present owner, Old Man Leekya's great granddaughter, brought it back to Zuni for the last night dance in 2013 and allowed me to photograph it. As for the production date, a Zuni artist friend of mine estimated that, based on the bezels and the stamped silver adornments on both sides of the central panel, it was made between the 1950s and the early 1960s. A high-domed turquoise cabochon is set in the center and surrounded by twelve smaller turquoise cabochons. Among these are twelve unstamped silver drops on both sides of the central medallion. Three turquoise cabochons flank a stamped silver platelet, followed by a turquoise cabochon with two unstamped silver drops.

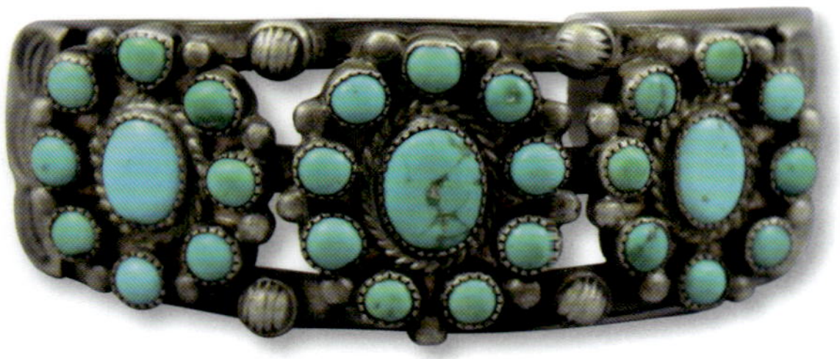

Turquoise bracelet, cluster work, Leekya Deyuse, no hallmark, 1940s, 0.88" × 0.94" central medallion, $10,000–15,000.

Lone Mountain turquoise Olla Maiden necklace, cluster work, Doris and Warren Ondelacy, D. & W., 1960s, 4.16" × 5.47" naja, $16,000–24,000.

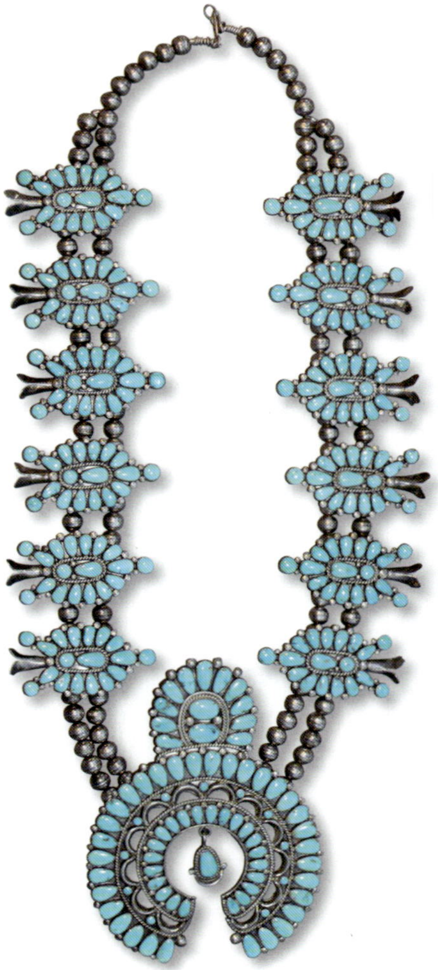

According to his granddaughter, Leekya Deyuse made the turquoise bracelet above. Three equally sized clusters are on the cuff, one oval turquoise cabochon is set in the center of each cluster, and the center stone is surrounded by nine snake-eye turquoise cabochons and nine unstamped silver drops. Two stamped silver drops are set between clusters. On both ends of all three clusters is one stamped silver platelet.

This Olla Maiden squash blossom necklace with Lone Mountain turquoise contains a 5.47-inch tall naja. While that is relatively large, it is not the Ondelacy's biggest; Tanner's Indian Arts in Gallup owns a much bigger squash blossom necklace by Doris and Warren in this same design. My necklace has six squash blossoms, with eighteen turquoise cabochons each, on both sides. The naja consists of sixty-five turquoise cabochons, excluding the olla on top, which is made up of two horizontally set turquoise cabochons, with eleven cabochons surrounding them. As this part resembles a pot on the head of a Zuni lady, it may accurately be called an olla necklace.

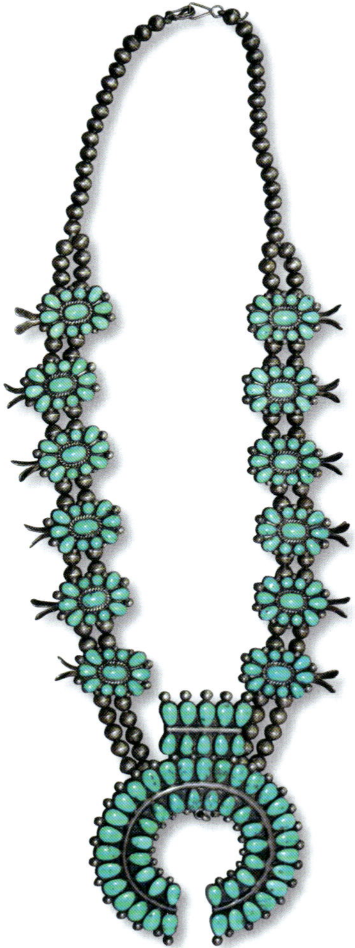

Lone Mountain turquoise squash blossom necklace, cluster work, Doris and Warren Ondelacy, no hallmark, 1940s–1950s, 3.52" × 4.30" naja, $10,000–15,000.

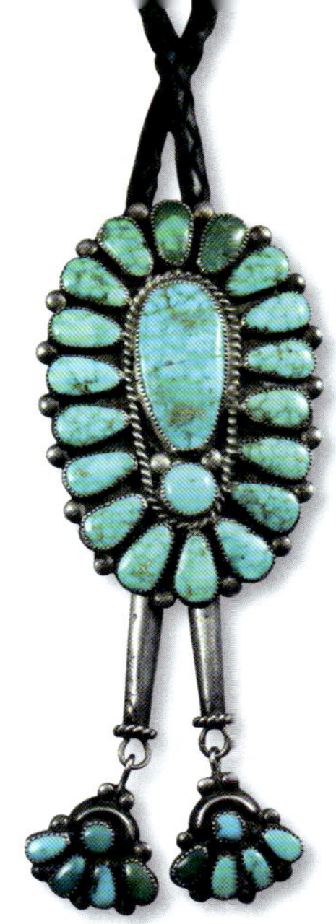

Lone Mountain turquoise bolo, cluster work, Doris and Warren Ondelacy, D & W in cursive, 1960s, 1.84 × 2.71", $1,000–1,500.

The necklace at left is not as large as the previous one, but its naja still measures 4.30 inches tall. The circular naja consists of forty-seven turquoise cabochons, plus two dangling, single-turquoise cabochons and ten cabochons over the circular naja. Each of the six squash blossoms on each side contains eleven turquoise cabochons.

The slide in the bolo above is made in the two-fold arrangement: a pear-shaped cabochon and a round turquoise cabochon are set in the center, and two unstamped silver drops are placed between them. The center stones are encircled by a twisted wire and eighteen turquoise cabochons. This bolo's turquoise tips are identical to the Ondelacys' earrings (p. 70).

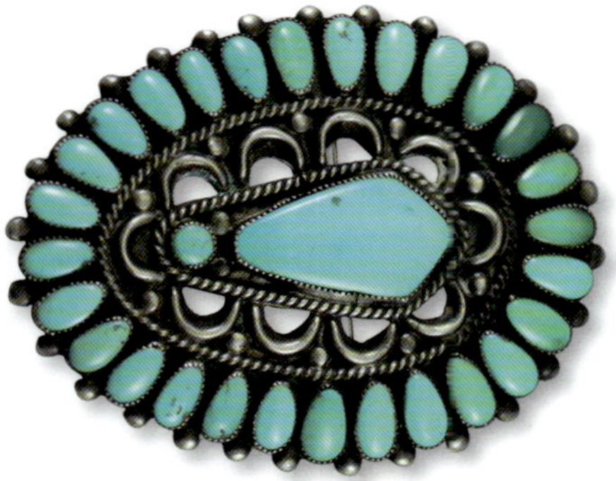

Lone Mountain turquoise pin converted from bolo, cluster work, Doris and Warren Ondelacy, D. & W., 1960s, 2.51" × 3.14", $2,000–3,000.

This pin, converted from a bolo, is made in the three-fold arrangement. Like the bolo slide, a large, unformed cabochon, a small, round cabochon, and two miniscule, unstamped silver drops are encircled by a twisted silver wire in the center. The second band consists of ten embossed silver crescents and ten unstamped silver drops, which are surrounded by a twisted silver wire. This second band is further encircled by twenty-eight turquoise cabochons and unstamped silver drops.

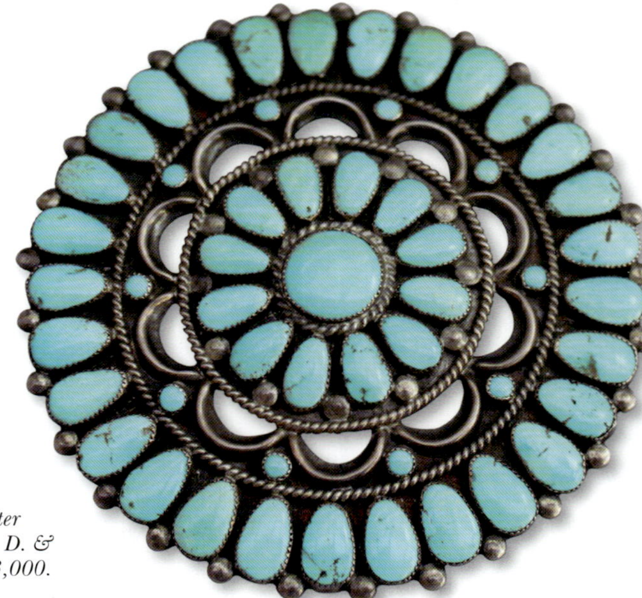

Lone Mountain turquoise pin, cluster work, Doris and Warren Ondelacy, D. & W., 1960s, 3.50" across, $2,000–3,000.

The pin above is made in the four-fold arrangement. Its center consists of one large, round cabochon and a twisted silver wire. This area is encircled by twelve pear-shaped turquoise cabochons and twelve unstamped silver drops that are encircled by a silver wire. The third circle consists of ten embossed silver crescents and ten small snake-eye cabochons contained in a twisted silver wire. Surrounding this band are twenty-nine pear-shaped turquoise cabochons and twenty-nine unstamped silver drops.

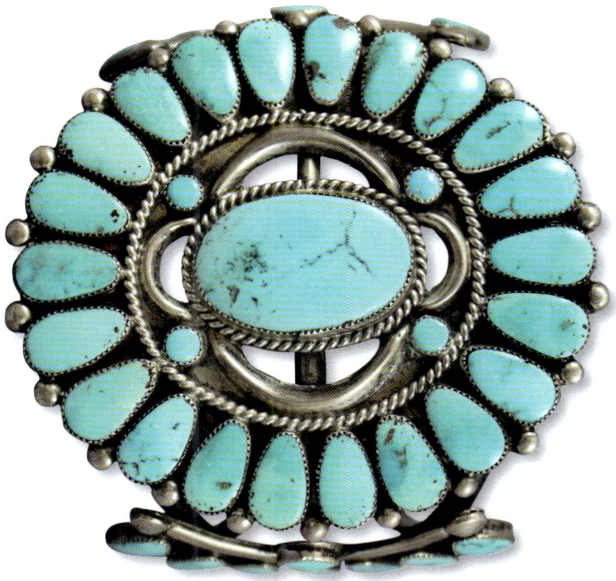

Lone Mountain turquoise bracelet, cluster work, Doris and Warren Ondelacy, D. & W., 1960s, 2.75" × 3.03" central medallion, $2,000–3,000.

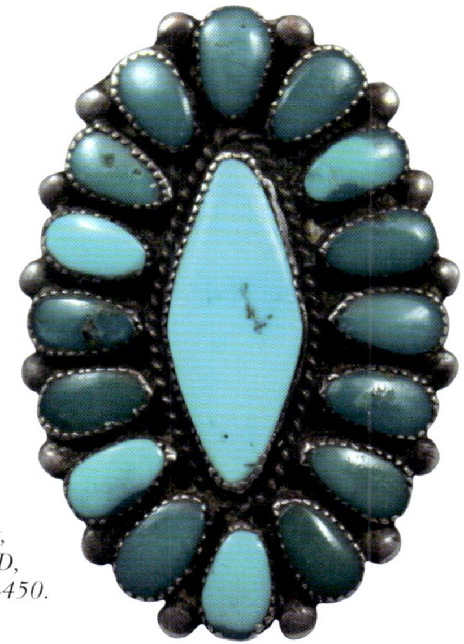

Lone Mountain turquoise ring, cluster work, Doris Ondelacy, D, 1970s, 1.25" × 1.83", $300–450.

In the same decade, Doris and Warren made this three-fold, Lone Mountain turquoise bracelet. A twisted silver wire encircles one large turquoise cabochon set in the center (band 1); then, two large and two small embossed silver crescents, four tiny snake-eye turquoise cabochons, and a twisted silver wire (band 2) surround band 1; twenty-two pear-shaped turquoise cabochons and twenty-two unstamped silver drops constitute band 3. On both sides of the central medallion, are two side panels, each consisting of one round and seven pear-shaped turquoise cabochons, eight unstamped silver drops, and a thick, V-shaped silver wire.

Doris made the two-fold ring above after Warren passed away. A twisted silver wire encircles a lozenge-shaped cabochon, while sixteen pear-shaped turquoise cabochons and sixteen unstamped silver drops surround the center.

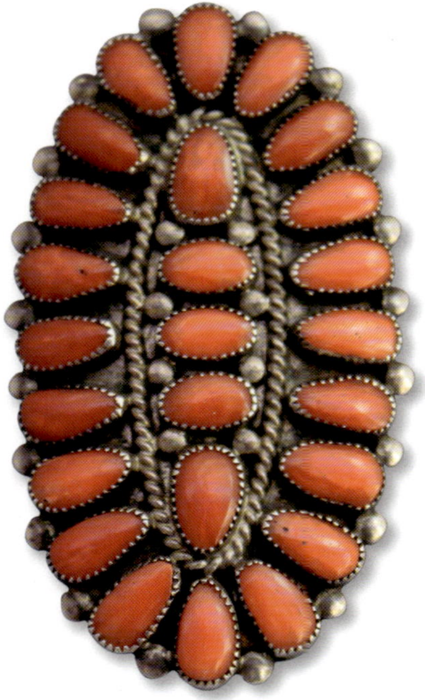

Coral ring, cluster work, Doris Ondelacy, D, 1970s, 1.50" × 2.60", $500–750.

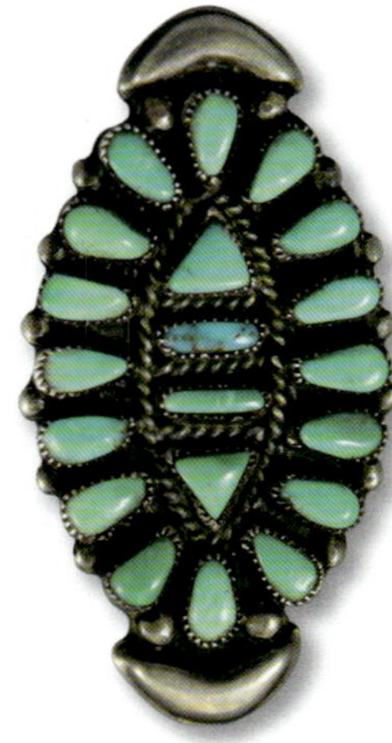

Lone Mountain turquoise ring, cluster work, Doris and Warren Ondelacy, no hallmark, 1950s–1960s, 0.92" × 1.78", $200–300.

Unusual in design, this two-fold coral ring consists of three oblong coral cabochons set horizontally in the center and one pear-shaped cabochon set vertically above and under each. Each cabochon is separated with two unstamped silver drops, and the center section is encircled by a twisted silver wire (band 1). This band is surrounded by twenty pear-shaped coral cabochons and unstamped silver drops (band 2).

Although this two-fold ring has no hallmark, Doris and Warren Ondelacy's granddaughter has attributed it to her grandparents. Two small rectangular and two triangular cabochons are set horizontally in the center. Each cabochon is then encircled by twisted silver wires (band 1). The center is surrounded by sixteen turquoise cabochons and sixteen unstamped silver drops. Finally, an embossed crescent is set over and under the complete cluster (band 2).

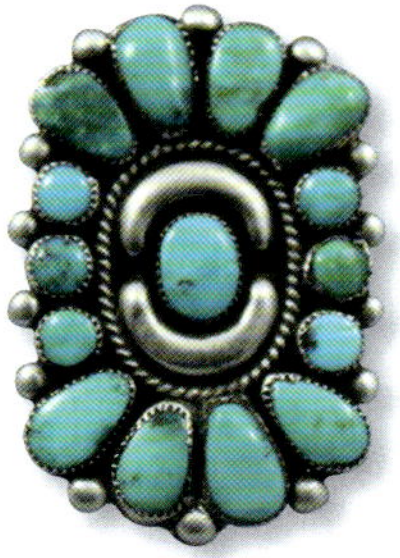

Lone Mountain turquoise ring (four cracked cabochons were replaced by Lorrain Waatsa), cluster work, Doris and Warren Ondelacy, no hallmark, 1940s, 1.01" × 1.49", $80–120.

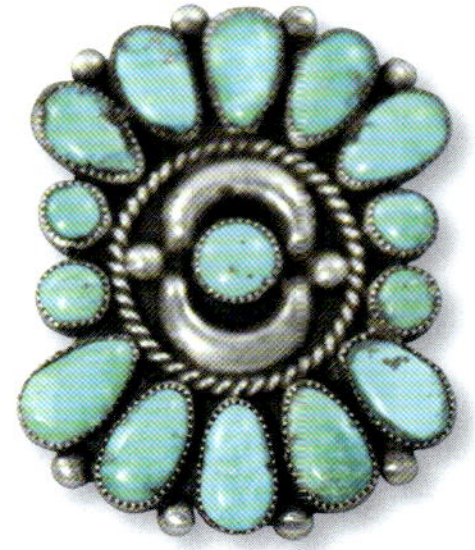

Lone Mountain turquoise ring (one cracked cabochon was replaced by Lorrain Waatsa), cluster work, Doris and Warren Ondelacy, no hallmark, 1940s, 1.16" × 1.53", $100–150.

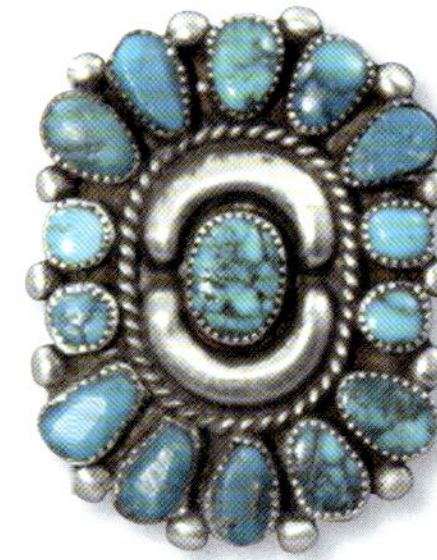

Lone Mountain turquoise ring (some cracked cabochons were replaced by Lorrain Waatsa), cluster work, Doris and Warren Ondelacy, no hallmark, 1940s, 0.94" × 1.22", $60–90.

The three rings on this page, all probably made in the 1940s, have required repair work due to damaged cabochons. Doris and Warren Ondelacy's granddaughter, who replaced the damaged turquoise cabochons with those of the matching colors in each ring, confirmed the attribution. The first is made in the two-fold arrangement. Embossed silver crescents are set over and under an oblong center cabochon and then encircled by a twisted silver wire. The center band is surrounded by two sets of four pear-shaped cabochons, two sets of three snake-eye cabochons, and fourteen unstamped silver drops separate these fourteen total cabochons.

In the next ring, a twisted silver wire encircles silver crescents, which are set over and under a snake-eye cabochon, and unstamped silver drops are added to both sides of the crescents. The center is surrounded by two sets of five pear-shaped cabochons, two sets of unstamped silver drops, and two sets of two snake-eye cabochons.

The central band of the third ring is shaped exactly like the first. Two sets of five pear-shaped cabochons are set over and under the center, two sets of two snake-eye cabochons are set on both sides, and fourteen unstamped silver drops are set between these cabochons.

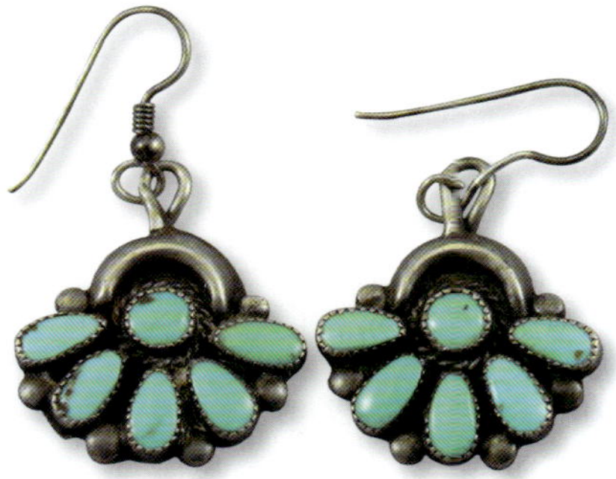

Turquoise earrings, cluster work, Doris and Warren Ondelacy, no hallmark, 1950s–1960s, 0.99 × 1.14" $300–450.

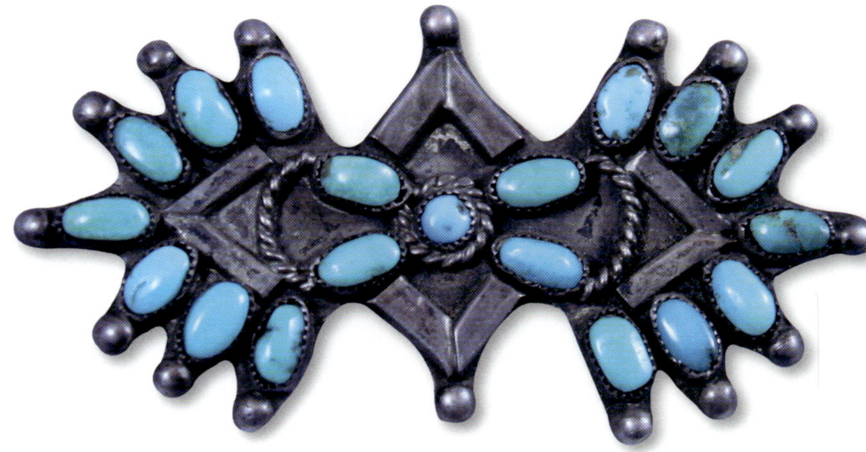

Lone Mountain turquoise pin, cluster work, Warren Ondelacy, no hallmark, 1940–1943, 2.11" × 1.09", $200–300.

The beautiful and well-made earrings above are almost identical to the Ondelacys' bolo tips described on page 65. A snake-eye cabochon is set in the center with a twisted silver wire, which is surrounded by an embossed silver crescent on the top and five pear-shaped cabochons and six unstamped silver drops in the lower section.

The turquoise pin above is unique in design. Based on the handmade silver chevrons, Warren Ondelacy's granddaughter estimates that he made it in the early 1940s. One snake-eye cabochon encircled by a twisted silver wire is set in the center, and two sets of pear-shaped cabochons with twisted wires are set on both sides of the center. These five cabochons and wires are surrounded by four silver chevrons.

On both sides of this medallion, two sets of seven pear-shaped cabochons are set, and sixteen unstamped silver drops are added on the tops of each outer cabochon and free silver chevron.

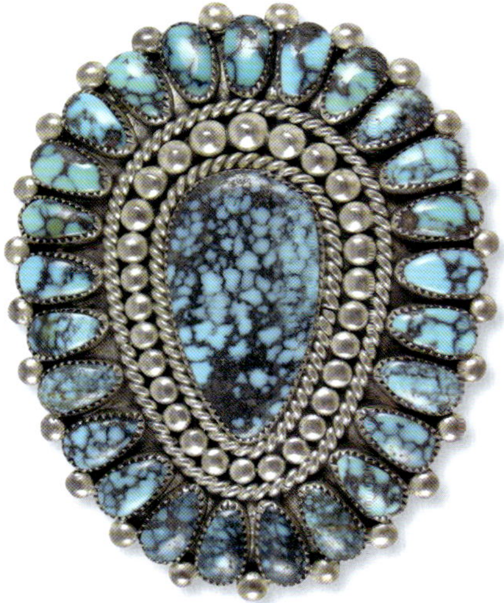

Lone Mountain spider web turquoise pin, cluster work, Alice Quam, A. Q., 1960s–1970s, 2.00" × 2.50, $3,600–5,400. Courtesy of Gloria Dollar Collection.

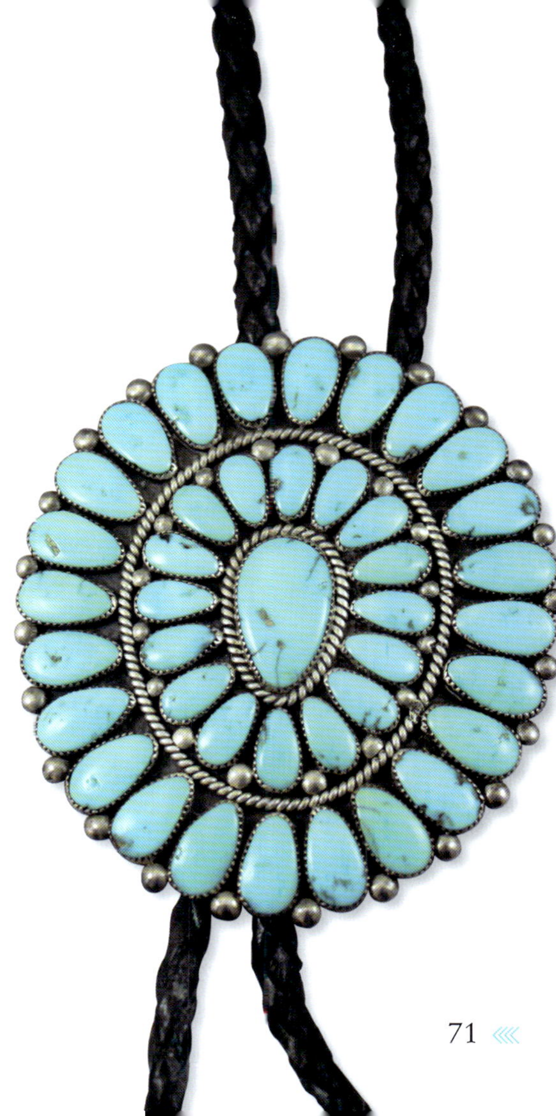

Sleeping Beauty turquoise bolo, cluster work, Alice and Duane Quam, A. Q., 1980s–1990s, 2.66" × 2.99", $1,000–1,500.

Alice and Duane Quam made this medium-size, Lone Mountain, spider web turquoise pin in the three-fold arrangement. An unusual design, the center consists of a large, pear-shaped cabochon encircled by a twisted wire (band 1).This band is surrounded by twenty-one silver beads and a twisted silver wire (band 2). The last band consists of twenty-five pear-shaped turquoise cabochons and twenty-five unstamped silver drops.

At this Sleeping Beauty bolo's center is a pear-shaped stone and a twisted silver wire (band 1) surrounded by sixteen pear-shaped turquoise cabochons, sixteen smaller, unstamped silver drops, and another wire (band 2). The outer band consists of twenty-four turquoise cabochons and twenty-four smaller, unstamped silver drops (band 3).

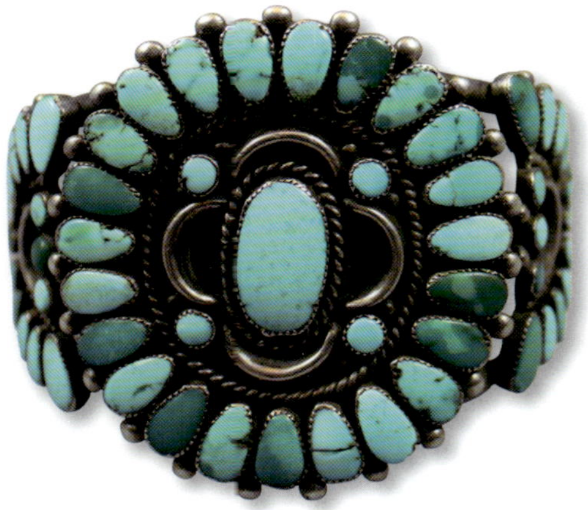

Lone Mountain turquoise bracelet, cluster work, Alice and Duane Quam, no hallmark, 1940s–1960s, 2.18" × 2.31" central medallion, $1,600–2,400.

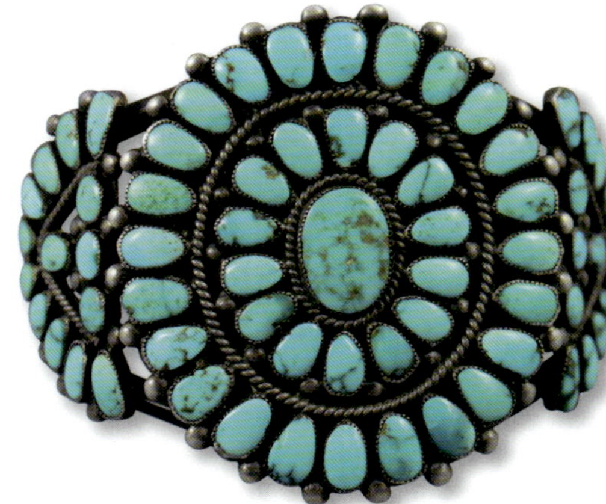

Turquoise bracelet, cluster work, Alice and Duane Quam, no hallmark, 1960s, 2.26" × 2.46" central medallion, $400–600.

The central medallion in the bracelet by Alice and Duane Quam above is an oblong stone encircled by a twisted silver wire (band 1). Four embossed silver crescents surround the center, as well as four snake-eye turquoise cabochons, eight unstamped silver drops, and a twisted silver wire (band 2). The last band consists of twenty-three pear-shaped turquoise cabochons and twenty-three unstamped silver drops. On Doris's work, the inside parts of the crescents are cut out, but on Alice's pieces they are not.

Next is a Kingman turquoise bracelet, also by Alice and Duane. The central medallion is made in the simple three-fold arrangement, and its oblong turquoise cabochon is bigger and crudely cut, but the pear-shaped cabochons in the second and third bands look like Zuni work.

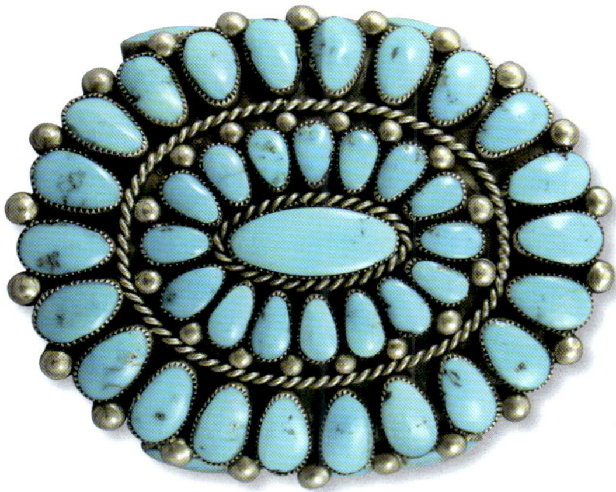

Sleeping Beauty turquoise bracelet, cluster work, Alice and Duane Quam, A. Q., 2001, 2.76" × 3.35" central medallion, $2,000–3,000.

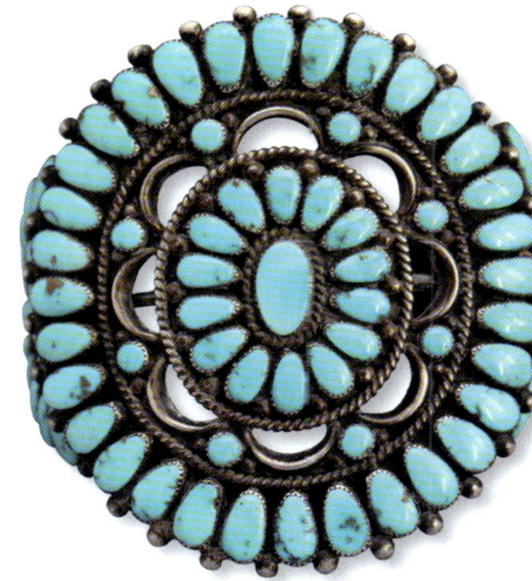

Sleeping Beauty turquoise bracelet, cluster work, Alice and Duane Quam, A. Q., 1970s, 2.76" × 3.35" central medallion, $2,000–3,000.

When I visited Alice Quam's home on December 29, 2001, I first met her husband, Duane, at his silver-work hatch. I asked him if he had some jewelry to sell. He said I had better ask his wife, Alice. She provided me with this gorgeous turquoise bracelet with a central medallion that measures 2.76 inches wide and 3.35 inches long. Its construction is almost the same as the bolo described on page 71. The only difference is that this piece's central stone is oblong instead of pear-shaped.

The center of Alice and Duane's large bracelet above contains a medallion made in the four-fold arrangement and an oblong turquoise cabochon encircled by a twisted silver wire. The second band consists of fourteen pear-shaped turquoise cabochons, fourteen unstamped silver drops, and a twisted silver wire. The third band consists of eight embossed silver crescents—inside of which eight snake-eye turquoise cabochons are cut out—sixteen unstamped silver drops, and a twisted silver wire. The fourth and final band consists of thirty-two pear-shaped turquoise cabochons and thirty-two unstamped silver drops.

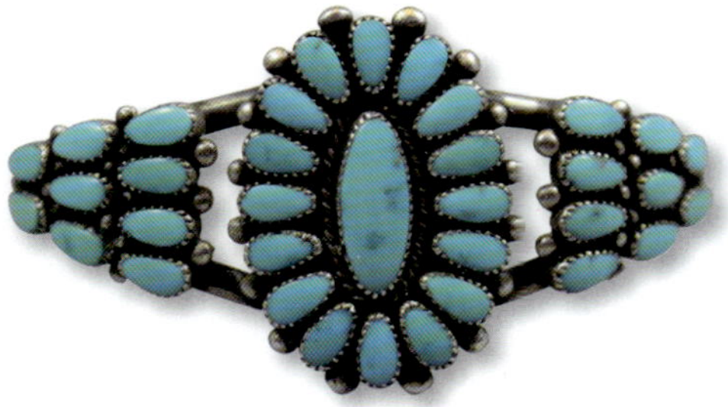

Sleeping Beauty turquoise bracelet, cluster work, Alice and Duane Quam, A. Q., 1980s–1990s, 0.96" × 1.39" central medallion, $300–450.

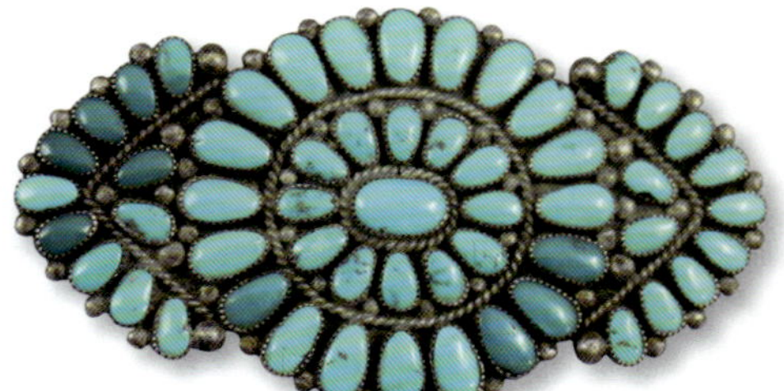

Lone Mountain turquoise manta pin, cluster work, Alice and Duane Quam, no hallmark, 1960s, 3.66" × 2.05", $1,000–1,500.

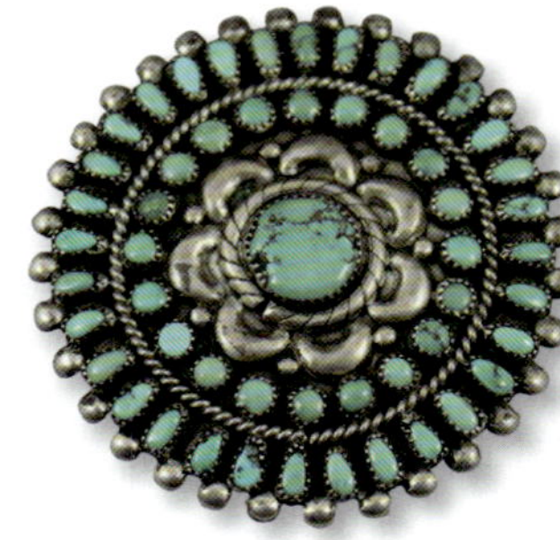

Fox turquoise pin, cluster work, Alice and Duane Quam, no hallmark, 1960s, 1.90 in diameter, $400–600.

The Quams' small turquoise bracelet above, made in the two-fold arrangement, contains an oblong center stone encircled by a twisted silver wire, which is surrounded by sixteen pear-shaped turquoise cabochons and sixteen unstamped silver drops. Each side medallion features nine cabochons set in quadruple, triple, and double formation down to the cuff end.

The central and side medallions in this manta pin are combined in this design, also seen in their buckle.

Although this small 1960s Fox turquoise pin is not hallmarked, Alice and Duane's daughter Lorraine Waatsa confirmed it as theirs. A round, green turquoise cabochon that is encircled by a twisted silver wire is surrounded by seven embossed silver crescents and seven unstamped silver drops that constitute the second band. These areas are surrounded by twenty snake-eye cabochons encircled again by a twisted silver wire, and all of these are surrounded by thirty-two turquoise cabochons and thirty-two unstamped silver drops. The inside areas of the embossed silver crescents are not cut out.

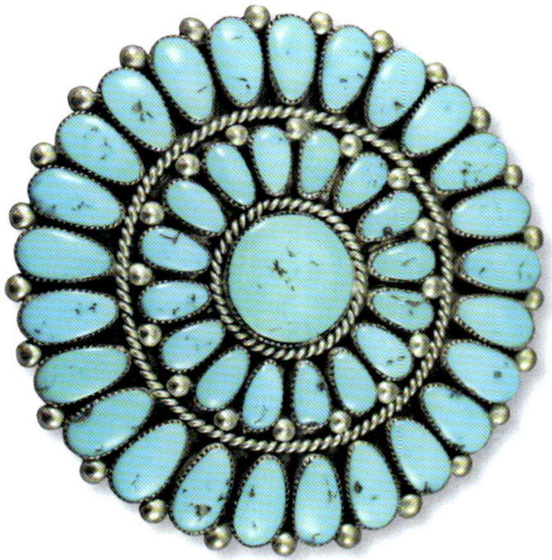

Sleeping Beauty turquoise pin, cluster work, Alice and Duane Quam, A. Q., 1980s–1990s, 2.85" in diameter, $800–1,200.

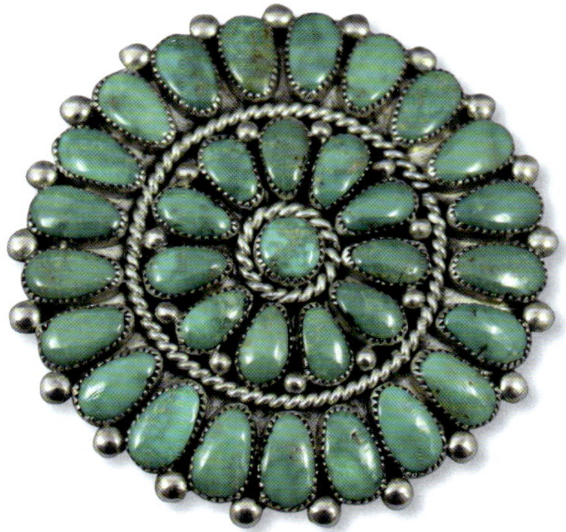

Fox turquoise pin, cluster work, Alice and Duane Quam, A. Q., 1980s–1990s, 2.23" in diameter, $700–1,050.

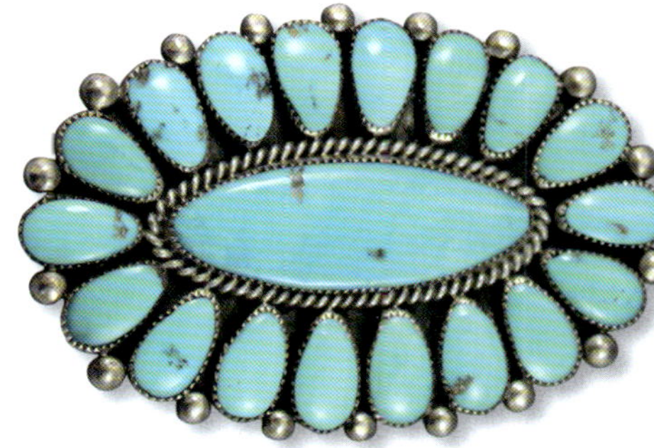

Sleeping Beauty turquoise ring, cluster work, Alice and Duane Quam, A. Q., 1980s–1990s, 1.72" × 2.53" for the ring face, $400–600.

Above is a Sleeping Beauty pin by Alice and Duane Quam. Turquoise cabochons are placed in the three-fold arrangement, in addition to two twisted silver wires and many unstamped silver drops. This design characterizes their round pins.

The Fox Turquoise pin in the middle, made at about the same time, is in the same three-fold arrangement as the one to its left.

The last pin, a Sleeping Beauty turquoise ring made in the simple two-fold arrangement, is quite large, measuring 2.53 inches tall. The center stone is the same shape as the one in their larger bracelet in my collection, quite possibly matching this ring.

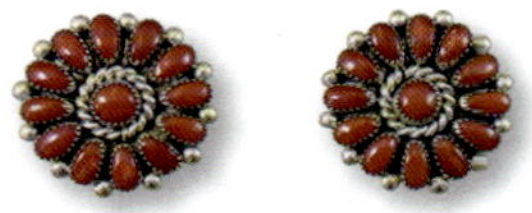

Coral earrings, cluster work, Alice and Duane Quam, A. Q., 1980s–1990s, 1.00" in diameter, $200–300.

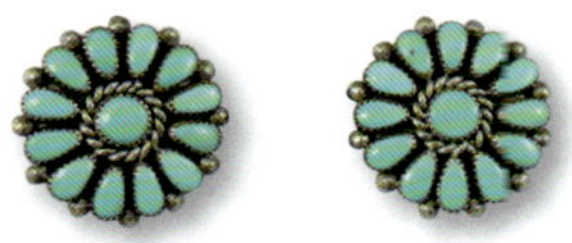

Turquoise earrings, cluster work, Alice and Duane Quam, A. q., 1970s–1980s, 1.01" in diameter, $200–300.

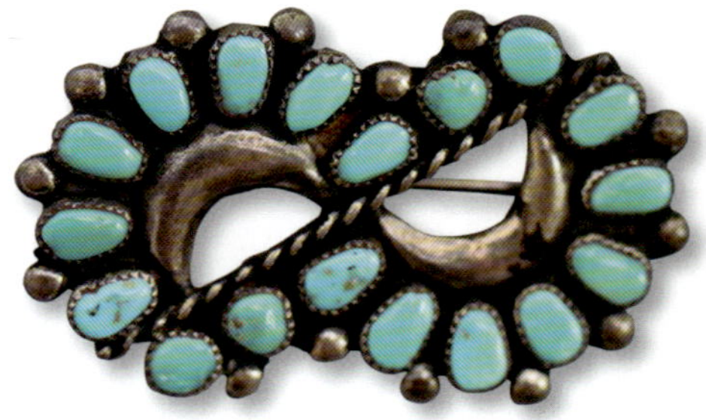

Lone Mountain turquoise pin, cluster work, Duane Quam, no hallmark, 1940s–1950s, 1.40" × 0.89", $100–150.

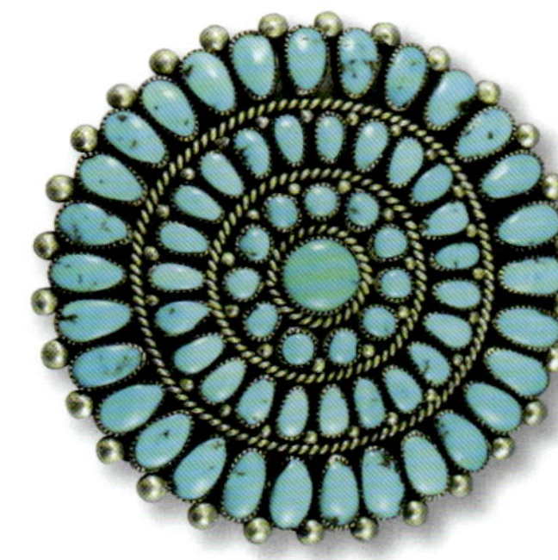

Sleeping Beauty turquoise pin, cluster work, Duane Quam, A. Q., 2003, 2.98" in diameter, $800–1,200.

Alice and Duane made the oxblood coral earrings above, on top. They are in the usual two-fold arrangement and have pin backs for pierced ears.

Next are Fox Turquoise earrings in the simple two-fold arrangement with clip backs.

The Quams also made the unusually small turquoise pin above, center, which measures only 1.40 inches wide. A twisted silver wire is set diagonally, with two embossed silver crescents set on both sides. Two sets of seven pear-shaped cabochons, two snake-eye Lone Mountain turquoise cabochons, and seven unstamped silver drops are set over and under the crescents and a wire.

Although this Sleeping Beauty turquoise pin bore the hallmark "A. Q.," Duane Quam made it after Alice died. When I purchased this four-fold-arranged pin from him on September 7, 2003, it was freshly made. Its turquoise stones are smaller than Alice's, and, although they are a little irregular due to Duane's deteriorated eye-sight and dexterity, it is still typical, authentic, and attractive Zuni cluster-work jewelry. After he sold this to me, he exercised at the Zuni health center!

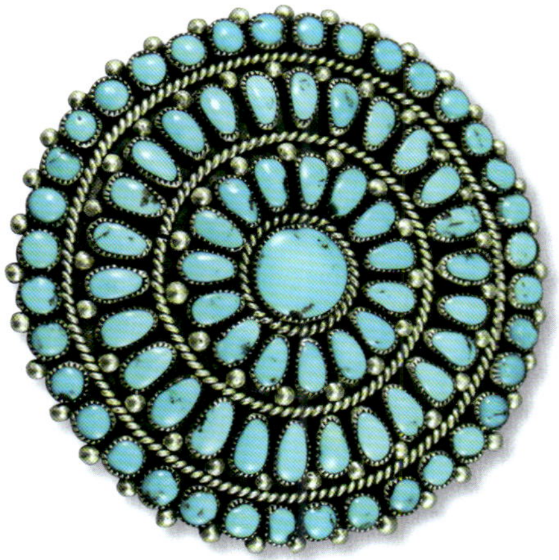

Sleeping Beauty turquoise pin, cluster work, Duane Quam, A. Q., 2003, 3.03" in diameter, $800–1,200.

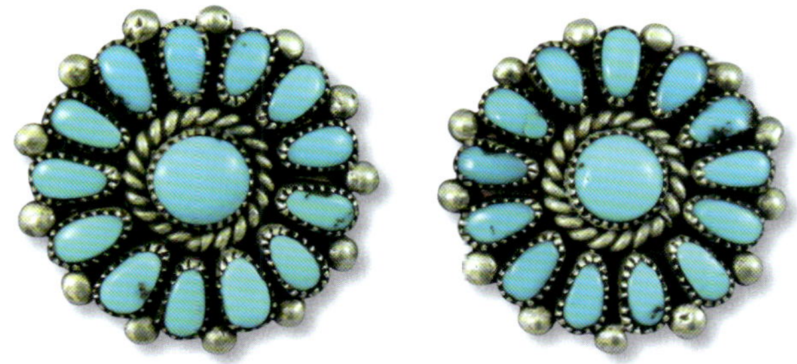

Sleeping Beauty turquoise earrings, cluster work, Duane Quam, A. Q., 2003, 1.05" in diameter, $100–150.

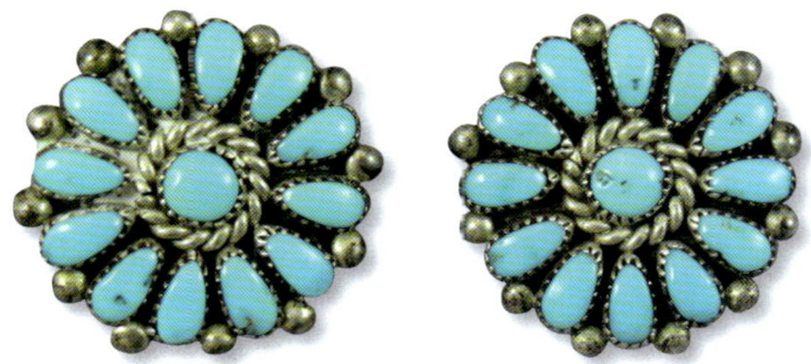

Sleeping Beauty turquoise earrings, cluster work, Duane Quam, A. Q., 2003, 0.94" in diameter, $100–150.

Duane's Sleeping Beauty pin above, which he made September 9, 2003, features the four-fold arrangement. This and the last pin have snake-eye turquoise cabochons in one of four bands.

On September 10, 2003, Duane Quam made the two pairs of Sleeping Beauty turquoise earrings above in the simple two-fold arrangement. The bottom pair's center stones are smaller than those in the top, and smaller than the two sets Alice and Duane worked on together, shown on the opposite page.

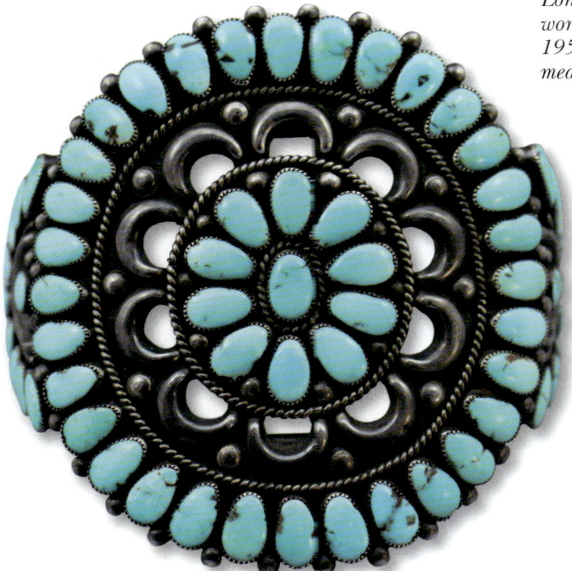

Lone Mountain turquoise bracelet, cluster work, Andy Ondelacy, no hallmark, 1950s–1960s, 2.58" × 2.86" central medallion, $2,000–3,000.

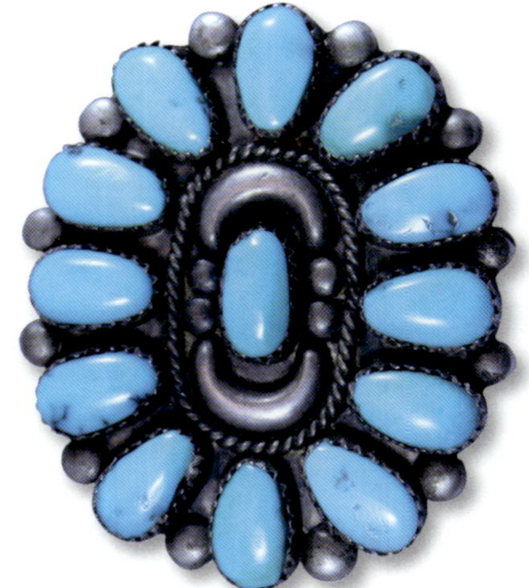

Turquoise pin/pendant, cluster work, Andy Ondelacy, no hallmark, 1960s, 1.57 × 1.85" $160–240.

Andy Ondelacy made the Lone Mountain turquoise bracelet above in the four-fold arrangement. One mid-size, oval turquoise cabochon is set in the center and encircled by a twisted silver wire (band 1). Ten pear-shaped cabochons and ten smaller, unstamped silver drops within a twisted silver wire constitute band 2. Ten embossed crescents, ten unstamped silver drops, and a twisted silver wire make up band 3. Lastly, the outer edge features thirty-two pear-shaped turquoise cabochons and thirty-two unstamped silver drops.

The same artist made the turquoise pin/pendant on the right in the two-fold arrangement. An oblong turquoise cabochon surrounded by two embossed silver crescents and four unstamped silver drops is encircled by a twisted silver wire (band 1). This central area is surrounded with twelve pear-shaped turquoise cabochons and twelve unstamped silver drops.

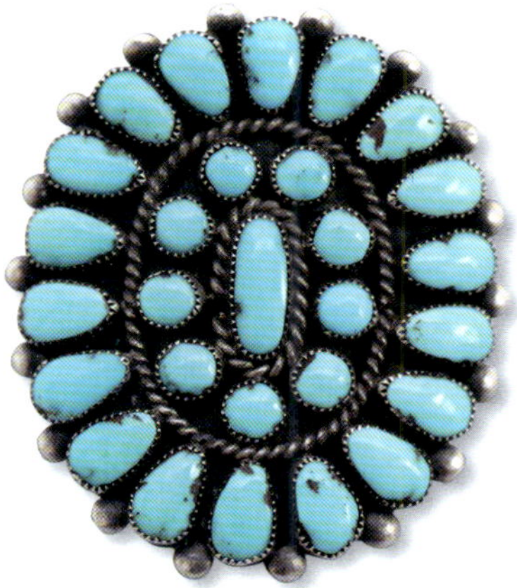

Turquoise ring, cluster work, Andy Ondelacy, no hallmark, 1960s, 1.51 × 1.76" $160–240.

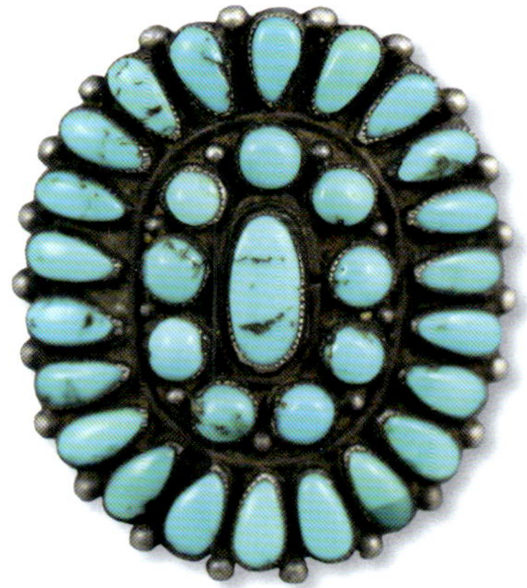

Kingman turquoise ring, cluster work, Andy Ondelacy, no hallmark, 1960s, 1.67" × 1.95" $160–240.

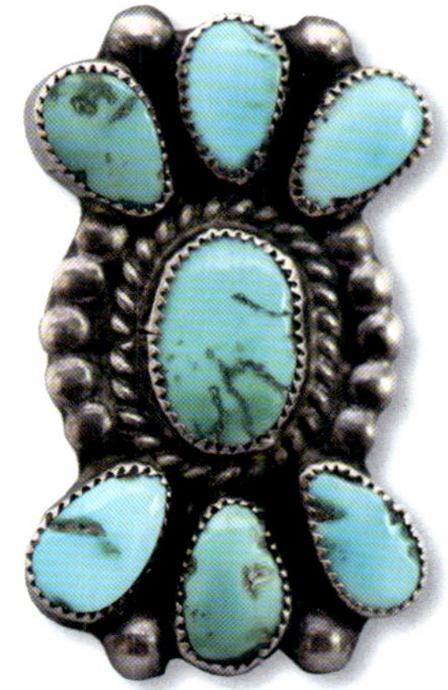

Turquoise ring, petite point, Andy and Fannie Ondelacy, no hallmark, 1950s–1960s, 1.67" × 1.95", $120–180.

The turquoise ring above is made in a typical three-fold arrangement: an oblong cabochon in the center with a twisted silver wire; nine snake-eye cabochons with a twisted wire in the middle band; and eighteen pear-shaped cabochons and eighteen unstamped silver drops in the outside band.

Above is Andy's three-fold turquoise ring, which consists of an oblong cabochon with a twisted wire in the center, nine snake-eye cabochons and nine smaller plain silver drops within a twisted wire in the second band, and twenty-one pear-shaped cabochons and twenty-one plain silver drops in the third band.

Finally, Andy and Fannie Ondelacy made the turquoise ring above, with one large oblong cabochon and a twisted silver wire in the center. Two sets of five unstamped silver drops surround the medallion on both sides and two sets of three pear-shaped cabochons are placed over and under it.

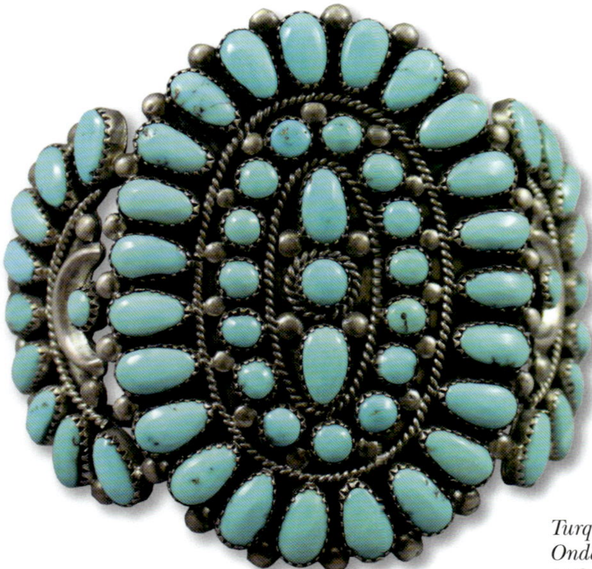

Turquoise bracelet, cluster work, Fannie Weebothee Ondelacy, F. W. O. in cursive, 1960s–1970s, 2.16" × 2.72" central medallion, $800–1,200.

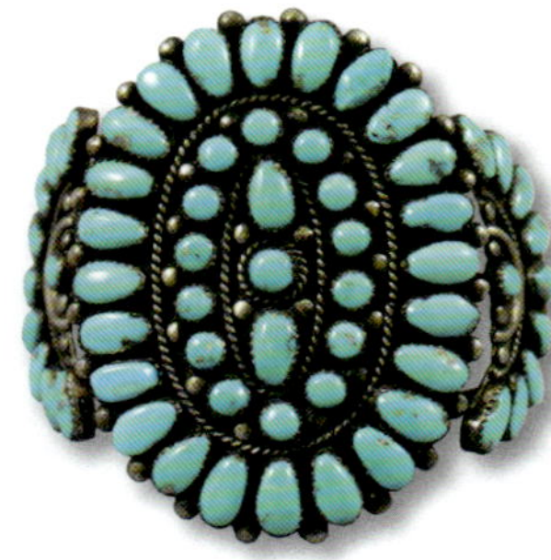

Turquoise bracelet, cluster work, Fannie Weebothee Ondelacy, F. W. Ondelacy, 1970s–1980s, 2.12" × 2.81" central medallion, $800–1,200.

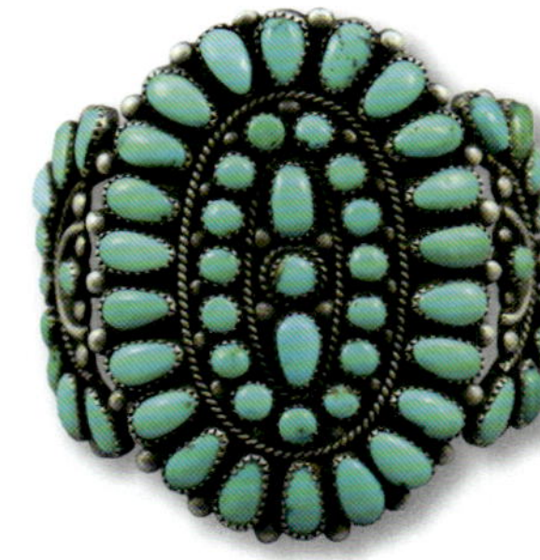

Turquoise bracelet, cluster work, Fannie Weebothee Ondelacy, F. W. Ondelacy, 1970s–1980s, 2.13" × 2.78" central medallion, $800–1,200.

I love this piece. This is my first cluster-work turquoise bracelet by Fannie Weebothee Ondelacy. I think it is one of the best examples of Zuni, cluster-work style jewelry. The blue turquoise and silver work demonstrate superb harmony. The central medallion is relatively small, measuring 2.16 inches wide and 2.72 inches long. This is her standard design: one round and two pear-shaped cabochons set vertically in the center, snake-eye cabochons placed in the middle band, and pear-shaped cabochons fixed on the outer layer with unstamped silver drops. The hallmark is a handwritten "FWO."

Fannie also made the next two identical bracelets above in her standard cluster-work design. They are a little wider than the previous example, and the turquoise cabochons are a deeper blue. They each have a silver plate stamped "F. W. Ondelacy" on their backs.

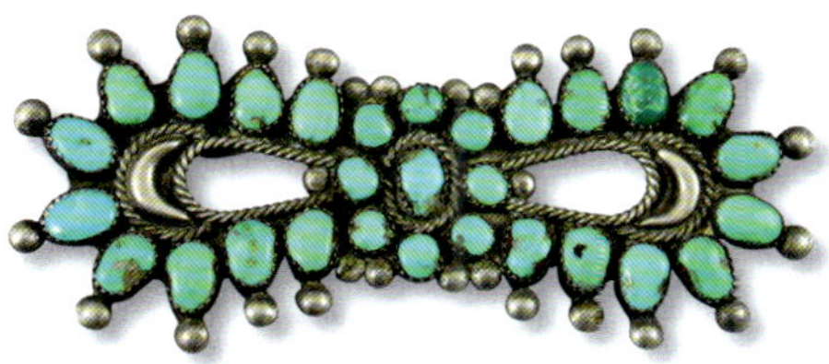

Turquoise bow pin, cluster work, Fannie Weebothee Ondelacy(?), no hallmark, 1940s–1950s, 1.68" × 3.94", $300–450.

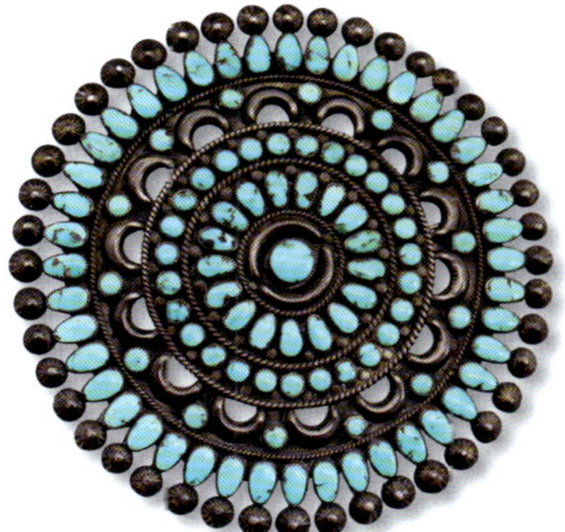

Turquoise pin, cluster work, Fannie Weebothee Ondelacy, no hallmark, 1950s–1960s, 4.17" in diameter, $1,200–1,800.

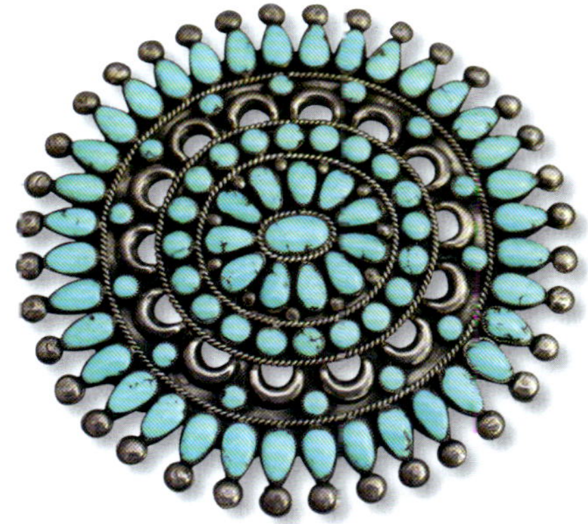

Lone Mountain turquoise pin, cluster work, Fannie Weebothee Ondelacy, no hallmark, 1950s–1960s, 4.30" × 4.21", $1,200–1,800.

Fannie Weebothee Ondelacy probably made the pin above. An oblong center stone with a twisted silver wire is surrounded by eight snake-eye cabochons. Two sets of ten pear-shaped turquoise cabochons are set on both sides of this two-fold cluster. Each set is adorned with two twisted silver wires, an embossed silver crescent, and eight unstamped silver drops.

The large turquoise pin above is made in the five-fold arrangement and includes an open-work fourth band, which consists of embossed silver crescents and snake-eye turquoise cabochons. The outer edge includes pear-shaped turquoise cabochons and stamped silver drops. It's reminiscent of the work of her brother Lee and his wife, Mary Weebothee, who used unstamped silver drops in this same design.

Above, on the right, is Fannie's large Lone Mountain turquoise pin, which has an oblong cabochon and a twisted silver wire in its center instead of the round cabochon and embossed silver crescents on the previous pin.

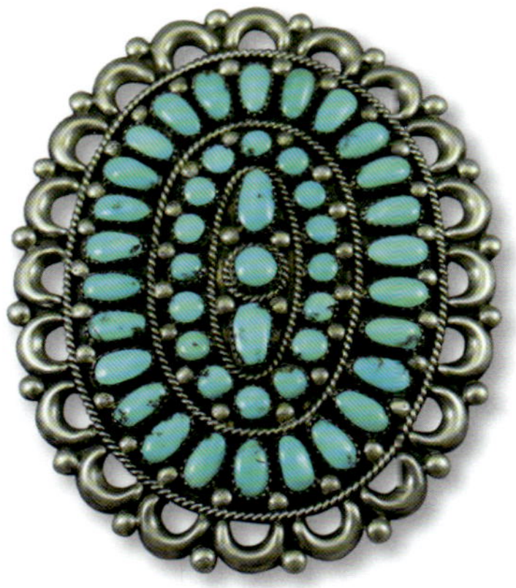

Lone Mountain turquoise manta pin, cluster work, Fannie Weebothee Ondelacy, no hallmark, 1950s–1960s, 3.75" × 3.03", $800–1,200.

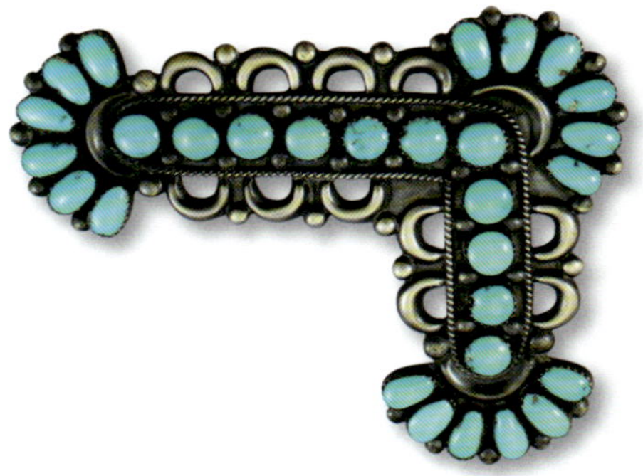

Lone Mountain turquoise manta pin, cluster work, Fannie Weebothee Ondelacy, no hallmark, 1950s–1960s, 3.93" × 3.19", $600–900.

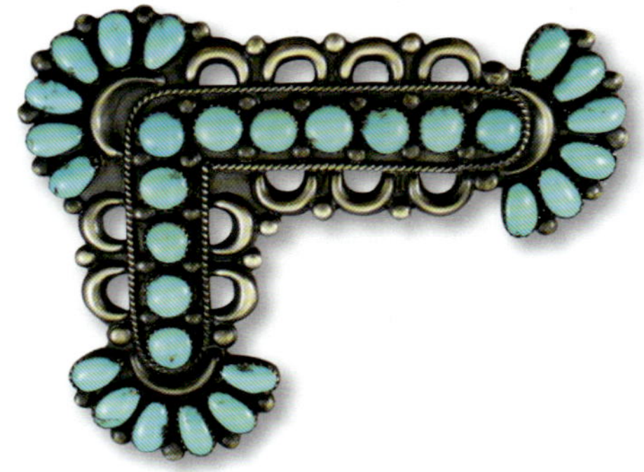

Lone Mountain turquoise manta pin, cluster work, Fannie Weebothee Ondelacy, no hallmark, 1950s–1960s, 3.74" × 3.03", $800–1,200.

Although there is no hallmark in the turquoise manta pin above, it appears to be Fannie's stone cutting style. It also shows her standard cluster-work design, except for the outer edge, which consists of open-work silver crescents and unstamped silver drops. With two loops for sewing on and a width of 3.75 inches, this pin is rather large.

The matching L-shaped pieces above each have a pin and two silver loops for sewing on. They consist of eleven snake-eye and eighteen pear-shaped turquoise cabochons, nine small and three large embossed silver crescents, and forty-eight unstamped silver drops.

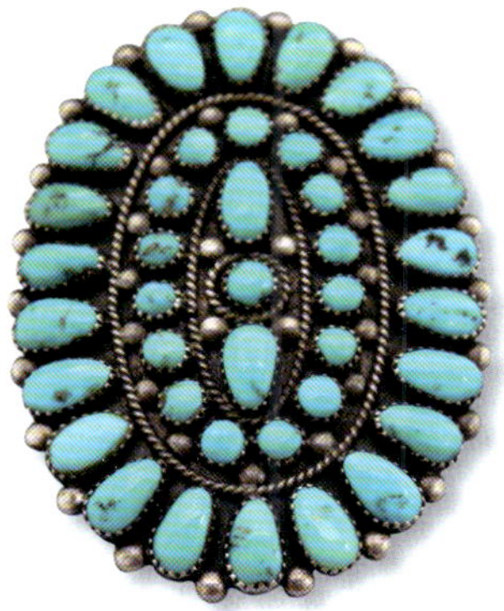

Turquoise ring, cluster work, Fannie Weebothee Ondelacy, no hallmark, 1950s–1960s, 2.10" × 2.75", $400–600.

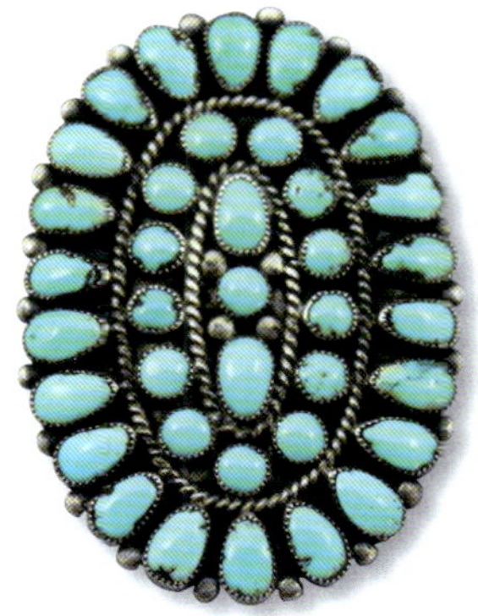

Turquoise ring, cluster work, Fannie Weebothee Ondelacy, no hallmark, 1950s–1960s, 1.56" × 2.15", $300–450.

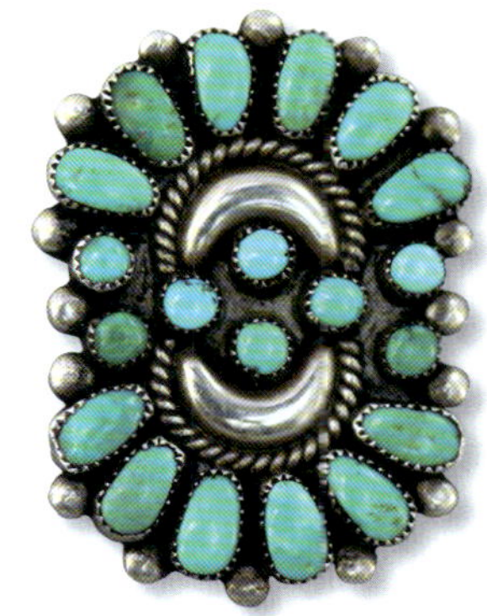

Lone Mountain turquoise ring, cluster work, Fannie Weebothee Ondelacy, no hallmark, 1950s–1960s, 1.21" × 1.70", $300–450.

The turquoise ring above is made in Fannie's standard design.

The second piece is smaller than the first, but it is still quite large, measuring 2.15 inches long.

The last ring design reminds me of the one her parents-in-law, Doris and Warren Ondelacy, created, except for the arrangement of four central turquoise cabochons.

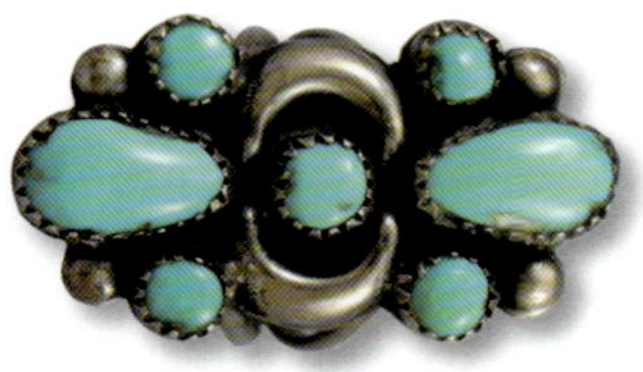

Turquoise ring, cluster work, Fannie Weebothee Ondelacy, F. W. Ondelacy, 1960s–1970s, 0.77" × 1.40", $120–180.

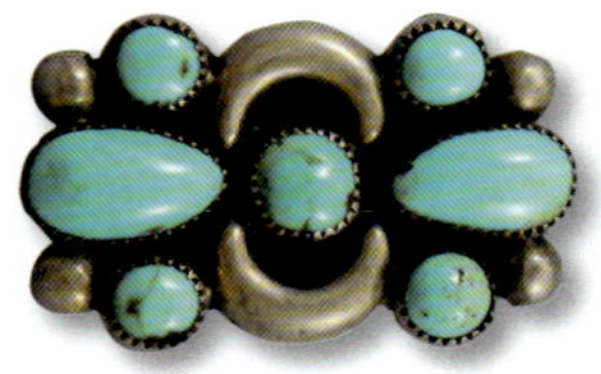

Turquoise ring, cluster work, Fannie Weebothee Ondelacy, no hallmark, 1950s–1960s, 0.79" × 1.26", $120–180.

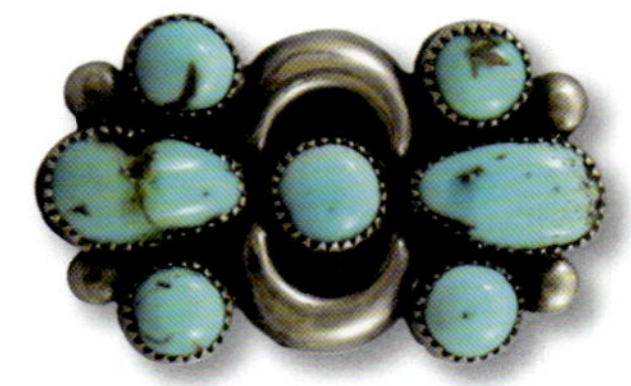

Turquoise ring, cluster work, Fannie Weebothee Ondelacy, no hallmark, 1950s–1970s, 0.81" × 1.30", $120–180.

The first turquoise ring above is a variation of Fannie's standard ring design. One snake-eye cabochon and two pear-shaped cabochons are set horizontally, and a snake-eye cabochon is set on both sides of the pear-shaped cabochons. Two additional embossed, silver crescents and four unstamped silver drops adorn this ring.

The next two rings were made in the exact same design. Neither of them is hallmarked, but they appear to be made by the same silversmith/lapidary—Fannie, of course.

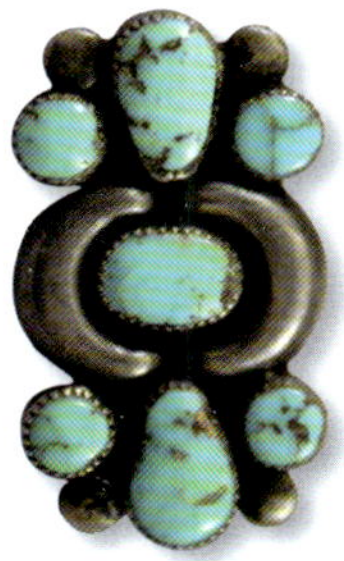

Turquoise pin, cluster work, Fannie Weebothee Ondelacy, no hallmark, 1960s–1970s, 1.10" × 0.62", $120–180.

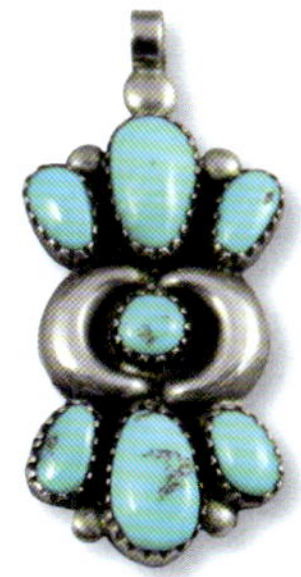

Turquoise pendant, cluster work, Fannie Weebothee Ondelacy, F. W. Ondelacy, 1970s–1980s, 0.75" × 1.66", $120–180.

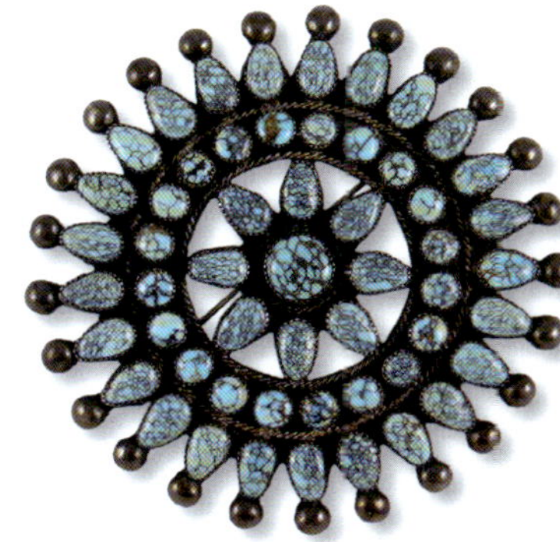

Number 8–spider web turquoise pin, cluster work, Fannie Weebothee Ondelacy(?), no hallmark, 1940s–1950s, 3.00" in diameter, $1,200–1800. Courtesy of the Gloria Dollar Collection.

The same design continues in the first pin above, only smaller, measuring just 1.10 inches wide. The second pin is a turquoise pendant hallmarked "F. W. Ondelacy."

Fannie probably made the piece above, a Number 8–spider web turquoise pin. One of my informants attributed it to Lee and Mary Weebothee, but their daughters Patsy and Darlene Weebothee denied this in December 2013. The second band from its center has only eight cabochons, leaving some desired open space.

Number 8–spider web turquoise pin, cluster work, Fannie Weebothee Ondelacy(?), no hallmark, 1940s–1950s, 3.05" in diameter, $1,000–1,500.

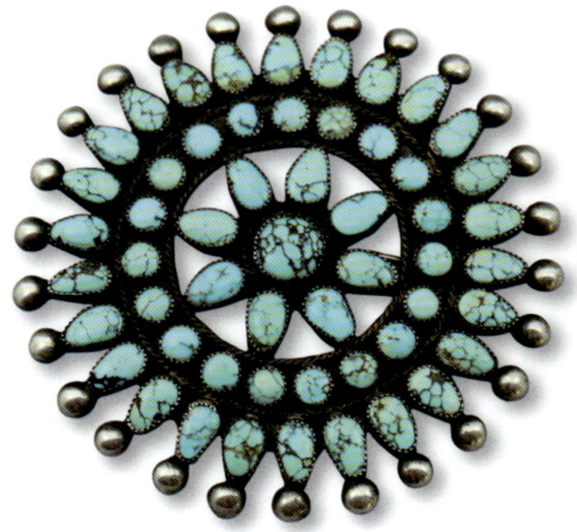

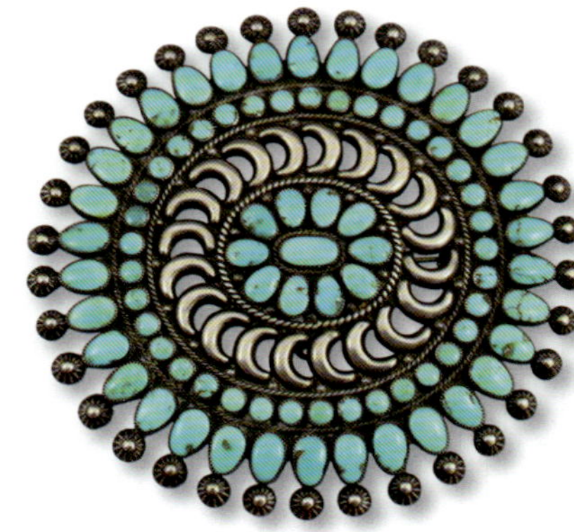

Turquoise pin, cluster work, Fannie Weebothee Ondelacy(?), no hallmark, 1950s–1960s, 4.01" × 3.87", $1,200–1,800.

Last is another Number 8–spider web pin. Several months after I received the photo of the previous pin from my collector friend Gloria Dollar, I found the next pin in an online auction. I noticed it was virtually identical to Gloria's, but the spider web pattern in my turquoise cabochons is not as evident as in Gloria's. Both of them have the same handwritten inscription, "RN." I visited some artists and tried to find out what the initials stood for, but failed—they might in fact be price codes. In March 2014 I took mine to Patsy and Darlene Weebothee, who denied it was their parents' and attributed both pins to their aunt Fannie, but said there was a slight possibility that mine was their uncle Leonard Weebothee's.

This sizable turquoise pin, above right, which measures 4.01 inches in width, was originally attributed to Lee and Mary Weebothee by my informant, but as its silver backing is very similar to the two previous pins, I visited Patsy and Darlene Weebothee once again. Patsy showed it to her father, Lee Weebothee, and told me Fannie probably made it. Again, there is a slight chance that it is the work of Leonard. This piece is made in the five-fold arrangement, and the third band from the oblong center stone consists of embossed crescents and small, unstamped silver drops. Each stone is carved a little flatter than in the previous bracelet, which might be Fannie's early stone-cutting style. The outermost silver drops are stamped and set on top of each pear-shaped cabochons.

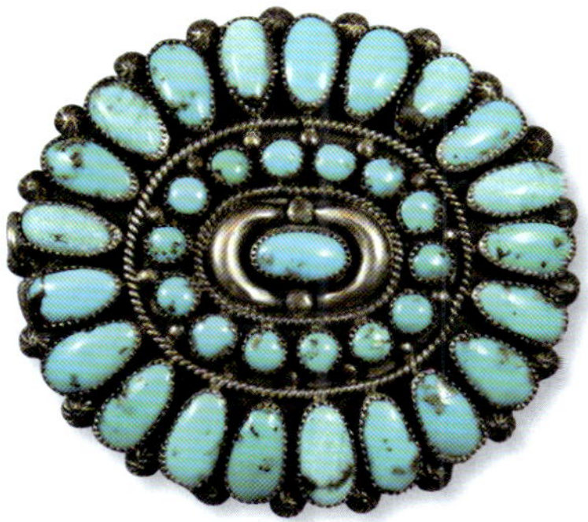

Turquoise pin/pendant, cluster work, Julie Ondelacy Lahi, Julie O. Lahi, 1970s–1980s, 2.40" × 2.13", $300–450.

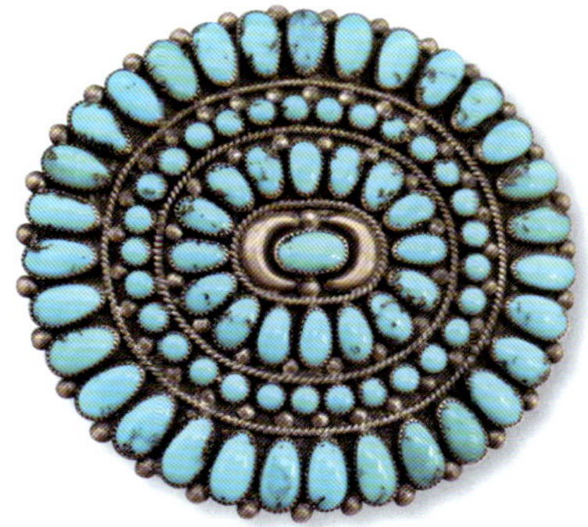

Kingman turquoise manta pin, cluster work, Julie Ondelacy Lahi, Julie O. Lahi, 1960s, 3.32" × 3.10", $400–600.

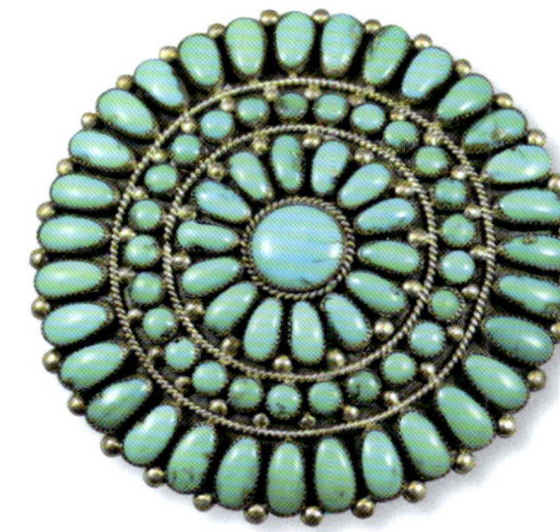

Turquoise manta pin, cluster work, Julie Ondelacy Lahi, Julie O. Lahi, 1970s–1980s, 3.12 in diameter", $400–600.

Above is a turquoise pin/pendant by Julie Ondelacy Lahi. It is reminiscent of the pieces by her father, Andy Ondelacy, on page 79, even if it is in the three-fold arrangement—his is two-fold.

She also made the Kingman turquoise manta pin above. Unlike the previous piece, it features a band of pear-shaped cabochons around the central medallion, making it a four-fold arrangement. It bears two pins on its back.

The third piece, a manta with two back pins, is similar to Julie's aunt Alice Quam's standard design.

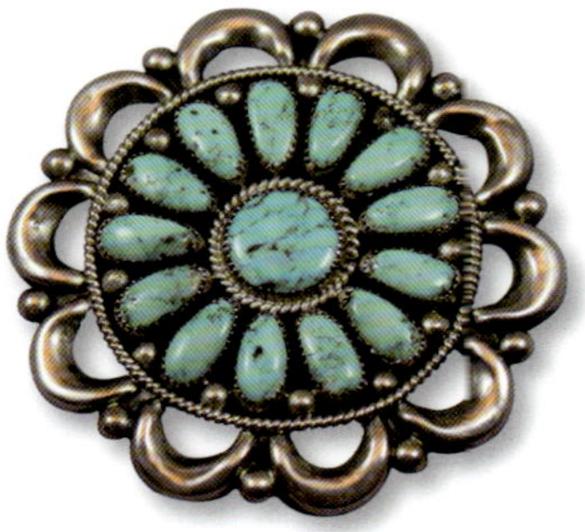

Turquoise pin/pendant, cluster work, Julie Ondelacy Lahi, Julie O. Lahi, 1970s–1980s, 2.11" in diameter, $240–360.

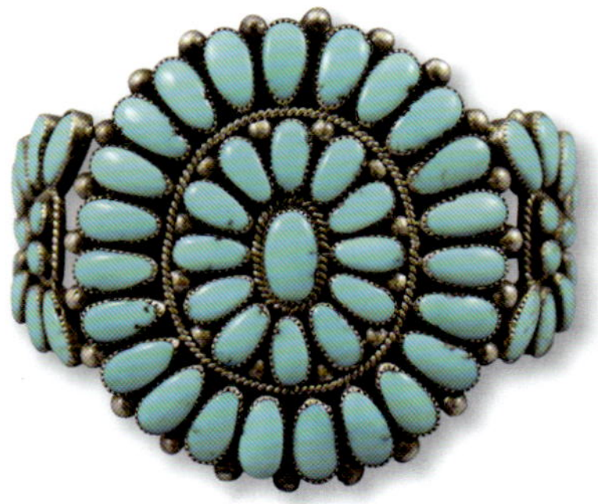

Turquoise bracelet, cluster work, Julie Ondelacy Lahi, Julie O. Lahi, 1970s–1980s, 2.19" × 2.35", $400–600.

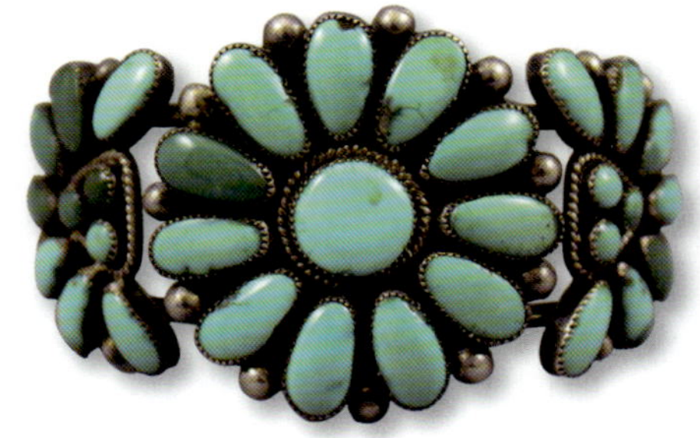

Turquoise bracelet, cluster work, Julie Ondelacy Lahi, Julie O. Lahi, 1970s–1980s, 1.66" in diameter central medallion, $400–600. Courtesy of Hisako Sueshige.

Next is Julie's turquoise pin/pendant in the three-fold placement, with the outermost layer consisting of open-work, embossed silver crescents and unstamped silver drops. This design is reminiscent of pieces made by her uncle Lee Weebothee, even though it does not have the long silver dangles frequently seen in Lee and Mary's work.

The first turquoise bracelet above is also in a three-fold design. The oblong center is set vertically, and two bands of pear-shaped cabochons and unstamped silver drops surround it. It is hallmarked "JULIE O LAHI."

The second, smaller, bracelet has a 1.66-inch central medallion and two side medallions. Some cabochons have turned deep green as time has gone by. Still, it maintains its attractiveness in this unique design. "JULIE O LAHI" is stamped on the back.

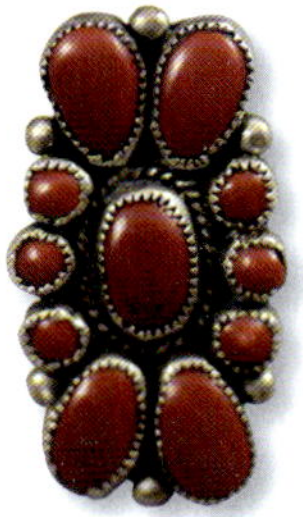

Coral ring, cluster work, Julie Ondelacy Lahi, Julie O. Lahi, 1970s–1980s, 0.81" × 1.50", $160–240.

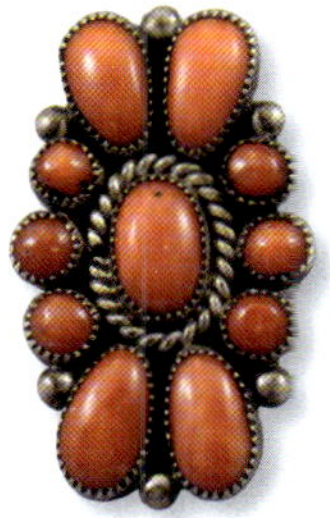

Coral ring, cluster work, Julie Ondelacy Lahi, Julie O. Lahi, 1970s–1980s, 0.89" × 1.51", $160–240. Courtesy of Hisako Sueshige.

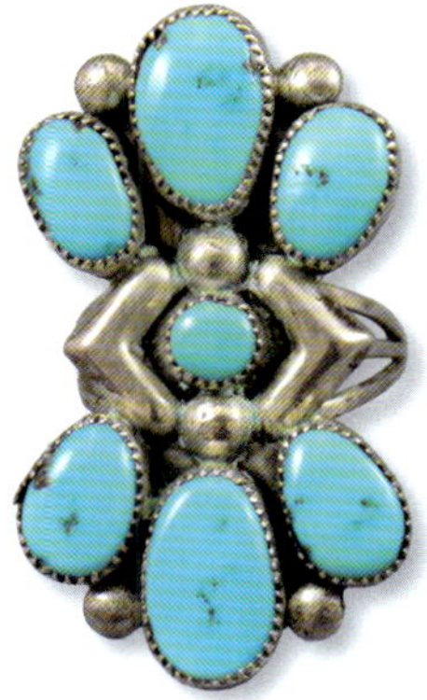

Turquoise ring, cluster work, Julie Ondelacy Lahi, Julie O. Lahi, 1980s–1990s, 0.93" × 1.65", $160–240.

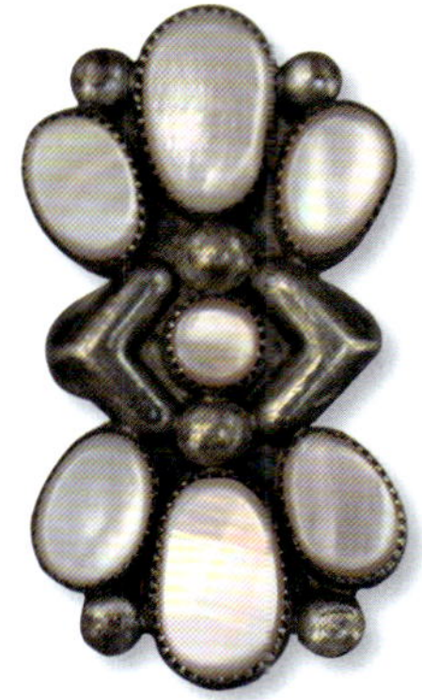

Mother-of-pearl ring, cluster work, Julie Ondelacy Lahi, Julie O. Lahi, 1980s–1990s, 0.89" × 1.68", $160–240.

The two oxblood coral rings above may be variations of those created by Julie's grandparents, Doris and Warren Ondelacy, but they are original and can be considered her own design.

A snake-eye cabochon is encircled by two chevrons and two unstamped silver drops in the third piece shown above, one of Julie's more recently designed turquoise rings. The center is adorned with two sets of three pear-shaped cabochons and two unstamped silver drops.

The pinkish mother-of-pearl ring on the right is made in the same design as the turquoise ring, but the stones appear flatter.

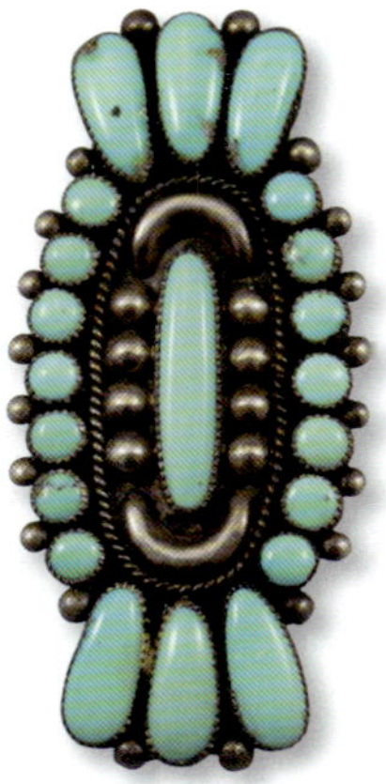

Turquoise ring, cluster work, Julie Or-delacy Lahi, Julie O. Lahi, 1970s–1980s, 1.27" × 2.77", $200–300.

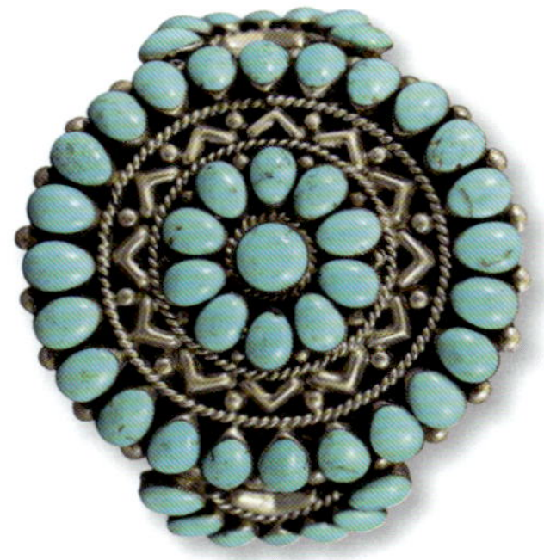

Turquoise bracelet, cluster work, Lee and Mary Weebothee, Lee & Mary, 1970s–1980s, 2.46" × 2.65" central medallion, $1,200–1,800.

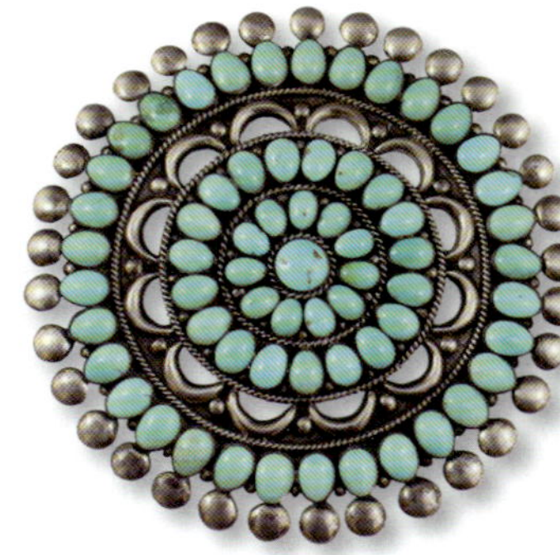

Turquoise manta pin, cluster work, Lee and Mary Weebothee, Lee & Mary, 1970s–1980s, 4.81" in diameter, $1,400–2,100.

The sheer length of Julie's ring above gives it its uniqueness. Its basic design elements, however, are reminiscent of the work of her mother, Fannie. "JULIE O LAHI" is stamped on the back.

Lee and Mary Weebothee made this turquoise bracelet in the four-fold arrangement. The third band from the center stone consists of embossed silver chevrons and unstamped silver drops. The roundness of the lapidary work, which gives the bracelet a kind of cubic effect, is unique to these artists. Their combination of lapidary and silver work is unique as well.

The Weebothee's turquoise, cluster-work manta pin, or concha, has a pin and a clasp for a belt on its back. The roundness of the stone carving and the presence of large, unstamped silver drops on the top of the outermost cabochons are characteristic of their later pieces.

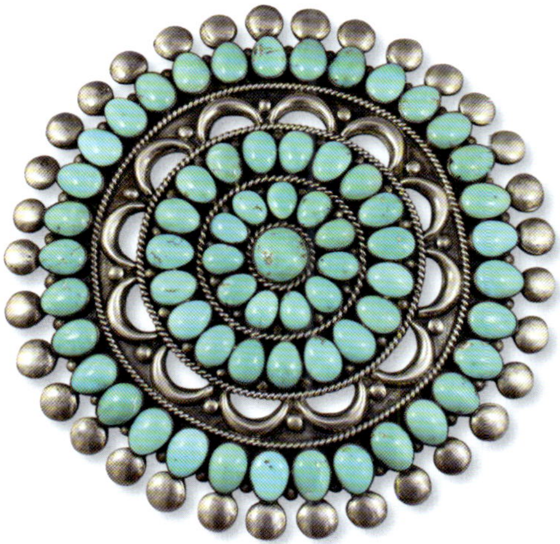

Turquoise manta pin, cluster work, Lee and Mary Weebothee, Lee & Mary, 1970s–1980s, 4.84' in diameter, $1,400–2,100.

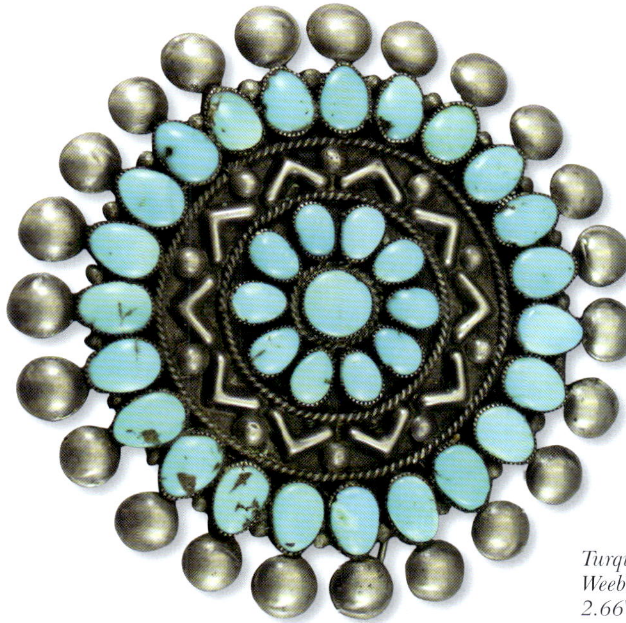

Turquoise pin, cluster work, Lee and Mary Weebothee, no hallmark, 1950s–1960s, 2.66" in diameter, $600–900.

The pin-less concha above and the identically designed previous example are so big that, when I asked what their purpose was, one of my collector friends joked that they could be bikini tops.

The medium-size pin above has no hallmark on its back, but the flat turquoise cabochons are characteristic of the Weebothees' early work. Also typical of their pieces is the placement of large, unstamped silver drops on top of pear-shaped cabochons. This outermost layer included, it has five bands in all. The third band consists of chevrons and unstamped silver drops.

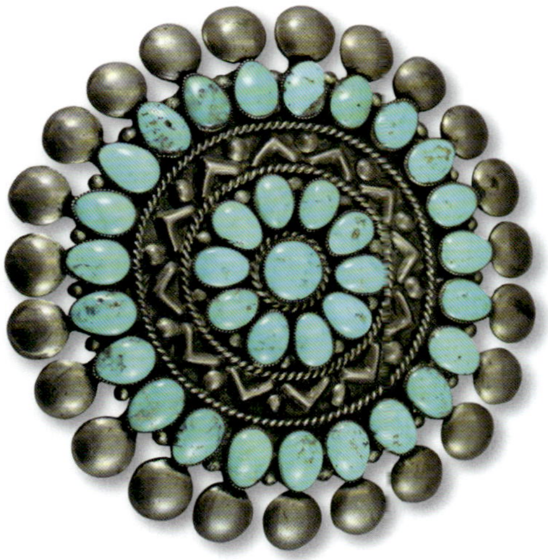

Turquoise pin, cluster work, Lee and Mary Weebothee, Lee & Mary, 1970s–1980s, 3.11" in diameter, $800–1,200.

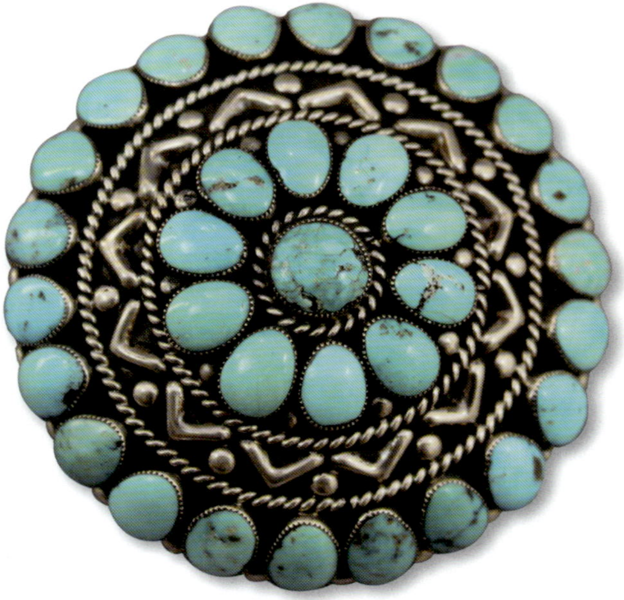

Domed turquoise pin, cluster work, Lee and Mary Weebothee, Lee & Mary, 1970s–1980s, 2.20" in diameter, $800–1,200.

Though identical in arrangement to the previous pin, the hallmarked example above is larger, measuring almost a half-inch longer in diameter. The round stone-cutting style clearly belongs to Lee and Mary.

A rare piece, this pin's silver backing is domed, measuring 2.20 inches in diameter and 0.71 inches in height. It also features miniscule, unstamped silver drops.

Turquoise pin/pendant, cluster work, Lee and Mary Weebothee, Lee and Mary, 1970s–1980s, 1.79" × 4.96", $800–1,200.

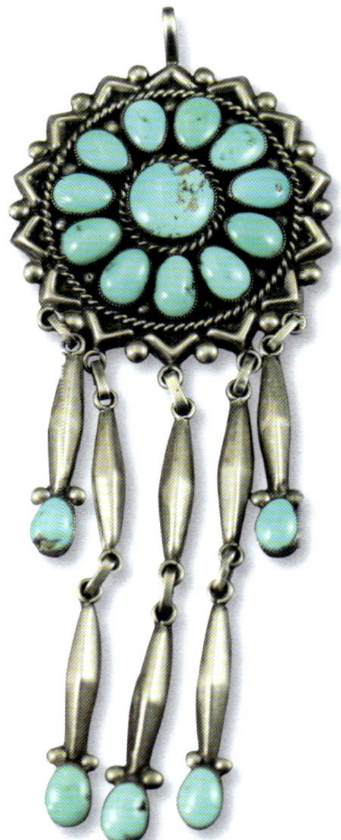

The first turquoise pin/pendant has three long and two short dangles. The main part consists of three bands: 1) a round cabochon with a twisted wire; 2) eleven cabochons and eleven smaller, unstamped silver drops within a twisted silver wire; 3) chevrons with unstamped silver drops. It measures 1.79 inches in diameter and the entire pendant stretches 4.96 inches from the bail to the bottom of the longest dangle. A pear-shaped turquoise cabochon is set on the tip of each silver dangle, a rare detail for their pieces with this particular embellishment.

The second piece's outermost silver work and dangles distinguish it from the last example. The artists used embossed silver crescents, and the applied dangles are their standard, without cabochon.

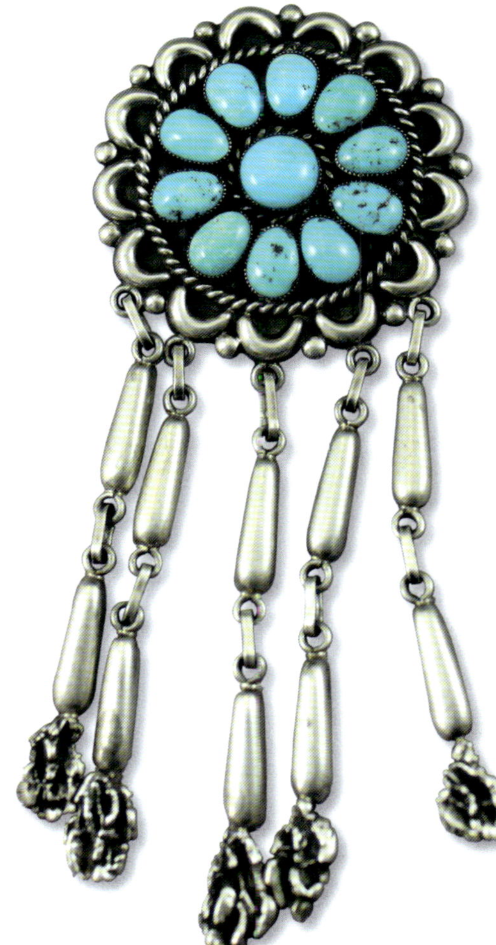

Turquoise pin/pendant, cluster work, Lee and Mary Weebothee, Lee and Mary, 1970s–1980s, 1.79" × 4.64", $800–1,200. Courtesy of Hisako Seto.

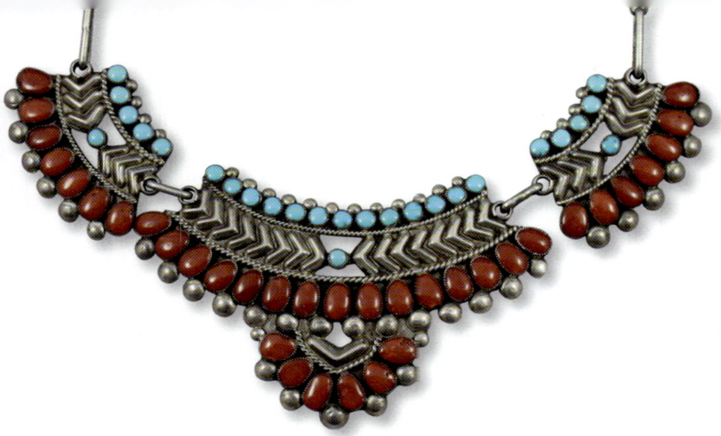

Turquoise and coral necklace, cluster work, Lee and Mary Weebothee, no hallmark, 1960s, 3.28" × 2.11" central medallion, $1,600–2,400.

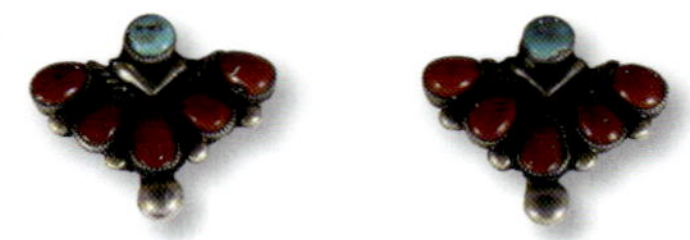

Turquoise and coral earrings, cluster work, Lee and Mary Weebothee, no hallmark, 1960s, 0.99" × 0.91", $300–450.

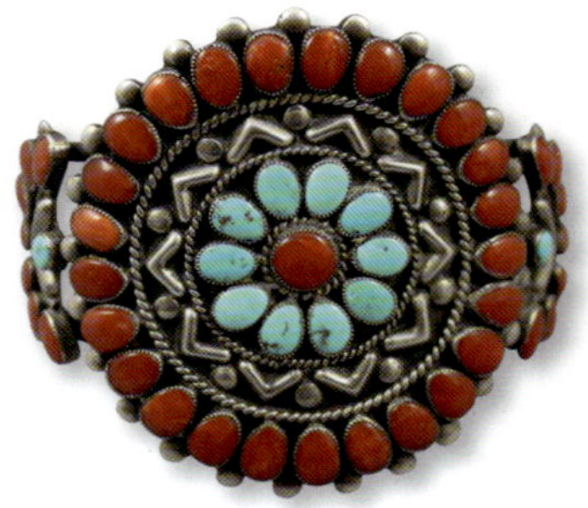

Turquoise and coral bracelet, cluster work, Lee and Mary Weebothee, no hallmark, 1960s, 2.22" × 2.29" central medallion, $1,600–2,400.

The necklace, bracelet, and earrings on this page are a set. The turquoise and coral choker necklace above has no hallmark, but their daughters Patsy and Darlene Weebothee confirmed it was Lee and Mary's. The most prominent stone is oxblood coral, and the artists made effective use of smaller, snake-eye turquoise cabochons as accents, and added vertically set chevrons and unstamped silver drops.

The matching turquoise and coral bracelet contains a main medallion with a round, red coral cabochon within a twisted wire in the center, wire-enclosed, pear-shaped turquoise cabochons in the second band, chevrons and smaller unstamped silver drops in the third, and pear-shaped, red coral cabochons and larger unstamped silver drops on the edge. As for its side medallions, embossed chevrons embrace a smaller, snake-eye, turquoise cabochon, and these parts are encircled by pear-shaped turquoise cabochons and unstamped silver drops.

Lastly, the turquoise and coral clip earrings above are almost identical in design to the bracelet's side medallions, except for the number of coral cabochons (five and seven, respectively).

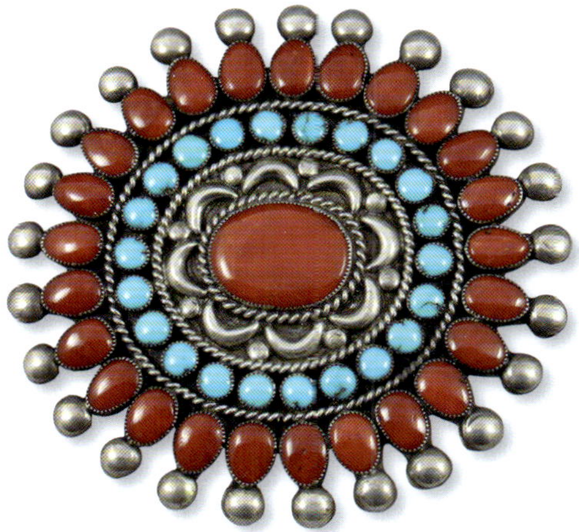

Turquoise and coral pin, cluster work, Lee and Mary Weebothee, no hallmark, 1960s, 2.68" × 2.56", $1,600–2,400.

Although this turquoise and coral pin by the Weebothees is not part of the set described on page 94, I got them as one package, and they seem to have been made around the same time. It exchanges the previous bracelet's round center stone for a large, oval-shaped red coral, and chevrons for embossed silver crescents. Another distinction is that unstamped silver drops are attached to the top of each pear-shaped coral cabochon in the pin, while the bracelet's cabochons are set in the reverse direction, and unstamped silver drops are set between each pair.

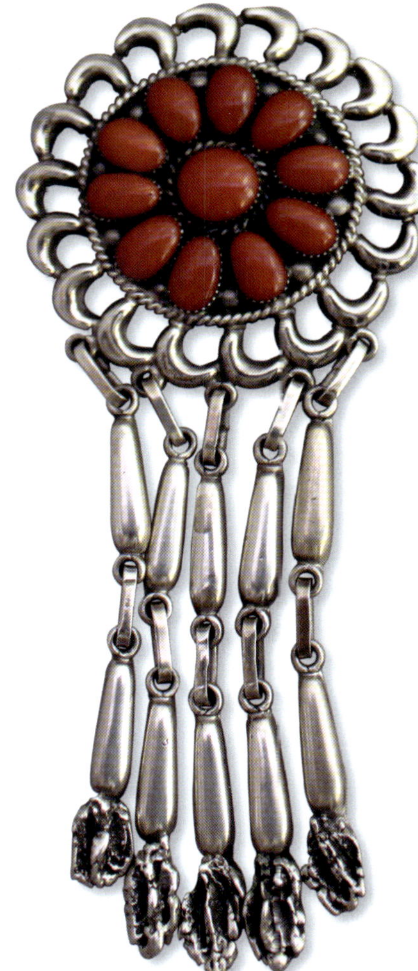

Coral pin/pendant, cluster work, Lee and Mary Weebothee, Lee & Mary, 1970s–1980s, 1.77" × 4.57", $1,200–1,800.

Like the second pin/pendant on page 93, the piece to the right has five silver dangles. One noticeable difference between the two is that the embossed silver crescents are set in different directions.

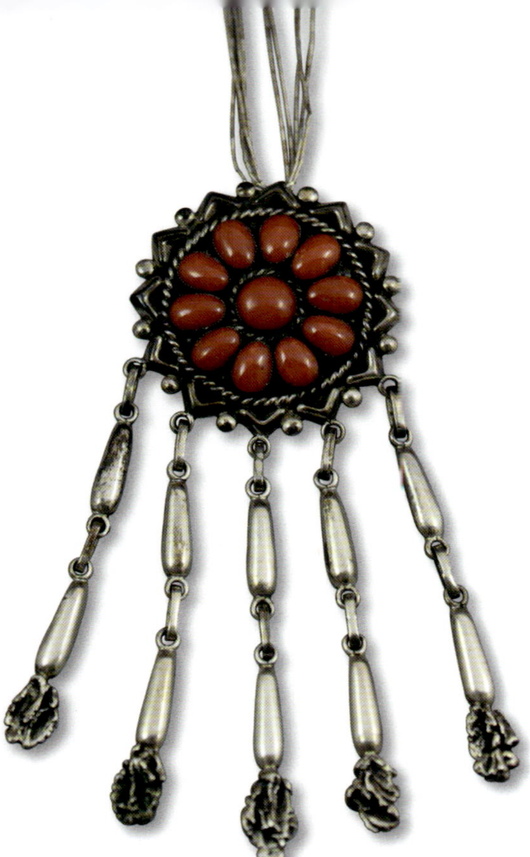

Coral pin/pendant, cluster work, Lee and Mary Weebothee, Lee & Mary, 1970s–1980s, 1.77" × 4.57", $1,200–1,800.

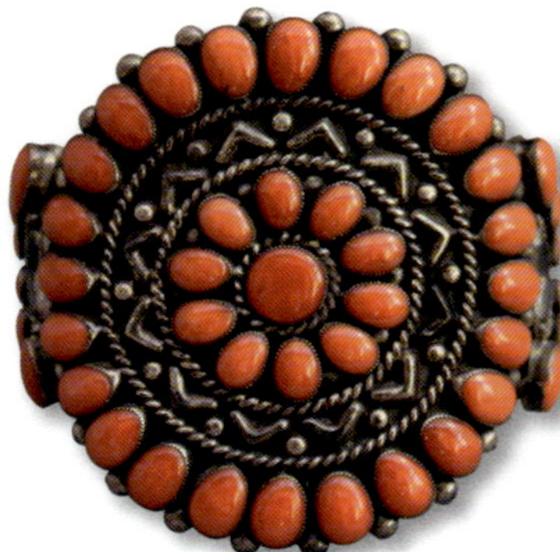

Coral bracelet, cluster work, Lee and Mary Weebothee, Lee & Mary, 1970s–1980s, 2.46" × 2.65" central medallion, $1,200–1,800.

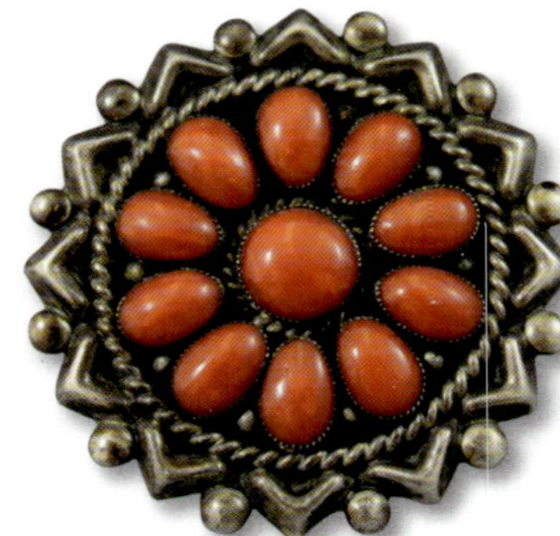

Coral ring, cluster work, Lee and Mary Weebothee, Lee & Mary, 1970s–1980s, 1.72" in diameter, $200–300.

The Weebothee's coral bracelet above is comparable to their turquoise bracelet on page 90. It also matches the pin/pendant to the left, embossed silver chevrons included. I bought them together from the one seller. The coral ring matches the pin/pendant and bracelet, even though I acquired this at a different time and their coral colors are slightly different.

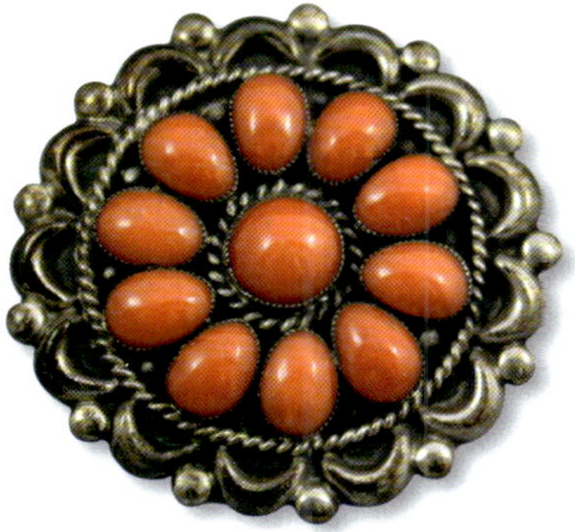

Coral ring, cluster work, Lee and Mary Weebothee, Lee & Mary, 1970s–1980s, 1.78" in diameter, $200–300.

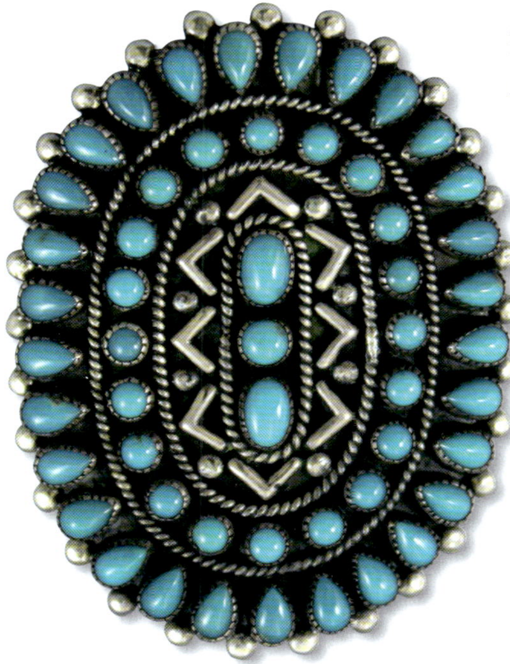

Turquoise ring, cluster work, Lee and Mary Weebothee, no hallmark, 1950s–1960s, 1.67" × 2.18", $200–300.

The coral ring above is similar to the previous example, but this piece incorporates silver crescents instead of chevrons.

Originally, I did not notice the Weebothees' characteristic lapidary style in the turquoise ring above. The silver ring set on the back of the piece, however, suggests it could be their work, as virtually no other silversmiths implement this specific detail.

I showed this ring to Darlene and Patsy Weebothee in March 2013, and they confirmed it was Lee and Mary's. Although they used small turquoise cabochons, it may be called cluster work because of the use of several pear-shaped cabochons.

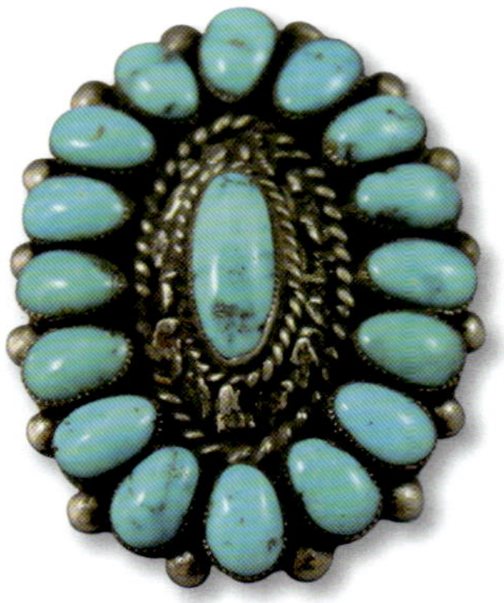

Turquoise ring, cluster work, Lee and Mary Weebothee, Lee & Mary, 1970s–1980s, 1.24" × 1.64", $200–300.

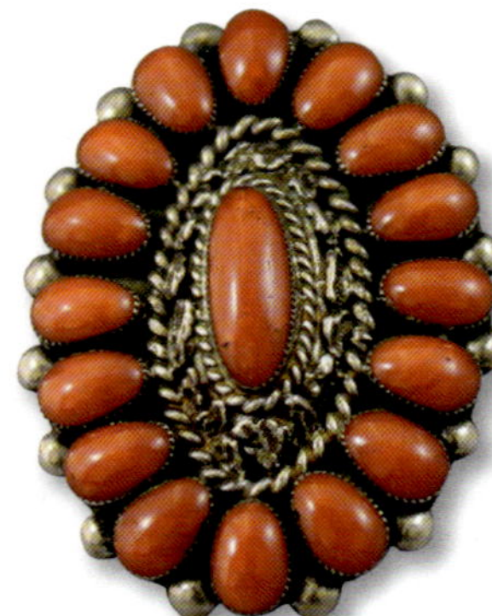

Coral ring, cluster work, Lee and Mary Weebothee, Lee & Mary, 1970s–1980s, 1.29" × 1.71", $200–300.

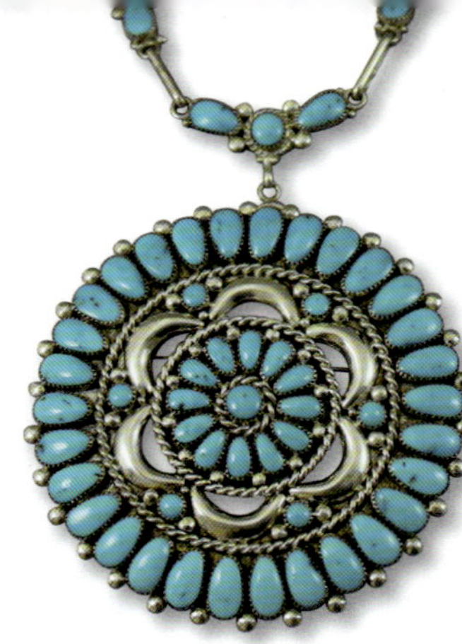

Turquoise necklace, cluster work, Lorraine Waatsa, LW, 2000s, 2.86" central medallion, $1,200–1,800.

The central, oblong, turquoise cabochon in the ring above is set high in the center. Lee and Mary's characteristic sloped silver work is present in the second band, and pear-shaped cabochons and unstamped silver drops are affixed on the outermost edge. The second piece, a coral ring, features exactly the same design.

After Alice Quam and Fannie Weebothee Ondelacy passed away, and Lee Weebothee and Julie Ondelacy Lahi retired due to deteriorating health, Lorraine and Luwayne Waatsa became the leading cluster-work artists. I only feature two pieces by them, however, because their jewelry development is actively ongoing, and the best is probably yet to come.

The Sleeping Beauty turquoise necklace above, which I bought from the Waatsas, is made in the traditional four-fold arrangement. A medallion that hangs from a matching turquoise chain features embossed silver crescents, snake-eye cabochons, and unstamped silver drops, with a twisted silver wire in the third band.

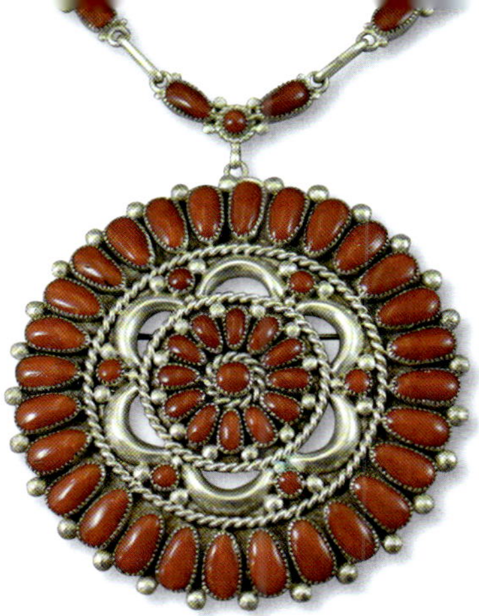

Coral necklace, cluster work, Lorraine Waatsa, LW, 1960s, 2000s, 3.06" central medallion, $1,200–1,800.

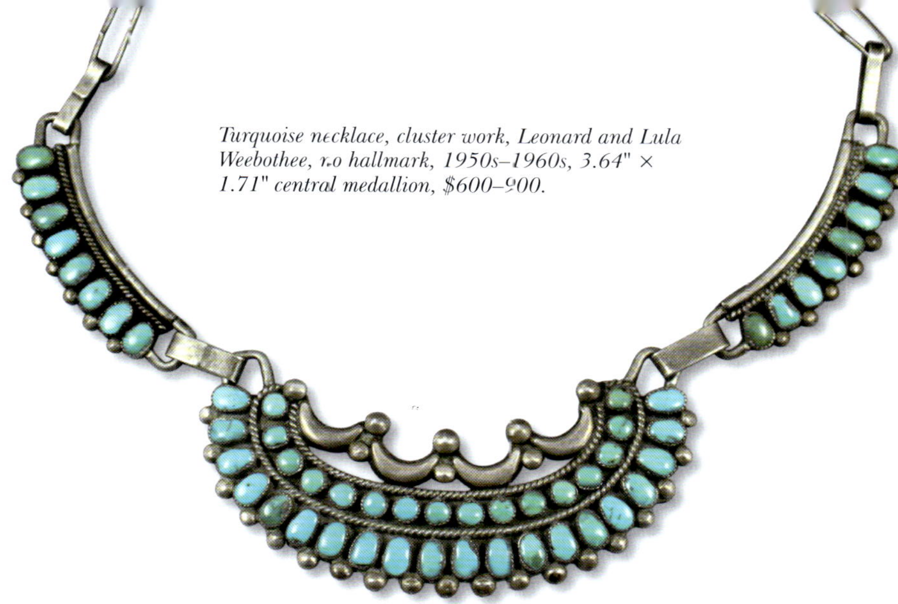

Turquoise necklace, cluster work, Leonard and Lula Weebothee, no hallmark, 1950s–1960s, 3.64" × 1.71" central medallion, $600–900.

I bought the oxblood coral necklace above from the Waatsas a few years after acquiring the turquoise one. They were made in exactly the same design.

Leonard and Lula Weebothee made this turquoise choker necklace. I noticed it was similar to other pieces made by the couple, but I wasn't certain this was their work. Patsy and Darlene Weebothee confirmed it had been made by Leonard and Lula. The center consists of pear-shaped and snake-eye turquoise cabochons, embossed silver crescents, unstamped silver drops, and two twisted silver wires, while each side panel features pear-shaped turquoise cabochons, a twisted wire, a plain wire, and unstamped silver drops.

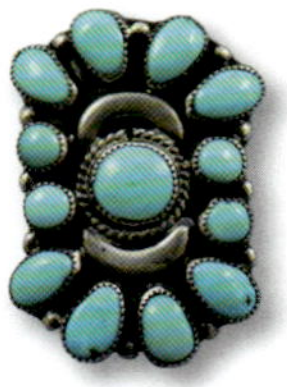

Turquoise ring, cluster work, Joe and Susan Tsabetsaye, J. Tsabetsaye, 1970s–1980s, 1.15" × 1.59", $200–300.

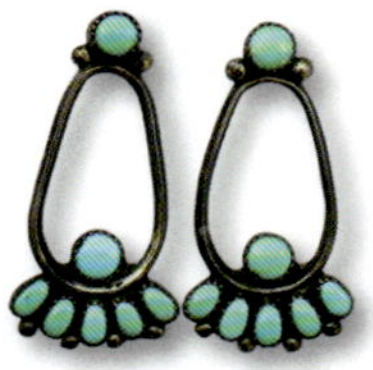

Turquoise earrings, cluster work, Roger Tsabetsaye Sr., R. Tsabetsaye with his the Knifewing shield, 1980s–1990s, 0.92" × 1.83", $200–300.

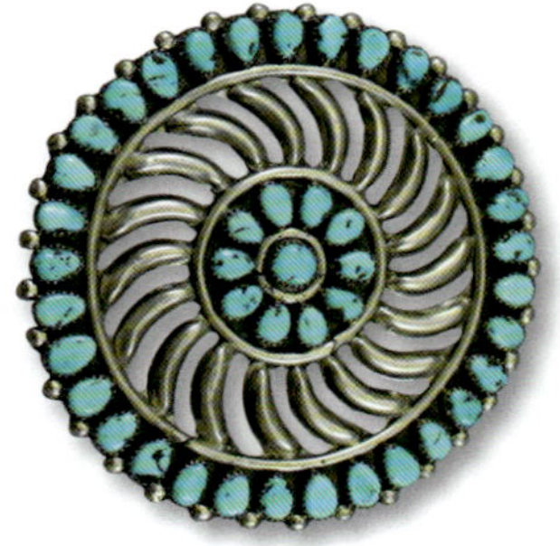

Turquoise pin, cluster work, Raymond Gasper, no hallmark, 1940s–1950s, 3.72" in diameter, $400–600.

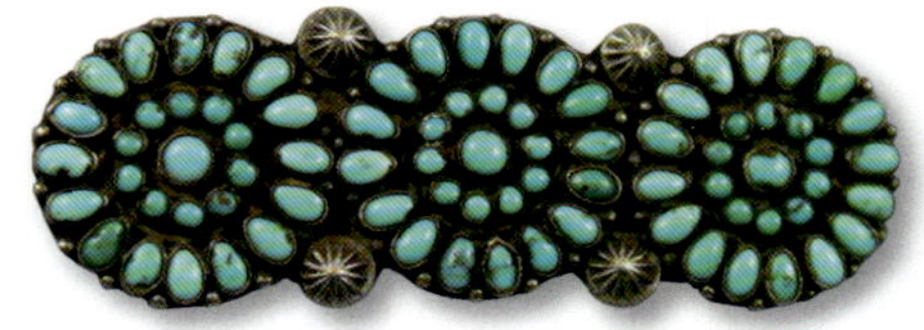

Turquoise pin, cluster work, Eva Solomon Sanchez(?), no hallmark, 1950s–1960s, 0.97" × 2.78", $200–300.

The design of the turquoise ring above, on top, by Joe and Susan Tsabetsaye, reminds me of the three rings made by Doris and Warren Ondelacy (p. 69).

Roger Tsabetsaye Sr. made the turquoise earrings above, on the bottom. Although they are not made in the traditional cluster work design in its strictest sense, the arrangement of turquoise cabochons is still reminiscent of a traditional flower-head pattern.

The original price tag on the Lone Mountain turquoise pin above read "Fannie Ondelacy" and "$180," but it turned out to be the work of Raymond Gasper, brother of Susan Gasper Tsabetsaye, and also a more valuable piece. A snake-eye cabochon with a plain silver wire is surrounded by ten pear-shaped cabochons accompanied. This central area is surrounded by an embossed silver crescent with a plain wire. The fourth band consists of thirty-three cabochons and thirty-three unstamped silver drops.

Eva Solomon Sanchez probably made the turquoise pin above. The three equally sized, horizontally set, three-fold clusters are divided by two stamped silver drops. The central and middle bands are set with snake-eye cabochons, while pear-shaped ones adorn the outer edge.

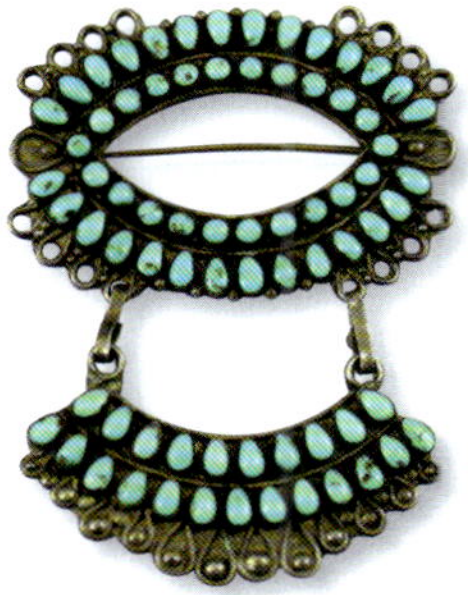

Kingman turquoise pin, cluster work, Alice Sanchez (?), No hallmark, 1950s–1960s, 2.34" × 3.13", $300–450.

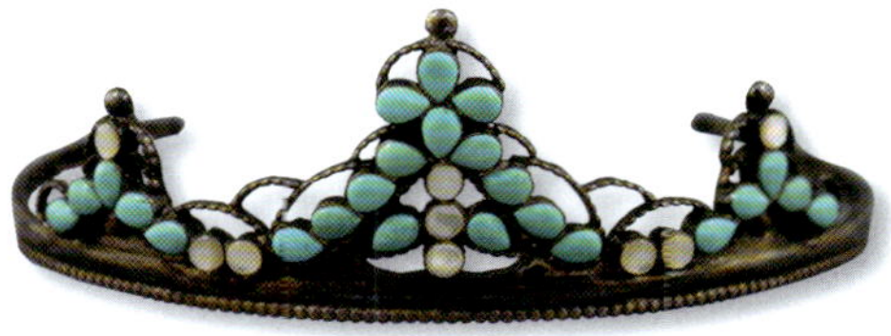

Turquoise and white mother-of-pearl tiara, cluster work, Veronica Poblano, Veronica, 1970s–1980s, 1.73" tall, $800–1,200.

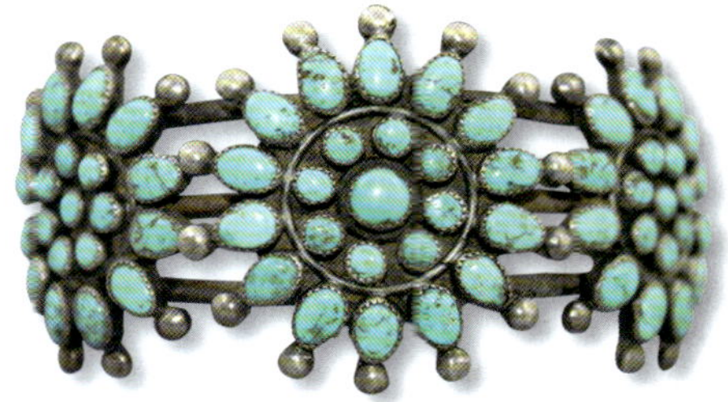

Turquoise bracelet, cluster work, artist unknown, no hallmark, 1940s–1950s, 1.59" in diameter central medallion, $300–450.

The upper part of the Kingman turquoise pin above is made with snake-eye and pear-shaped cabochons, while the lower part is made with solely pear-shaped stones. Although each cabochon is very tiny, this style is still considered cluster work, because the pear-shaped cabochons are dominant.

Veronica Poblano made the turquoise and white mother-of-pearl tiara above for Miss Zuni in the annual Zuni Pueblo Head Start program. Two matching combs came with it but have been lost.

The maker of the three-fold turquoise bracelet above is unknown. One of my Zuni informants attributed it to Douglas Lesansee, but Douglas is more famous for needle point than cluster work. The center and second band consist of snake-eye cabochons, and the outer edge features pear-shaped stones and unstamped silver drops.

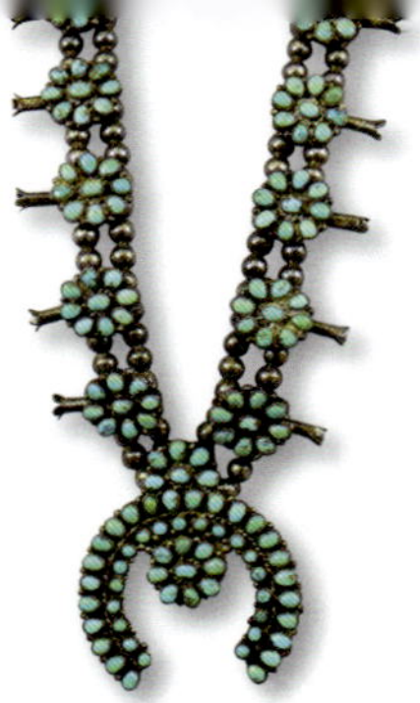

Kingman turquoise squash blossom necklace, cluster work, artist unknown, no hallmark, 1940s–1950s, 1.96" × 2.20" naja, $600–900.

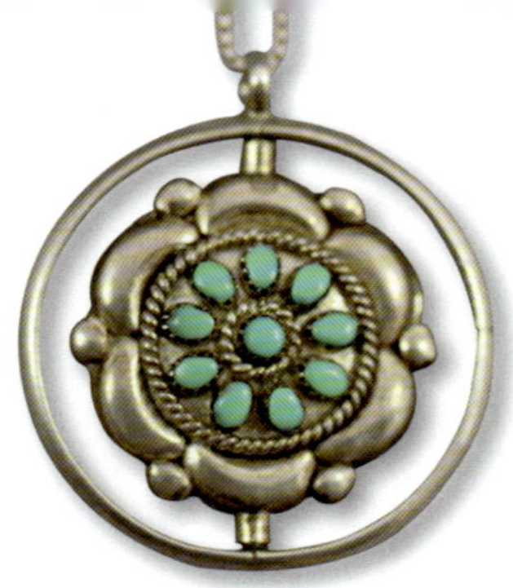

Turquoise and coral swivel pendant, cluster work, Fred and Elsie Laconsello, Fred and Elsie, 1980s–1990s, 1.28" × 1.45", $100–150.

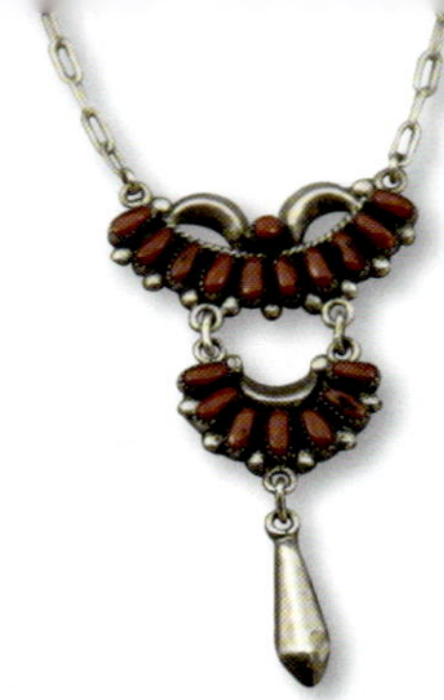

Coral necklace, cluster work, Billy and Lucinda Laweka, Bill and Lou, 1970s–1980s, 1.41" × 2.56", $300–450.

One of my informants attributed the tiny Kingman turquoise squash blossom necklace above to Roosevelt and Bernice Tekala, but the Tekalas are more famous for Dishta-style inlay than cluster work.

Fred and Elsie Laconsello made this double-sided, three-fold, turquoise and coral swivel pendant. Its central and middle bands consist of turquoise cabochons on one side and coral ones on another side, and the outer edge is made with embossed silver crescents and unstamped silver drops on both sides.

The top part of Billy and Lucinda Laweka's well-executed coral necklace above consists of one snake-eye and ten pear-shaped cabochons, in addition to two embossed silver crescents and twelve plain silver drops. The mid-section consists of seven pear-shaped cabochons, one embossed silver crescent, and nine plain silver drops, and hangs from the top section. Lastly, a silver embossed dangle hangs from the middle. This couple's pear-shaped cabochons are always longer than those made by almost all cluster-work lapidaries.

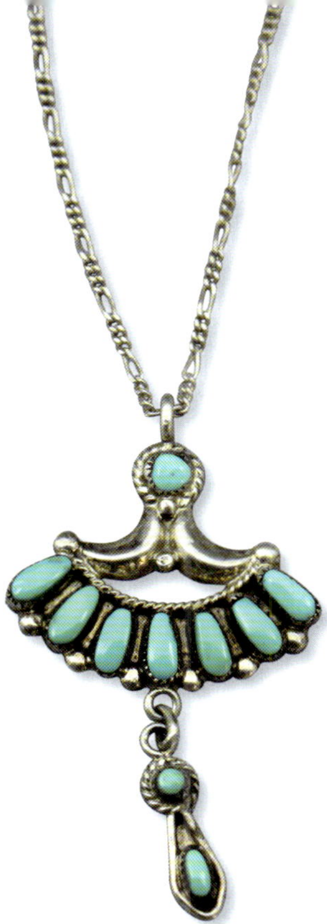

Turquoise and pendant, cluster work, Billy and Lucinda Laweka, Bill & Lou, 1970s–1980s, 1.28" × 2.30", $160–240.

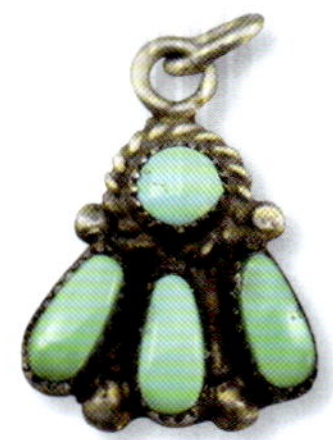

Turquoise pendant, cluster work, Billy and Lucinda Laweka, Bill & Lou, 1980s–1990s, 0.57" × 0.80", $100–150.

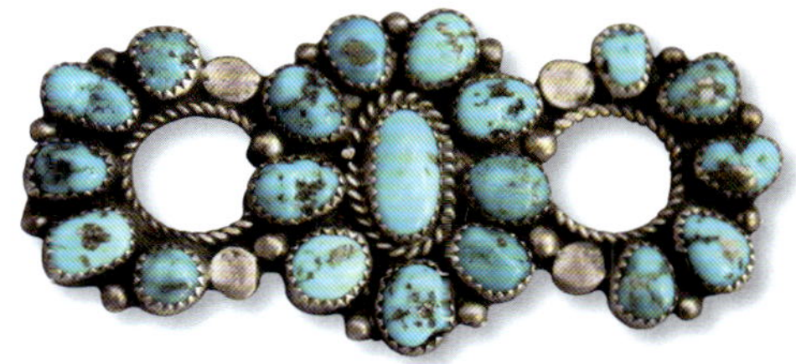

Turquoise bow pint, cluster work, Louise Paywa (?), no hallmark, 1980s–1990s, 2.90" × 1.38", $150–225.

Except for the dangles in the turquoise pendant at left, this piece by Billy and Lucinda is similar to their coral pendant featured in *Who's Who in Zuni Jewelry* (Levy, 1980, p.54). The dangle in the piece in Gordon Levy's book has an embossed silver part, while mine consists of one snake-eye and one pear-shaped cabochon, each encircled by twisted silver wire. Above is a simple, but attractive, turquoise pendant from the 1980s or '90s, which measures 0.80 inch long.

My friend, a Zuni artist, attributed this turquoise bow pin, to Bowman Paywa's wife, Louise. An oblong center cabochon is set vertically and encircled by a twisted wire. This is encircled by nine turquoise cabochons accompanied by nine unstamped silver drops. On both sides of this central cluster, two sets of flat silver drops, five turquoise cabochons, and five smaller unstamped silver drops are placed in the form of a bow.

2. Petite-Point Style

The name "petite point' derives from the way in which a turquoise cabochon is cut. If it is cut in the pear-shape, it is cluster work. If one end of a cabochon has a sharp point, it is petite point. The arrangements of cabochons in both styles are almost identical and resemble flower heads.

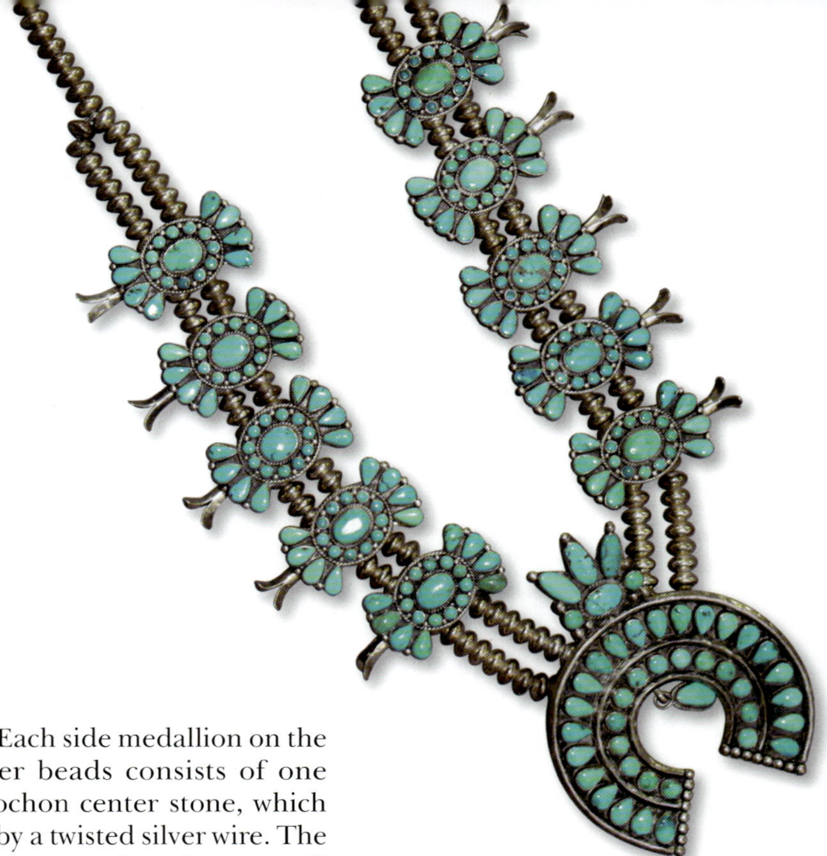

Thelma Sheche made this Lone Mountain turquoise squash blossom necklace for her mother, Susie Kucate, under the guidance of Thelma's aunt, Doris Ondelacy. Its naja consists of twenty-two pear-shaped and fourteen snake-eye cabochons, and above this naja sit four oblong and two snake-eye cabochons. Each side medallion on the double-silver beads consists of one oblong cabochon center stone, which is encircled by a twisted silver wire. The next band out contains eleven small cabochons, and two sets of four cabochons adorn both sides of each respective, surrounding wire.

Lone Mountain turquoise squash blossom necklace, cluster work, Thelma Sheche, no hallmark, late 1940s, 3.83" × 4.93" naja, $6,000–9,000.

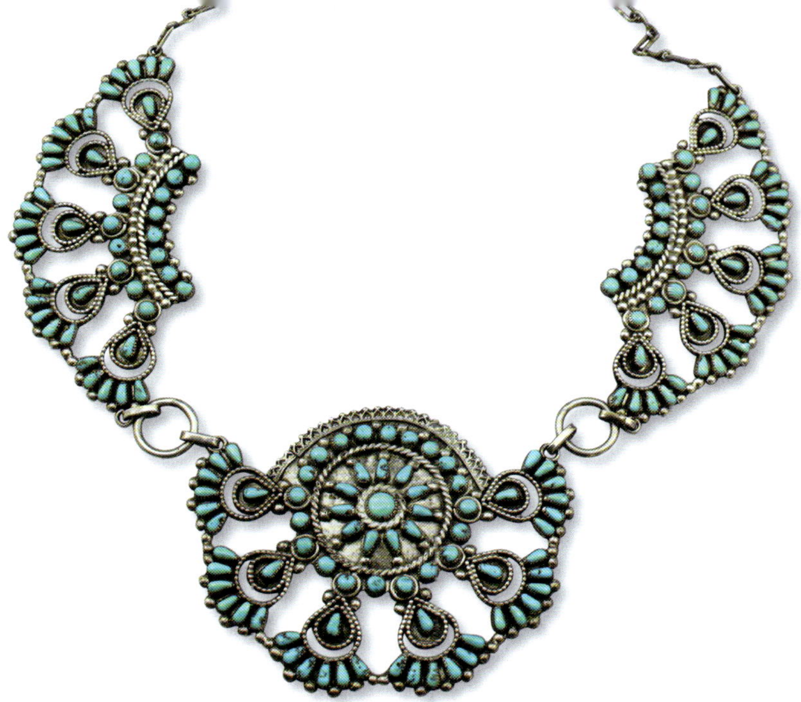

Turquoise necklace, petite point/cluster work, Pesancio and Ramona Lasiloo, P. L. Z. N. M., late 1970s, 3.75" × 3.04" central medallion, $600–900.

Pesancio and Ramona Lasiloo made this turquoise necklace in the 1970s. It is one of the most elegant necklaces I have ever seen—its highly refined silver work and lapidary work are among the best examples in Zuni jewelry.

I heard the names Pesancio and Ramona Lasiloo for the first time when a young potter named Jaycee Nahohai stayed with me to observe and learn Japanese pottery making. One day, he told me his maternal grandmother, Ramona Lasiloo, and her husband, Pesancio Lasiloo, made jewelry. He promised me he would introduce me to her the next time I visited Zuni.

A few weeks later, this necklace showed up in an online auction. As its design and execution were superb, I decided to acquire it without knowing who made it. There is a hallmark, "P. L., Z. N. M.," in addition to a handwritten message, "The former governor of Zuni tribe." This turned out to be the work of the Lasiloos. Pesancio was the lieutenant governor, however, not the governor.

Its central medallion consists of seventy-four turquoise cabochons, and each side medallion has sixty-four stones. Two different sizes of snake-eye turquoise cabochons surround the center, with those touching each fan-shaped cluster carved a little larger than the others.

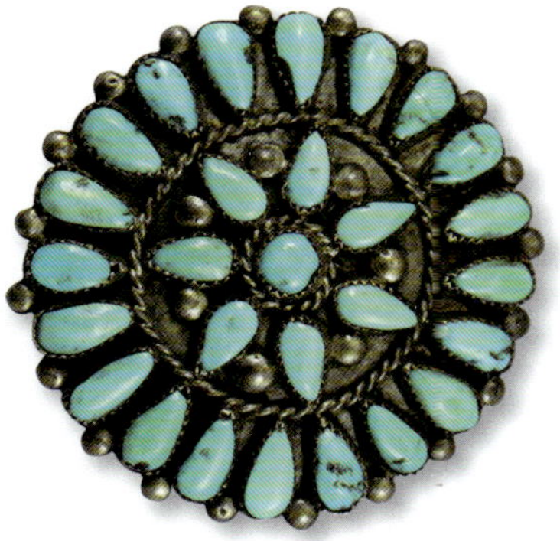

Turquoise pin/pendant, petite point, artist unknown (Tammie Simplicio?), 1970s–1980s, 1.84" in diameter, $100–150.

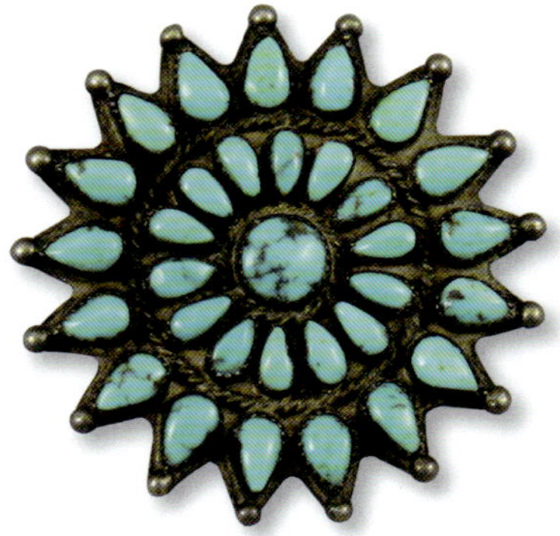

Turquoise pin, petite point, Eva Solomon Sanchez (?), no hallmark, 1950s–1960s, 1.67" in diameter, $160–240.

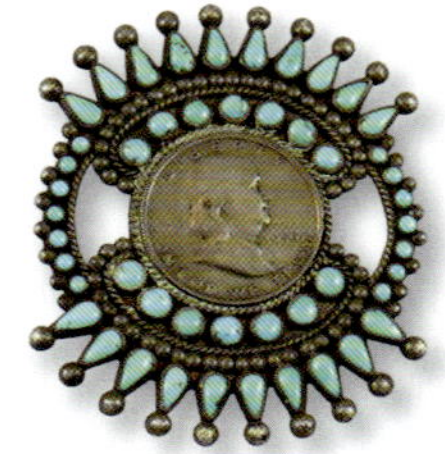

Turquoise bolo converted from pin, petite point, artist unknown, no hallmark, 1950s, 2.61" × 3.12", $400–600.

The medium-size turquoise pin/pendant above is made in the three-fold arrangement. As the turquoise cabochons in the second and third bands from the center clearly have sharp points, it should be classified as petite point jewelry.

Eva Solomon Sanchez is probably the artist responsible for this turquoise pin above, made in the three-fold arrangement. The first band consists of a round turquoise cabochon; the second, cabochons with sharp points that direct inward; and the third, stones with sharp points directing outward, with unstamped silver drops on each point. It is a small, but beautiful, delicate, and appealing piece.

The large turquoise bolo above, measuring 3.12 inches long and converted from a pin, was made in the three-fold arrangement. A half-dollar coin produced in 1950, encircled by a twisted silver wire, is set in the center, and two sets of seven snake-eye turquoise cabochons are set over and under its center in the second band, with a cut-out on both sides. Two sets of ten petite-point cabochons with unstamped silver drops are set over and under the bolo slide, and two sets of small snake-eye cabochons with small unstamped silver drops are set in the third layer. One of my informants has attributed this well-executed piece to Annie Quam Gasper.

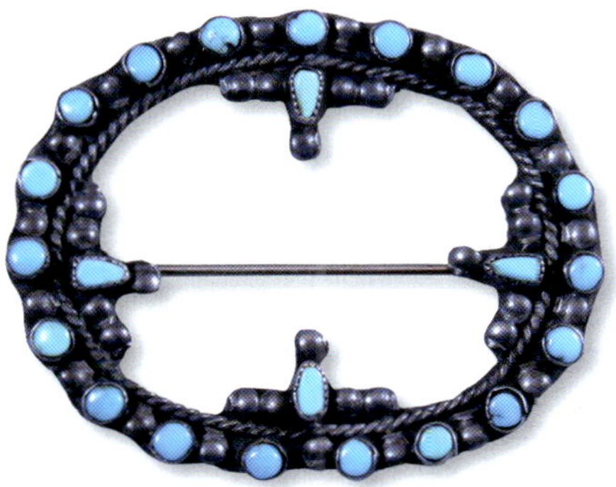

Turquoise pin, petite point, artist unknown, no hallmark, 1950s–1960s, 1.88" × 1.52", $100–150.

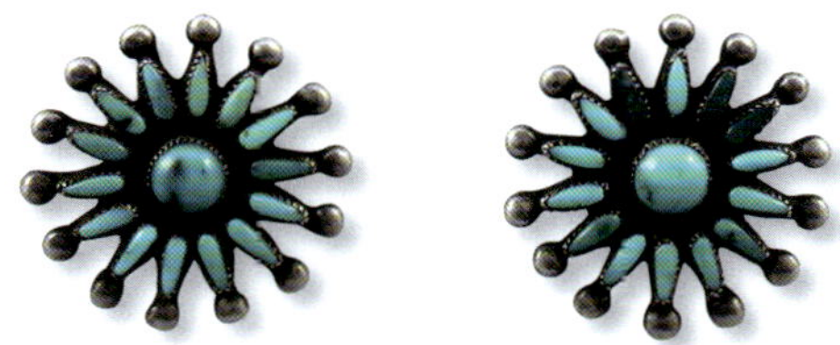

Turquoise earrings, petite point, Jennie Eustace (?), no hallmark, 1950s–1960s, 0.81" in diameter, $120–180.

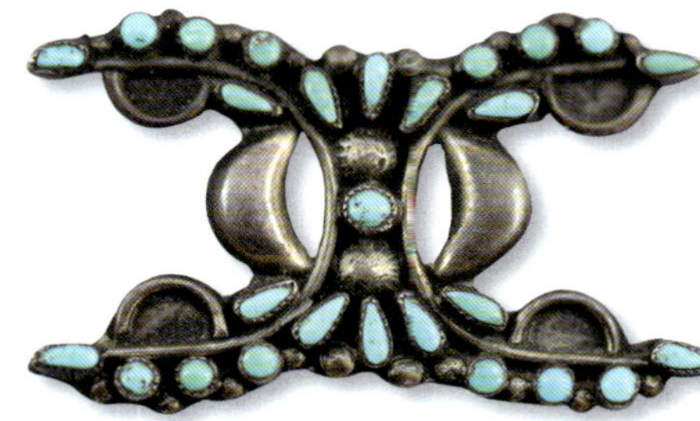

Turquoise pin, petite point, artist unknown, no hallmark, 1950s–1960s, 1.48" × 0.90", $100–150.

Snake-eye turquoise cabochons are set in the outer rim of the unique pin above, and four petite-point cabochons are set inward—two horizontally and two vertically.

Jennie Eustace probably made the tiny turquoise earrings above. A snake-eye cabochon is set in the center without a twisted silver wire, and fourteen petite-point cabochons with unstamped silver drops are pointed outward.

One of my informants attributed this tiny, complexly designed turquoise pin to Virgil Dishta Sr.

3. Needle Point

In needle point, both ends of a cabochon have sharp points. These cabochons are placed in the flower-head pattern or row pattern, a straight-lined arrangement.

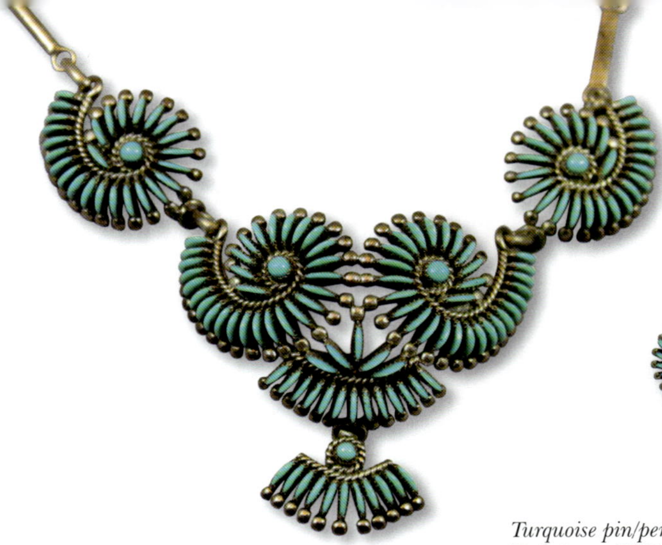

Turquoise necklace, needle point, Edith Tsabetsaye, EZT with barrel, 1980s–1990s, 1.83" × 1.78" central medallion, $3,000–4,500.

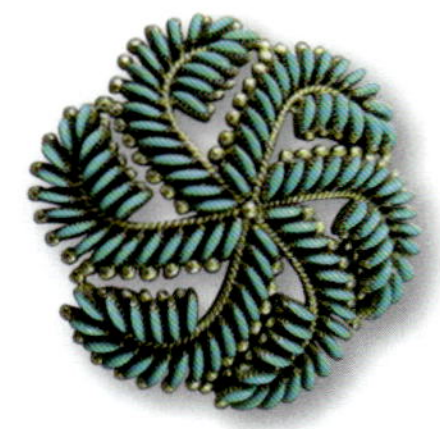

Turquoise pin/pendant, needle point, Edith Tsabetsaye, EZT with barrel, 1990s–2000s, 1.84" × 1.78", $1,000–1,500.

Edith Tsabetsaye made the Sleeping Beauty turquoise necklace above. Usually, matching earrings come with her originally designed necklaces, such as this one, but the pair that had once completed a set had been lost before I bought it. Several half moon–shaped cabochons are set in the raised swirl pattern on silver backings, giving this necklace a cubic impression.

Each cabochon in the Sleeping Beauty turquoise pin above is carved in the shape of a half-moon, polished, and set on a three-dimensional, swirled silver backing, or flower head. This is also Edith's original design.

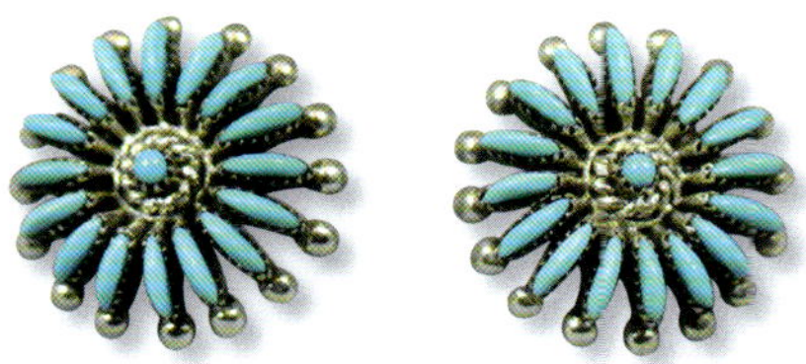

Turquoise earrings, needle point, Edith Tsabetsaye, EZT on the rectangular silver platelet, 1990s–2000s, 0.71" in diameter, $200–300.

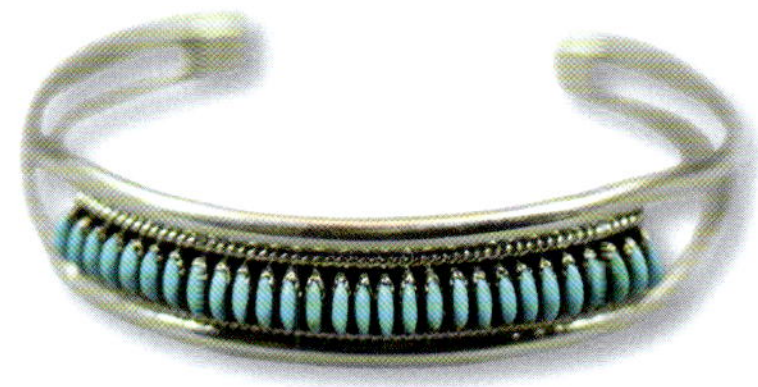

Turquoise bracelet, needle point, Edith Tsabetsaye, EZT with barrel, 1990s–2000s, 0.52" wide, $300–450.

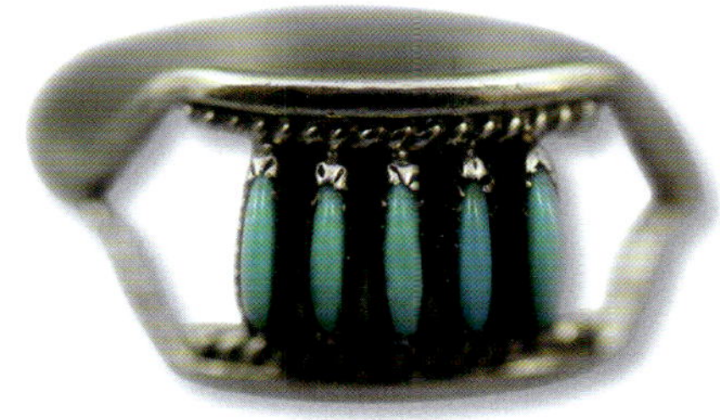

Turquoise ring, needle point, Edith Tsabetsaye, EZT with barrel, 1990s–2000s, 0.36" wide, $160–240.

At around the same time, Edith made these Sleeping Beauty turquoise earrings. They look like simple flower heads, but they are three-dimensional, with domed silver backing and half-moon cabochons, just like the necklace and pin on the previous page.

The simple, beautiful bracelet above is made in a cabochon arrangement called row work. The half-moon shape is characteristic of Edith's personal style.

Next is a Sleeping Beauty turquoise ring, also made in the row work style. It looks similar to the bracelet, but I am not sure whether they are matching pieces.

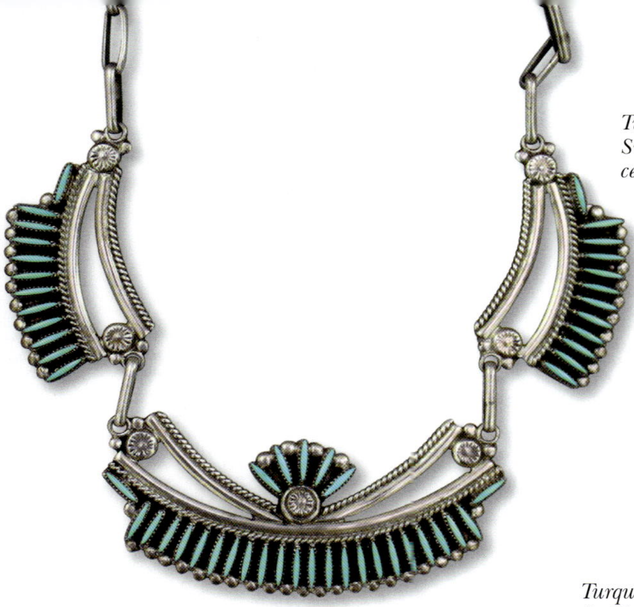

Turquoise necklace, needle point, Bryant Waatsa Sr., B. Waatsa, 1970s–1990s, 2.33" × 1.02" central medallion, $400–600.

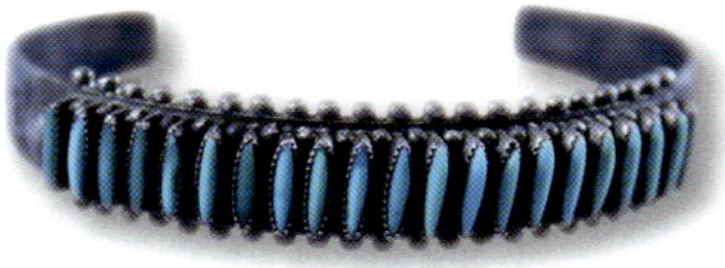

Turquoise bracelet, needle point, Bryant Waatsa Sr., B. W., 1970s–1980s, 0.48" wide, $300–450.

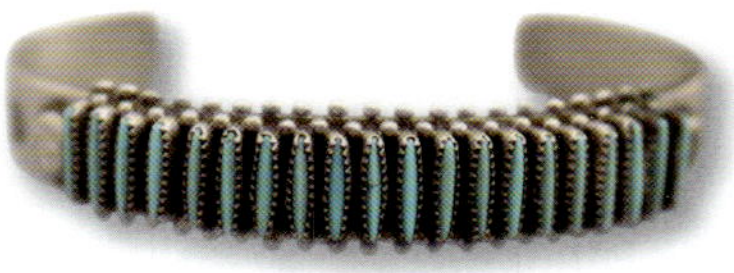

Turquoise bracelet for a baby, needle point, Bryant Waatsa Sr., B. Waatsa, 1990s, 0.41" wide, $120–180.

The overall composition of Bryant Waatsa Sr.'s turquoise necklace above is clean, simple, and attractive. The center panel in this three-panel composition consists of twenty-nine cabochons, twenty-seven plain silver drops, three stamped silver drops, and three twisted and three plain silver wires.

The row-work turquoise bracelet above consists of twenty-one cabochons and forty-two small and two large unstamped silver drops. Both ends of the bracelet are stamped with two different dies: the crescent and the flower head. They might be clues to identifying Bryant Waatsa Sr.'s unsigned jewelry.

Next is a turquoise baby bracelet from the mid-1990s. Bryant's granddaughter asked me to take it, because it was of no use to her. The silver cuff has two stamps and stamped silver drops.

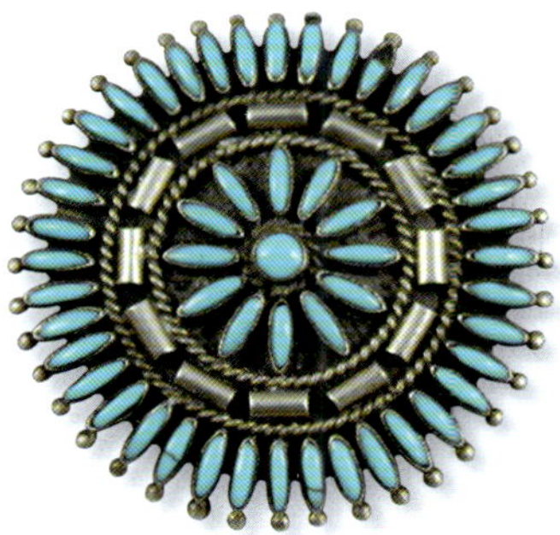

Turquoise pin/pendant, needle point, Aaron Sheche, no hallmark, 1950s–1960s, 2.05" in diameter, $100–150.

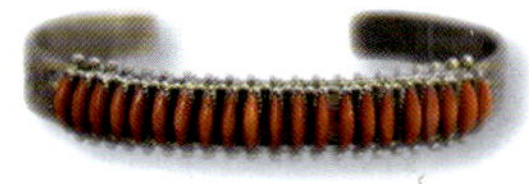

Coral bracelet, needle point, Hugh and Agnes Bowekaty, H. & A. Bowekaty, 1980s–1990s, 0.89" wide, $200–300.

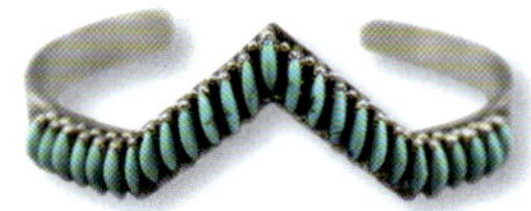

Turquoise bracelet, needle point, Hugh and Agnes Bowekaty, H. & A. Bowekaty, 1980s–1990s, 0.89" wide, $200–300.

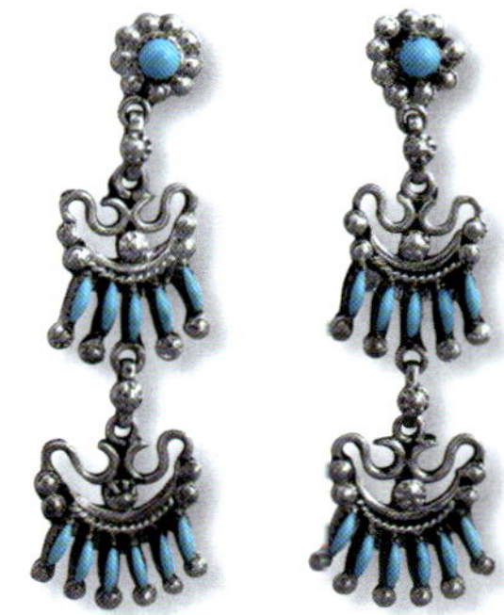

Turquoise earrings, needle point, Hugh and Agnes Bowekaty, H. & A. Bowekaty, 1980s–1990s, 0.50" × 2.35", $120–180.

Thelma Sheche gave me this turquoise pin/pendant on September 7th, 2013. She told me her late husband, Aaron Sheche, made it. Although one cabochon is broken and another one is cracked, it is an invaluable tool for studying his work before he switched from silver and lapidary works to fetish carving. It is made in the four-fold arrangement, with silver tubes set in the third band.

The turquoise bracelet on top, by Hugh and Agnes Bowekaty, is a variation of row work in which turquoise cabochons are set in the form of a house's roof. Like Bryant Waatsa's bracelets, both ends of the silver cuff are stamped with two different dies. It is no wonder their silver works are so similar—they worked side by side for a long time.

Hugh and Agnes made the coral bracelet on the bottom around the same time. The half-moon shaped cabochons is characteristic of their later pieces. The stampings on the surface on the cuff are the same as on the first bracelet.

Notice the delicate harmony of the silver and lapidary work in the unique "chandelier" earrings above.

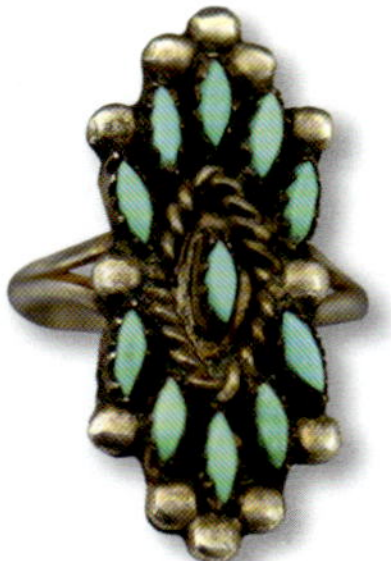

Turquoise ring, needle point, Eva Solomon Sanchez, no hallmark, 1940s–1950s, 0.52" × 1.16", $120–180.

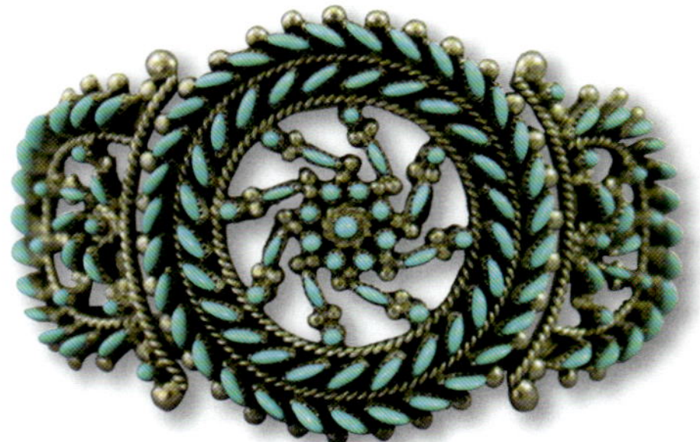

Turquoise bracelet, needle point, Octavius and Irma Seowtewa, Octavius & Irma S. in cursive, 1970s–1980s, 1.57" wide, $400–600.

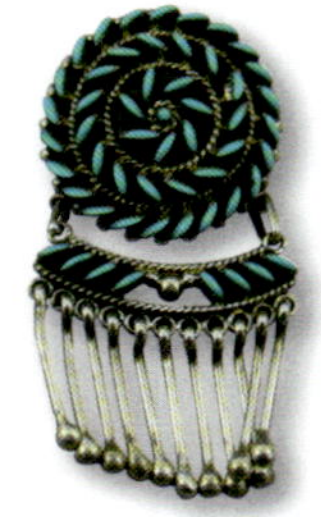

Turquoise pin/pendant, needle point, Octavius and Irma Seowtewa, Octavius Irma, 1990s–2000s, 1.12" × 2.35", $200–300.

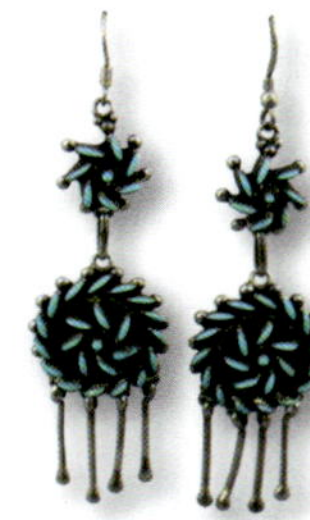

Turquoise earrings, needle point, Octavius and Irma Seowtewa, OIS, 1990s–2000s, 0.82" × 2.62", $160–240.

Although the turquoise cabochons in Eva Solomon Sanchez's ring above are carved a little thicker than average, they are still considered needle point, as they have two sharp ends.

Octavius and Irma Seowtewa's pieces are unique and easily identified by the presence of half-moon cabochons set diagonally in the flower-head pattern. The unnecessary background of the well-executed bracelet above has been cut out, making it a combination of needle point and open work.

The background of the silver backing on the Seowtewas' turquoise pin/pendant above, on top, is blackened due to oxidization as a result of the use of some type of acid. The main round part is domed and gives this pin, which measures 1.12 inches in diameter, a three-dimensional effect. The matching, delicate earrings feature two domed, silver backings connected by a handmade link.

4. Snake-Eye style

If small, round cabochons are used in the main part of a piece of jewelry, it is called snake-eye style.

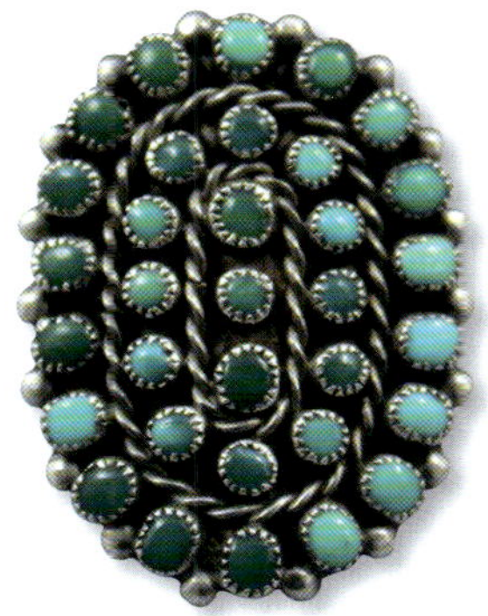

Turquoise ring, snake eye, Duane Quam, no hallmark, 1940s–1950s, 0.94" × 1.25", $160–240.

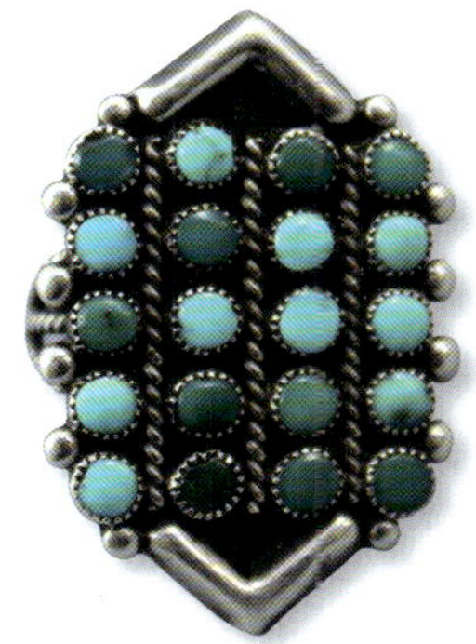

Turquoise ring, snake eye, Fannie Weebothee Ondelacy, no hallmark, 1940s–1960s, 0.91" × 1.35", $160–240.

Duane Quam made the turquoise ring shown in the center of the page in a simple, three-fold arrangement. Three cabochons within a twisted wire are set vertically in the center, twelve cabochons are fixed in the second band, and twenty cabochons and twenty small unstamped silver drops are used in the outermost band.

The cabochon arrangement of Fannie Weebothee Ondelacy's ring above is considered row work. Its stamped silver chevrons are common among works by the Weebothees, including Lee and Mary, Fannie, and Julie.

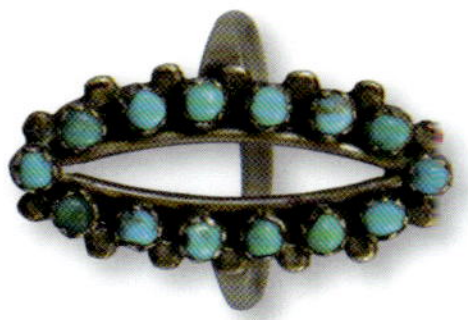

Turquoise ring, snake eye, Bernice Tekala (?), no hallmark, 1940s–1960s, 0.52" × 1.05", $160–240.

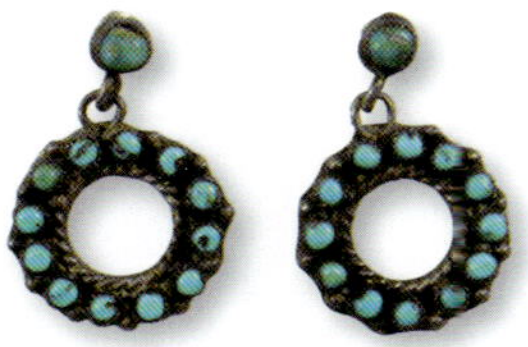

Turquoise earrings, snake eye, Bernice Tekala (?), no hallmark, 1940s–1960s, 0.76" × 1.07", $160–240.

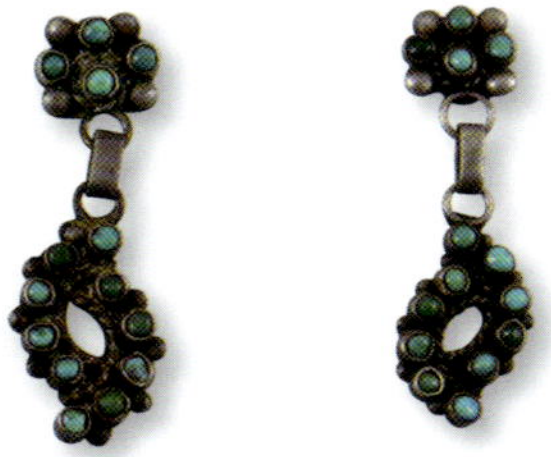

Turquoise earrings, snake eye, Bernice Tekala (?), no hallmark, 1940s–1960s, 0.61" × 1.05", $80–120.

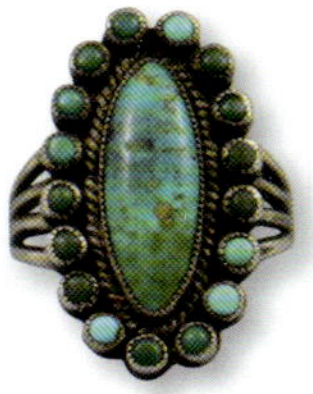

Turquoise ring, snake eye, Bernice Tekala (?), no hallmark, 1940s–1960s, 0.52" × 1.05", $160–240.

Bernice Tekala probably made the simple turquoise ring above that measures 1.05 inches long and the screw-back turquoise earrings below it.

The next pair of earrings also have screw-backs. The cabochon arrangement is reminiscent of the Yin and Yang pattern.

Last is a turquoise ring, presumably by Bernice. A large cabochon is set with a very fine, hand-cut, saw-tooth bezel and is surrounded by a twisted silver wire. Seventeen snake-eye cabochons surround the centerpiece. Its shank is a silver platelet with ends in a rare four-split design.

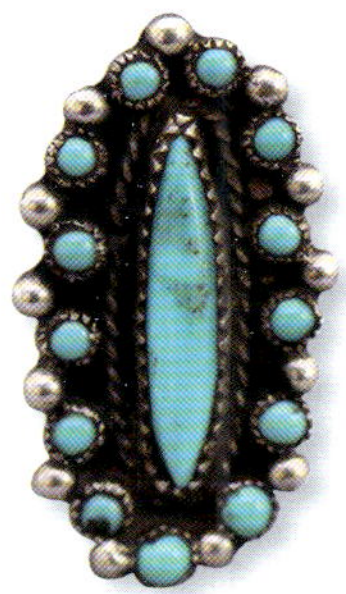

Blue Gem turquoise ring, snake eye, artist unknown, no hallmark, 1950s–1960s, 0.74" × 1.36", $160–240.

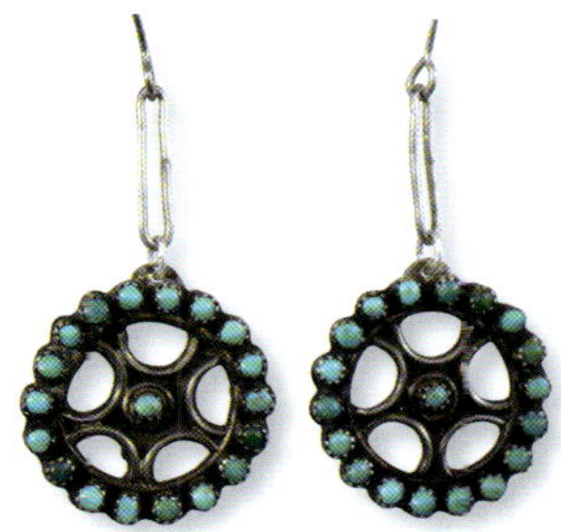

Turquoise earrings, snake eye, artist unknown, no hallmark, 1950s–1960s, 0.82" × 0.89', $160–240.

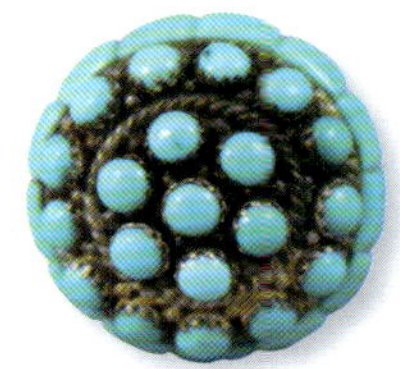

Turquoise ring, snake-eye and mosaic inlay, Lee and Mary Weebothee, Lee & Mary, 1980s–1990s, 0.85" in diameter, $300–450.

One of my informants attributed this Blue Gem turquoise ring to Annie Quam Gasper. A thin turquoise cabochon is set with a hand-cut, saw-tooth bezel, and surrounded by a twisted silver wire, which is encircled by thirteen snake-eye cabochons and unstamped silver drops.

An informant attributed the turquoise earrings above, which resemble a wheel pattern, to Virgil Dishta Sr. They originally had screw-backs, which at some later time, were converted to French hooks.

The shank (not pictured) of the ring above is a characteristic feature of Lee and Mary Weebothee's work. This and the following five rings each have a band arranged just outside the outer edge that consists of rectangular turquoise cabochons in the mosaic inlay style, but I put them in this section because they have groups of seven or more snake-eye cabochons as centerpieces.

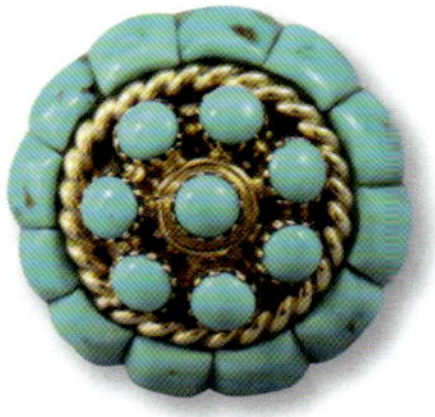

14K gold and turquoise ring, snake-eye and mosaic inlay, Lee and Mary Weebothee, Lee & Mary, 1980s–1990s, 0.78" in diameter, $400–600.

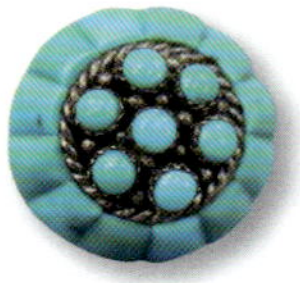

Turquoise ring, snake-eye and mosaic inlay, Lee and Mary Weebothee, Lee & Mary, 1980s–1990s, 0.74" in diameter, $200–300.

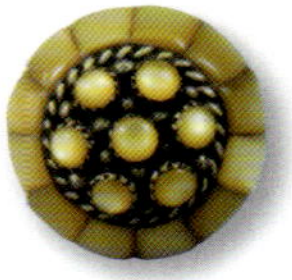

Gold lip mother-of-pearl ring, snake-eye and mosaic inlay, Lee and Mary Weebothee, Lee & Mary, 1980s–1990s, 0.74" in diameter, $200–300.

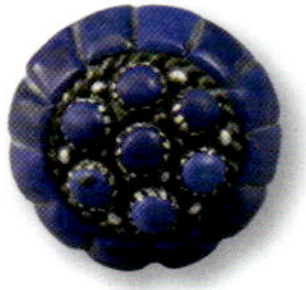

Lapis lazuli ring, snake-eye and mosaic inlay, Lee and Mary Weebothee, Lee & Mary, 1980s–1990s, 0.73" in diameter, $200–300.

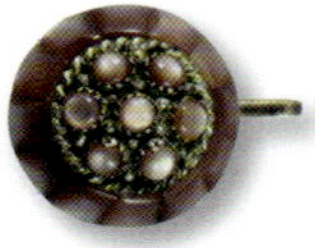

Purple lip mother-of-pearl pendant, snake-eye and mosaic inlay, Lee and Mary Weebothee, Lee & Mary, 1980s–1990s, 0.73" in diameter, $200–300.

Seven snake-eye cabochons surround one in the center in the piece above, the only ring on this page with eight cabochons and the only example here of gold and turquoise jewelry—the twisted metal wiring is 14K gold. Its simple shank is different from more complex shanks frequently seen in their rings. The ring measures 0.78 inch across and the central snake-eye cabochon is 0.41 inch tall from its base, giving the ring a three-dimensional effect.

The snake-eye cabochons surrounding the center in the ring on top, above, total six. Its ring ends are characteristic to their style, in which both ends are split into two and extended 180 degrees wide. The lapis lazuli ring underneath is nearly identical in design and size.

Row work is so named not for the method of stone cutting, but of stone arrangement. Usually, rectangular- or square-cut cabochons are arranged in a straight row or multiple straight rows.

5. Row Work

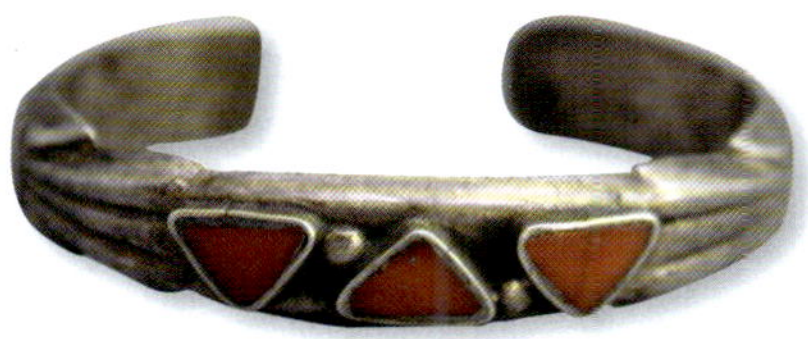

Coral bracelet, cast and row works, artist unknown, no hallmark, 1930s–1940s, 0.45" wide, $200–300.

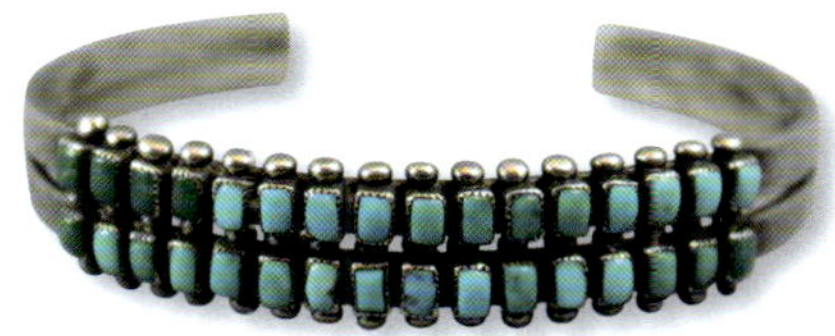

Turquoise bracelet, row work, Clark and Bessie Couyancy, no hallmark, 1950s–1960s, 0.50" wide, $200–300.

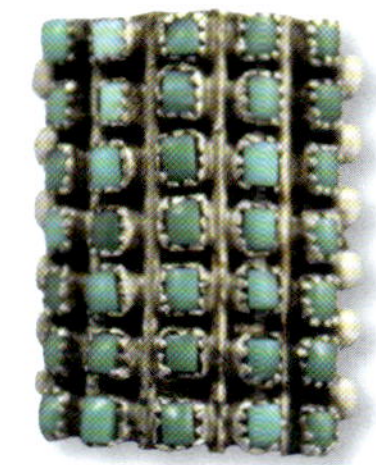

Turquoise ring, row work, Clark and Bessie Couyancy, no hallmark, 1950s–1960s, 0.72" × 1.01", $160–240.

The small child's bracelet above has three triangular corals in the cast and row work styles. Leonard Martza attributed it to his father's uncle, Juan de Dios. I bought it from an older, active Zuni silversmith.

The turquoise bracelet above features the incredibly intricate silver and lapidary work that is characteristic of Clark and Bessie Couyancy. It consists of sixteen cabochons in two rows, and each cabochon is extremely tiny—only 0.10 inches wide and 0.16 inches long.

Their turquoise ring above contains thirty-five cabochons arranged in five rows by seven columns, four plain silver wires, and six plain silver drops on both sides. The ends of the ring shank are split into two.

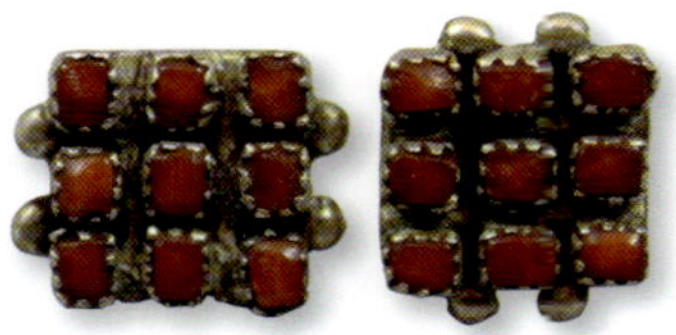

Coral earrings, row work, artist unknown, no hallmark, 1960s–1970s, 0.41" × 0.50", $80–120.

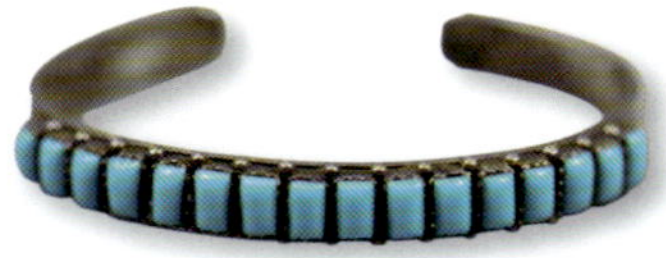

Turquoise bracelet, row work, Eleanor Wallace Ahiyite, no hallmark, 1960s–1970s, 0.33" wide, $200–300.

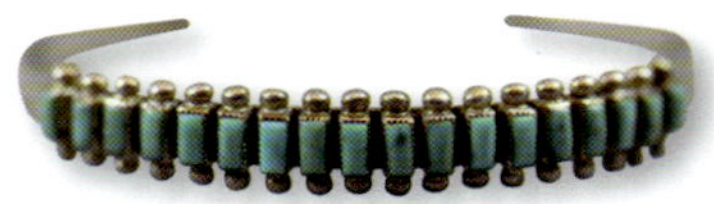

Turquoise bracelet, row work, Eleanor Wallace Ahiyite, E. A., 2012, 0.58" wide, $200–300.

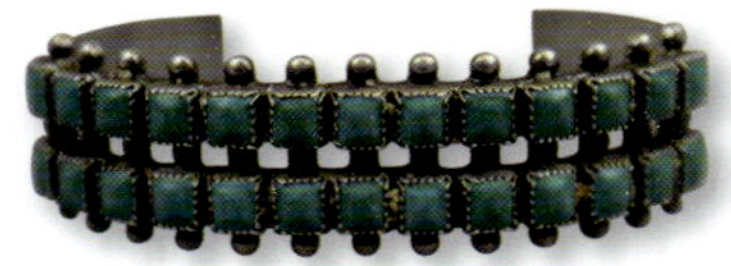

Turquoise bracelet, row work, Carrie Katsenih, no hallmark, 1960s–1970s, 0.70" wide, $200–300.

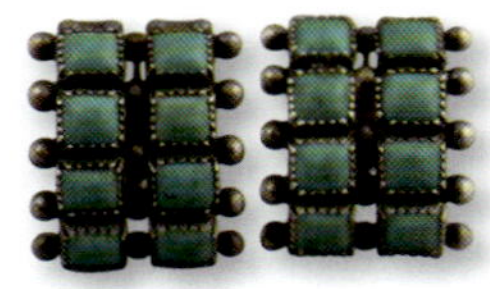

Turquoise earrings, row work, Carrie Katsenih, no hallmark, 1960s–1970s, 0.65" × 0.78", $120–180.

An informant attributed these tiny coral earrings to Irma Unkestine.

Eleanor Wallace Ahiyite made both bracelets above. The one on top consists of sixteen cabochons and fifteen tiny, plain silver drops on both sides of the cuff. She cut her rectangular cabochons longer than the Couyancys usually do.

She also made this Sleeping Beauty turquoise bracelet, underneath, in October 2012. It is signed "E. A." with an electric pencil. The newer bracelet has larger cabochons and silver drops.

Carrie Katsenih's turquoise bracelet above consists of thirteen square-cut cabochons in two rows on a split silver plate/cuff, and thirteen plain silver drops on the top, bottom, and middle of the cuff.

Underneath are her turquoise earrings, with eight square-cut cabochons and twenty-three plain silver drops each.

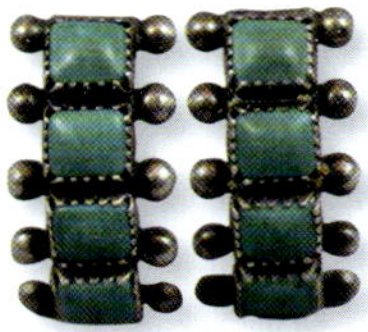

Turquoise earrings, row work, Carrie Katsenih, no hallmark, 1960s–1970s, 0.39" × 0.74", $100–150.

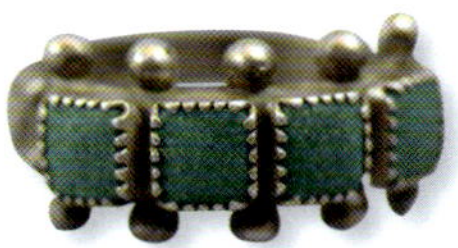

Turquoise ring, row work, Carrie Katsenih, no hallmark, 1960s–1970s, 0.75" × 0.39", $100–150.

In the pair above, each earring has four square-cut cabochons and twelve plain silver drops.

Finally, underneath is a ring with four turquoise cabochons and eighteen plain silver drops.

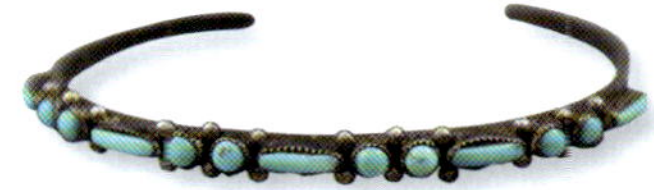

Turquoise bracelet, dot and dash, Tony Chopito Sr., no hallmark, 1960s–1970s, 0.22" wide, $100–150.

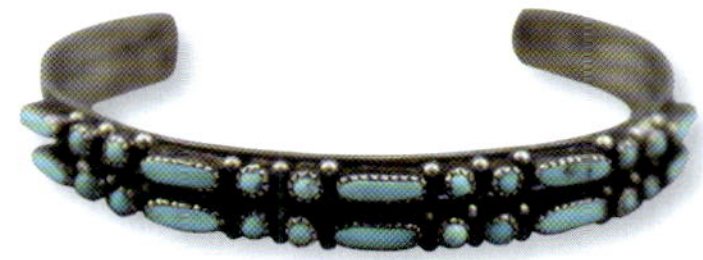

Turquoise bracelet, dot and dash, Tony Chopito Sr., TC, 1970s–1980s, 0.35" wide, $160–240.

Tony Chopito Sr. made both pieces above. The row-work bracelet on top can also be called dot-and-dash because of the combination of eight snake-eye and five long cabochons. Set around the cabochons is a total of twenty-four small plain silver drops.

Two silver cuffs of the same arrangement as the previous piece are welded together in the bracelet underneath.

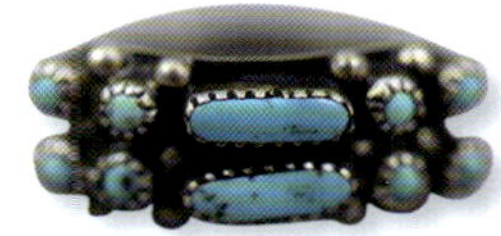

Turquoise ring, dot and dash, Tony Chopito Sr., no hallmark, 1970s–1980s, 0.34" × 0.83", $80–120.

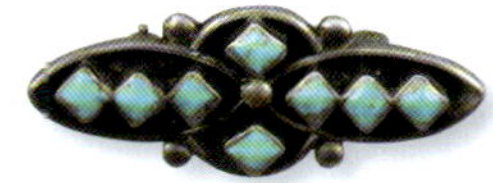

Turquoise pin, row work, Jennie Salvador, no hallmark, 1950s–1960s, 1.63" × 0.65", $100–150.

Eight snake-eye cabochons, two long cabochons, and twelve plain silver drops adorn Tony's bracelet above.

Jennie Salvador made the pin underneath, which consists of eight diamond-shaped cabochons and five plain silver drops, in a variation of the row work style. The edges of the pin, fanned with silver wires, give this piece a shadowy, box-like effect.

CHAPTER IV

CHANNEL WORK

Where silver work is concerned, there is no difference between mosaic inlay and channel work. First, a silversmith creates a silver backing with multiple channels, and then a lapidary cuts and polishes individual stones and shells to fit into each channel. Usually, in channel inlay, stones and shells of the same color are set in whole channels, while mosaic inlay is usually marked by variously colored stones and shells. In some cases, in a work of mosaic inlay, a few different colors of stone and shell are set in the same channel.

There are several prolific Zuni artists in the channel work style, including Alice Leekya Homer and Bernard Homer Sr., Annie Quam Gasper and her sister Ellen Quam Quandelacy, Frank Dishta and his son Virgil Dishta Sr.

1. Random Pattern

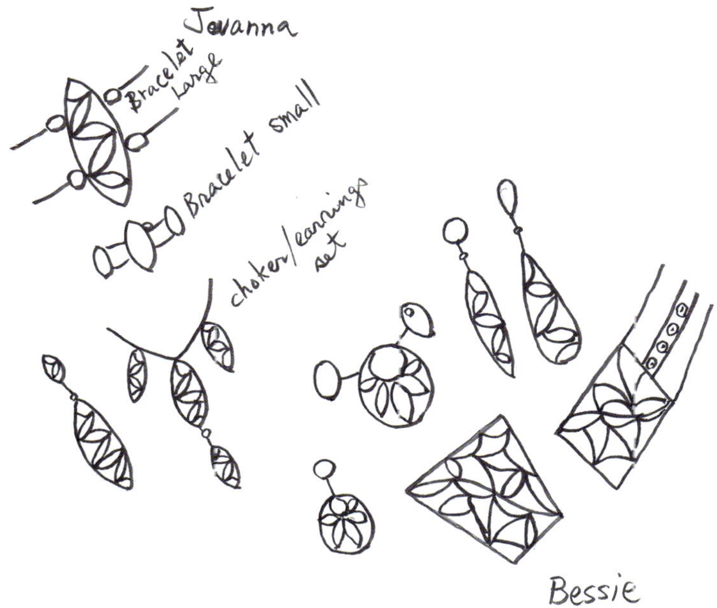

Drawing of her jewelry in random pattern design.

Alice Leekya Homer, daughter of Old Man Leekya, is a silversmith/lapidary who creates her designs in channel work. As her husband, Bernard Homer Sr. is not a silversmith, but a lapidary, or stone cutter, their pieces are either attributed to them both or to Alice alone. Her design is unique in that she set and welded a long silver wire in an S-shape or reverse-S-shape, and as a result, created several small channels or compartments. Her niece Bessie Vacit called the design the random pattern.

Bessie Vacit drew this sketch of her and her sister Jovanna's jewelry styles. Bessie learned silversmithing from her aunts Sarah Leekya and Alice Leekya Homer, so it is no wonder their designs are so similar. In the trapezoidal bolo design in the bottom right, a reverse-S-shaped line runs from the upper left corner down to the bottom right, and several flower petals are drawn along this line. Even though her random pattern design is similar to Alice's, Bessie told me this pattern is her own design and that Alice's S-shaped line patterns resemble ginkgo leaves rather than a flower petals.

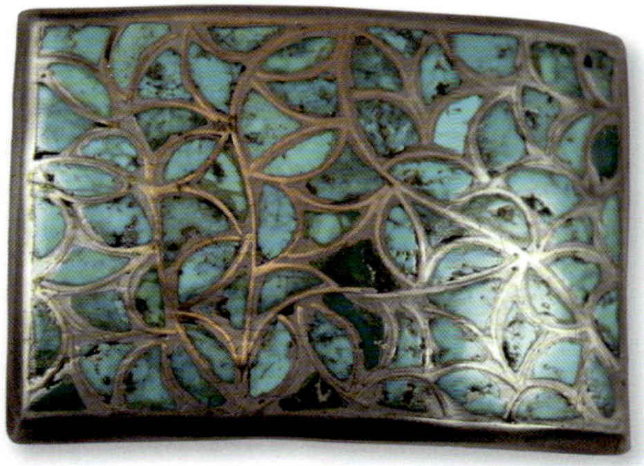

Turquoise buckle, channel inlay, Alice Leekya Homer, no hallmark, 1950s–1960s, 2.97" × 2.12",, $500–750.

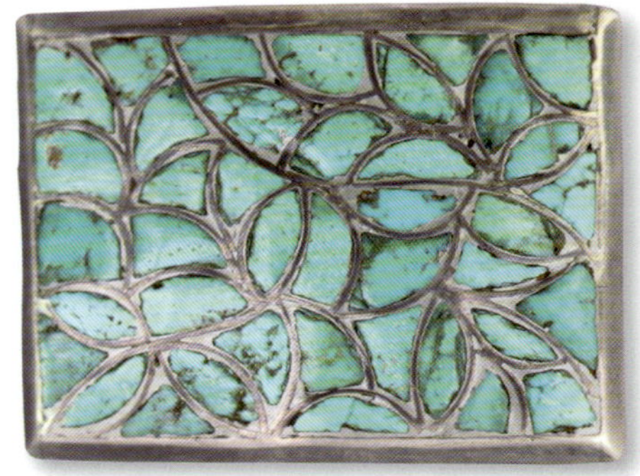

Turquoise buckle, channel inlay, Alice Leekya Homer, no hallmark, 1940s–1950s, 2.77" × 1.78", $300–450.

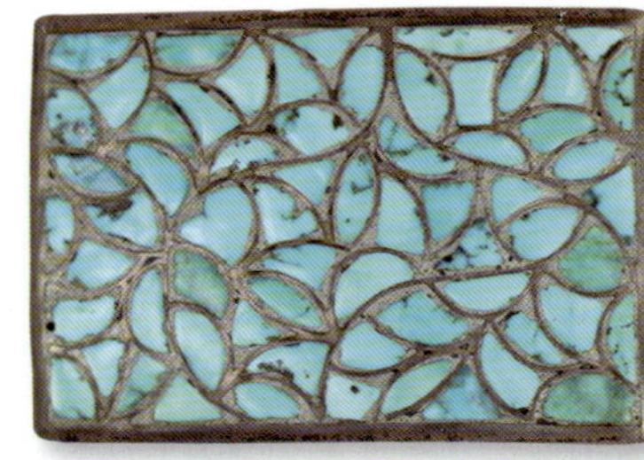

Turquoise buckle, channel inlay, Alice Leekya Homer, no hallmark, 1940s–1950s, 2.15" × 1.51", $240–360.

In Alice Leekya Homer's large turquoise buckle above, a long, S-shaped line runs from top center down to the bottom right corner, creating numerous channels. The surface of the buckle is slightly bumpy because each turquoise part is cut and polished to fit.

In the next example above, a long, S-shaped line runs from the upper left side down to the middle right, creating channels in the shapes of crescents and ginkgo leaves.

A long S-shaped line runs from the upper middle side down to the middle right in this smaller piece.

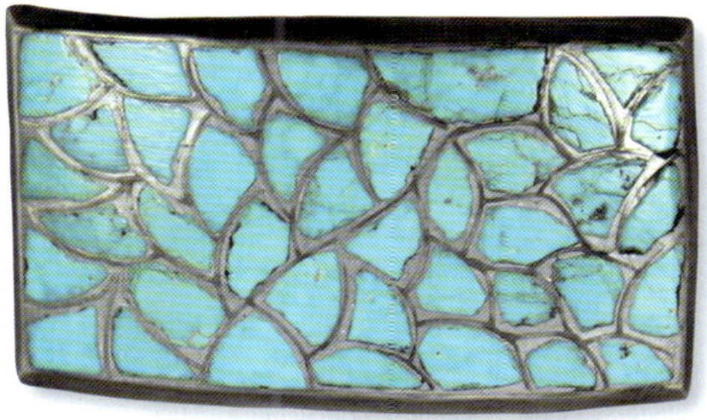

Turquoise buckle, Alice Leekya Homer, no hallmark, 1950s–1960s, 2.19" × 1.29", $200–300.

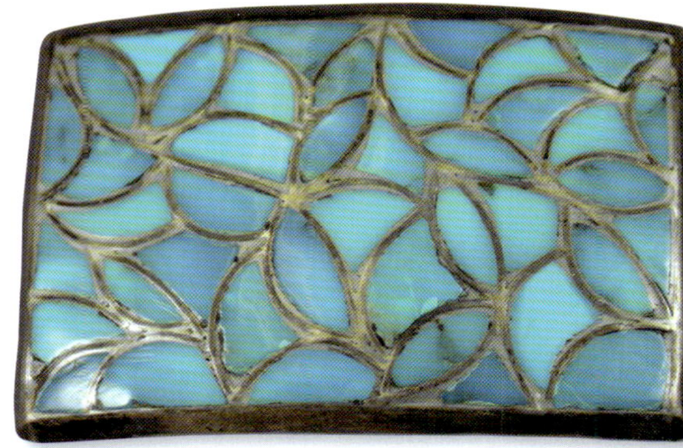

Turquoise buckle, channel inlay, Alice Leekya Homer, ALH, 1970s–1980s, 2.60" × 1.79", $400–600.

This small buckle piece features many ginkgo leaf patterns, but does not have Alice's characteristic long, S-shaped line running from one side down to the other. Bessie Vacit has confirmed it, however, as her aunt Alice's.

The last turquoise buckle here by Alice has an S-shaped line running from the upper middle down to the bottom right, along which flower petal–shaped channels take shape, a design very similar to Bessie's. The presence of the hallmark "ALH," however, proves that this piece is Alice's.

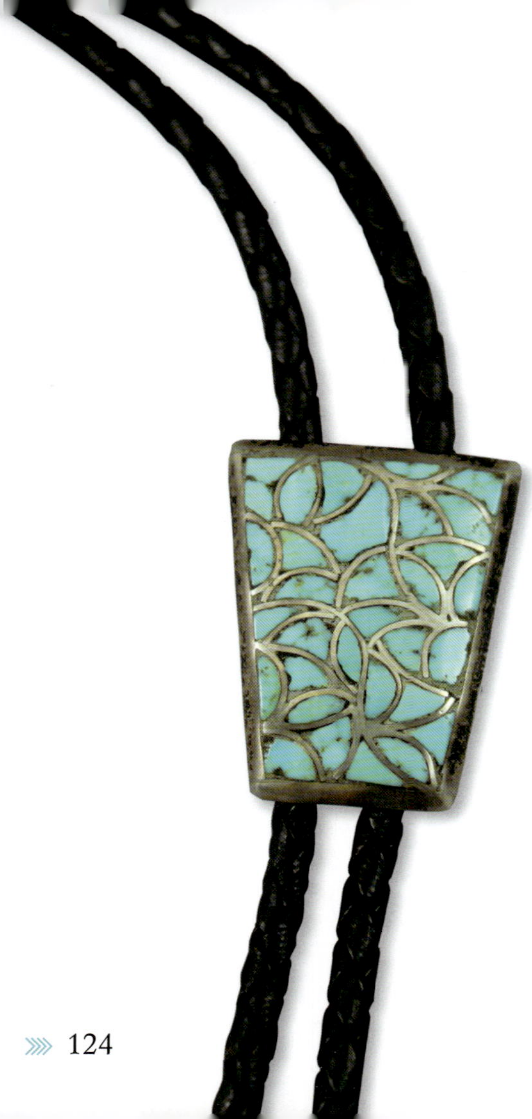

One September morning in 2003, I visited the Homers intending to identify the maker of one of my Hopi bird bracelets. I asked one of the children if he could ask his father, Bernard Homer Sr., if the bracelet had been made by his brother, Lambert Homer Sr. After consulting Bernard, he confirmed the maker was his uncle Lambert.

All the children there also agreed that their mother, Alice, probably made the bolo seen here, and their father once again confirmed our belief.

This turquoise bolo is fairly small, measuring only 1.01 inch at its widest point and 1.29 inches long. It was probably designed with a female wearer in mind. The presence of many silver compartments means each turquoise part is miniscule. The piece has a feature that is distinctive of Alice Leekya Homer's jewelry: two continuous silver lines from one side to the other and shorter, ginkgo leaf–shaped silver lines. Minutely cut turquoise parts are inlaid in each of these compartments. Despite the size of these compartments, this bolo bears an explicit resemblance to the bracelet attributed to Bernard Homer Sr. in *Southwest Silver Jewelry* from the 1940s (Baxter, 2001, p. 136).

I met Sarah Leekya and Juana Homer (Alice's sister and daughter, respectively) on different occasions. They both confirmed that Alice made my similar looking bolos and also told me that Alice often did most of her own silver and lapidary work, and that Bernard helped her finish her pieces.

Turquoise bolo, channel inlay, Alice Leekya Homer, no hallmark, 1940s–1950s, 1.01" × 1.29", $200–300.

Alice's turquoise bolo here, which is a little larger than average, has a reverse-S line running from the middle of the upper side down to the middle of the right side. This creates large channels, where cut and polished turquoise parts are inlaid.

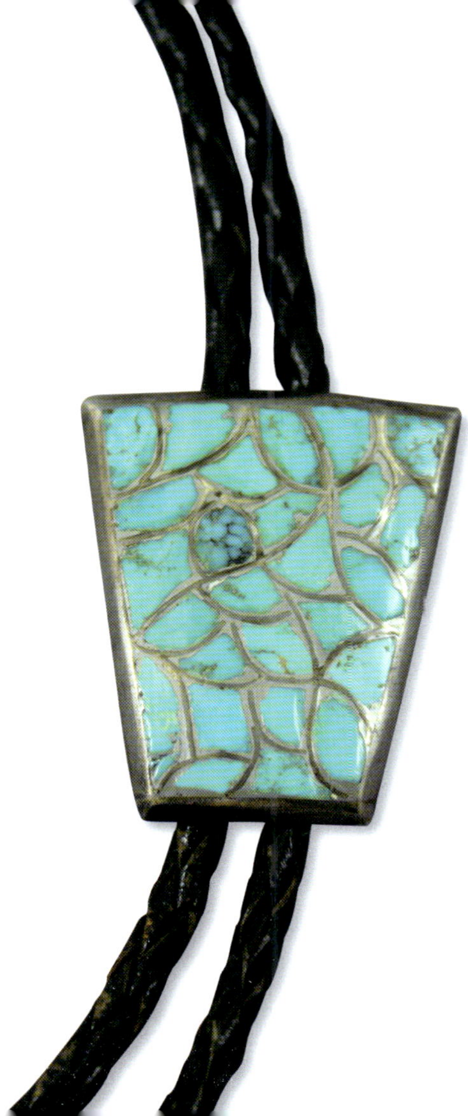

Turquoise bolo, channel inlay, Alice Leekya Homer, no hallmark, 1940s–1950s, 1.35" × 1.57", $240–360.

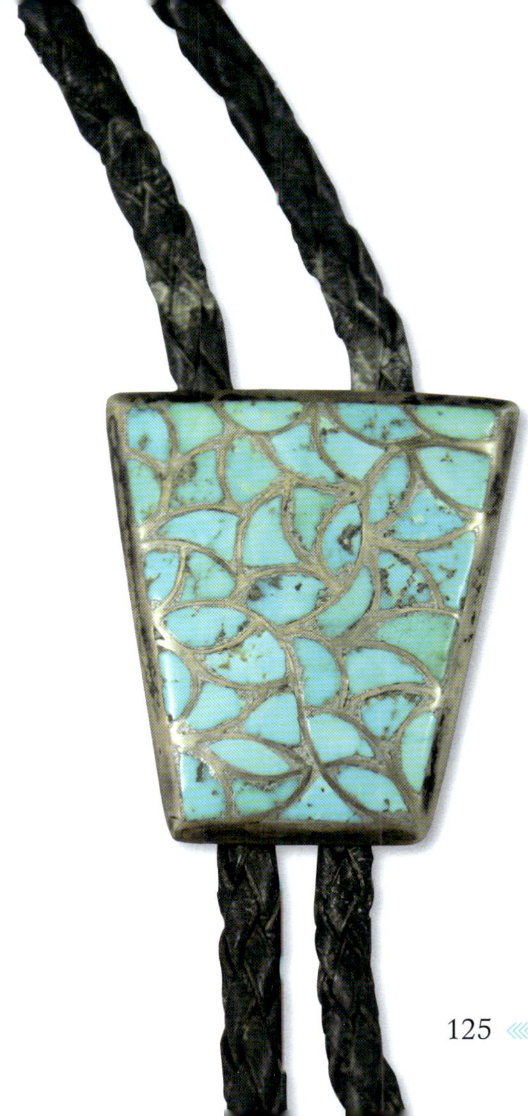

Turquoise bolo, channel inlay, Alice Leekya Homer, no hallmark, 1940s–1950s, 1.45" × 1.65", $240–360.

A reverse-S line runs from the middle of the left side down to bottom right corner in the next example, resulting in several small channels filled with cut and polished turquoise stones.

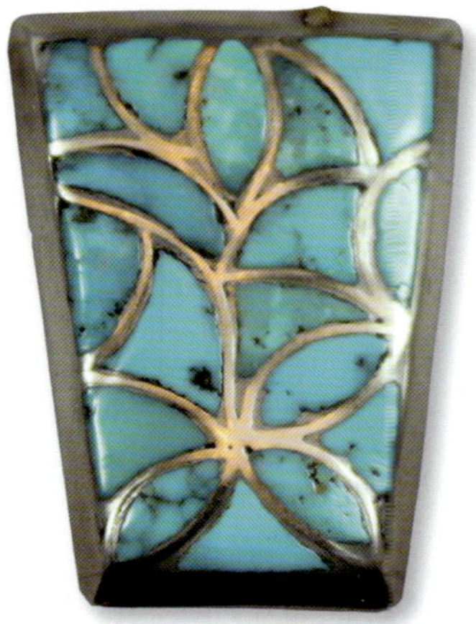

Turquoise bolo, channel inlay, Alice Leekya Homer, no hallmark, 1940s–1950s, 0.97" × 1.33", $200–300.

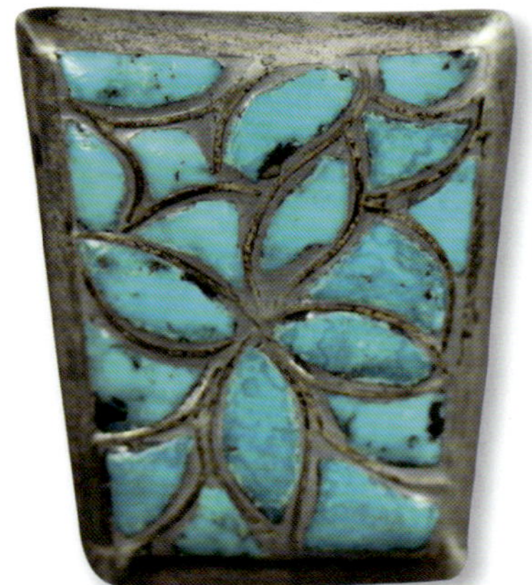

Turquoise bolo, channel inlay, Alice Leekya Homer, no hallmark, 1940s–1950s, 0.95" × 1.16", $200–300.

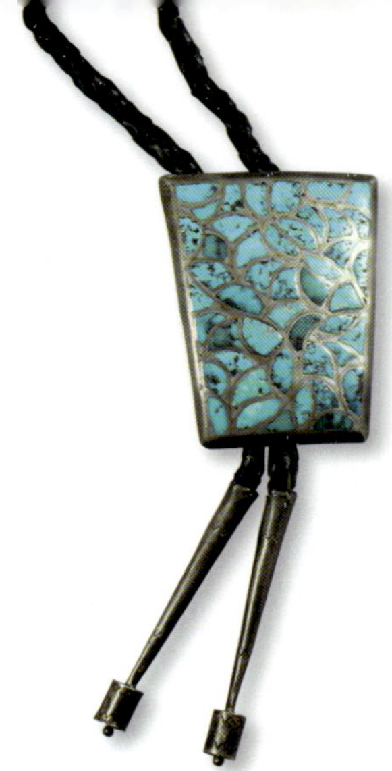

Turquoise bolo, channel inlay, Alice Leekya Homer, no hallmark, 1950s–1960s, 1.91" × 2.40", $400–600.

The first bolo, featuring seventeen channels in the shapes of ginkgo leaves and flower petals, is the second smallest one in my collection, measuring 0.97 inch wide and 1.33 inches long.

We have yet another example of Alice's bolo work here, the smallest one from my collection, also with a reverse-S line running from the middle of the left to the lower right and seventeen channels.

This bolo's surface is slightly bumpy and has an S-line running from the middle of the upper side down to the middle of the right, creating forty-five channels in the shapes of leaves and petals.

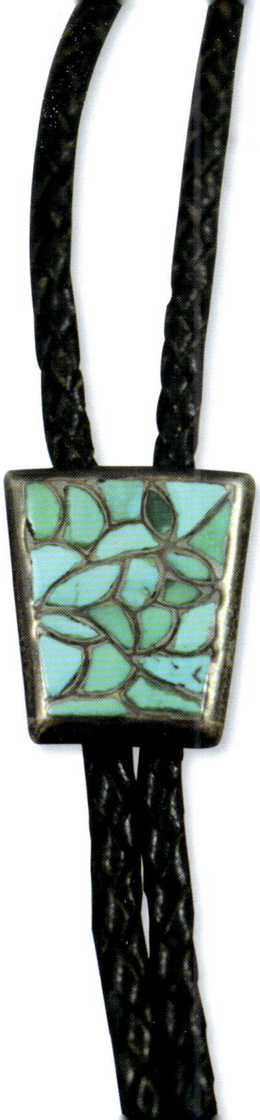

Turquoise bolo, channel inlay, Alice Leekya Homer, no hallmark, 1950s–1960s, 0.97" × 1.14", $200–300.

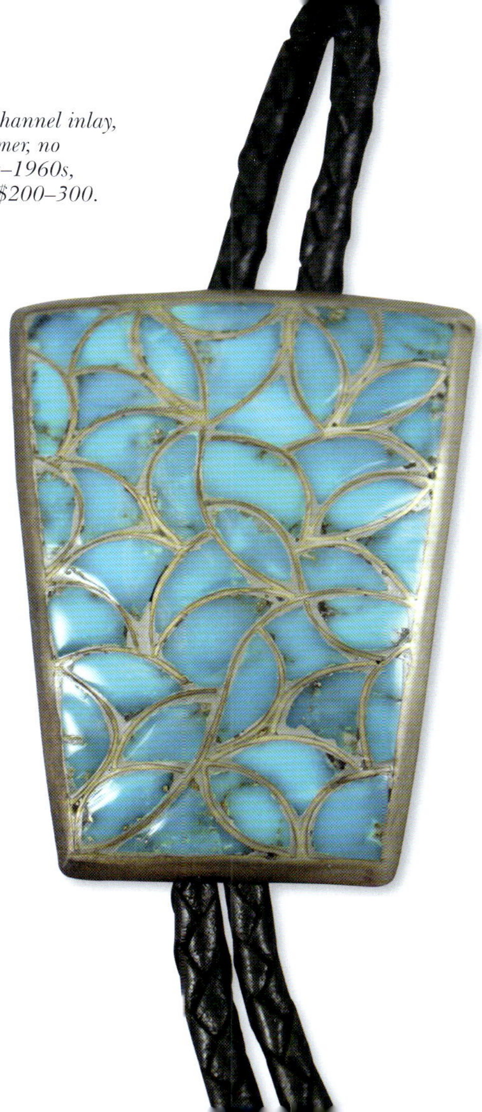

A reverse-S line runs from the middle of the left down to the lower right. It has a slightly bumpy surface and twenty-one channels.

Alice made this bolo with an S-line running from the middle of the left side to the lower left corner. It has forty channels, a slightly bumpy surface, and an "ALH" hallmark, and is the largest of my collection, measuring 2.02 inches wide and 2.63 inches long.

Turquoise bolo, channel inlay, Alice Leekya Homer, ALH, 1970s–1980s, 2.02" × 2.63", $400–600.

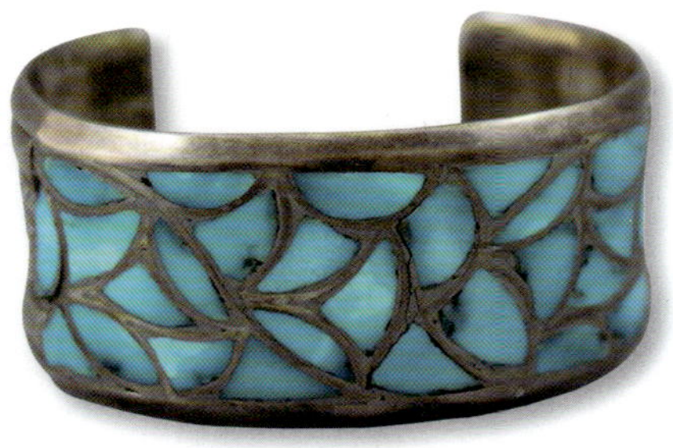

Turquoise bracelet, channel inlay, Alice Leekya Homer, ALH, 1970s–1980s, 1.14" wide, $400–600.

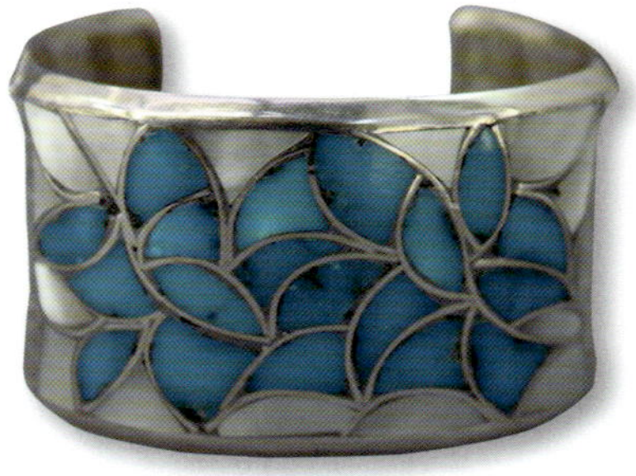

Turquoise bracelet, channel inlay, Alice Leekya Homer, ALH, 1970s–1980s, 1.53" wide, $500–750.

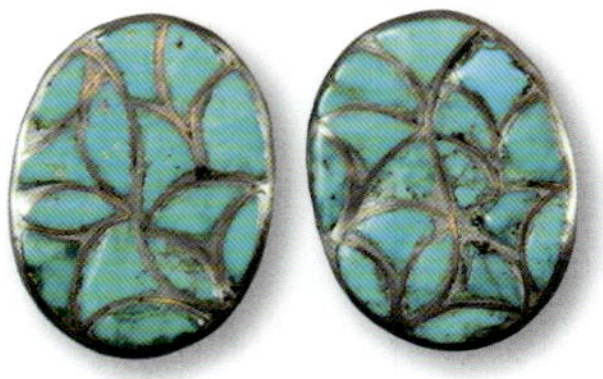

Turquoise earrings, channel inlay, Alice Leekya Homer, no hallmark, 1950s–1960s, 0.82" × 1.12", $140–210.

This bracelet bearing the "ALH" hallmark is narrow, measuring 1.14 inches wide. It has a reverse-S line running from the middle of the upper side to the lower right corner. Twenty-seven channels are created, and it has a slightly bumpy surface. This piece has V-shaped stamps on the surface of the silver cuff.

A reverse-S line runs from the middle of the upper side to the lower right side of this turquoise and white mother-of-pearl bracelet, which bears the "ALH" hallmark. The bracelet has a bumpy surface and thirty-four ginkgo leaf and flower petal–shaped channels. A wide bracelet, it measures 1.53 inches. Like the last example, this bracelet also has V-shaped stamped bands on the surface of the silver cuff.

In these turquoise earrings, an S-line runs on one, while a reverse-S line runs through another, and each earring has sixteen channels with cut and polished turquoise parts inlaid.

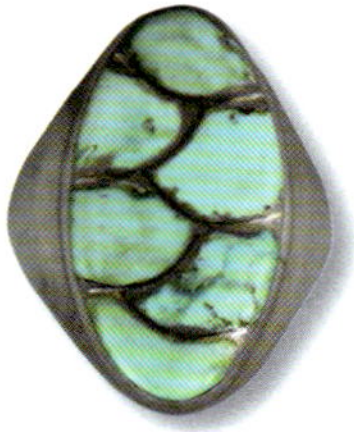

Turquoise ring, channel inlay, Alice Leekya Homer, no hallmark, 1950s–1960s, 0.58" × 1.09", $100–150.

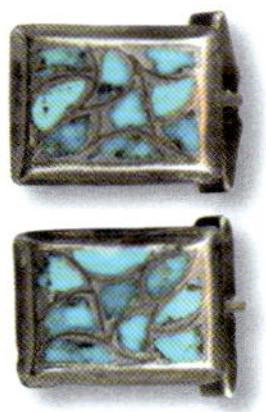

Turquoise cuff links, channel inlay, Alice Leekya Homer, no hallmark, 1950s–1960s, 0.63" × 0.82", $140–210.

Turquoise and coral bolo, channel inlay, Francis Leekya, no hallmark, 1940s–1950s, 2.02" × 2.39", $600–900.

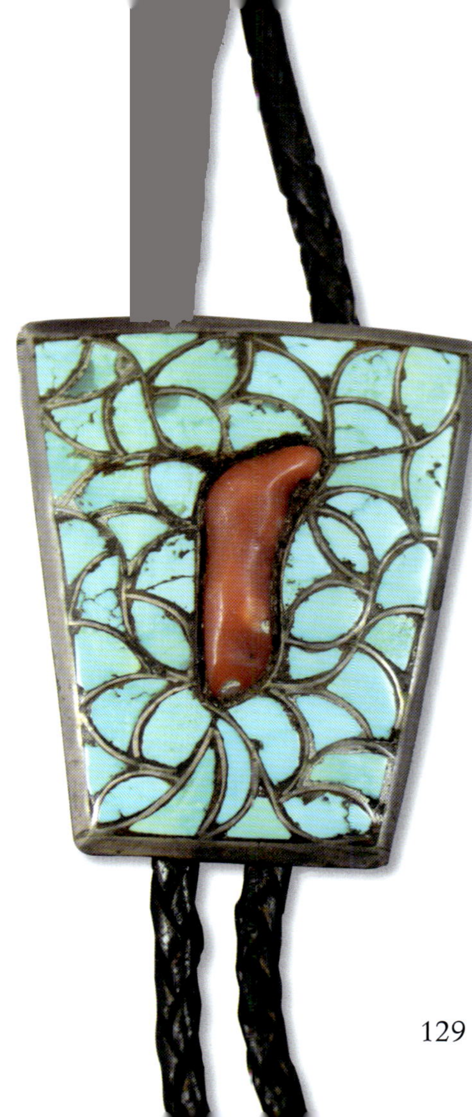

Next is a turquoise ring probably made by Alice. It has neither an S- nor a reverse-S line, but one of Alice's close relatives has attributed the ring to her. It's possible, however, that one of her brothers made it.

There is no doubt that Alice made the turquoise cuff links above. A reverse-S line runs on both pieces, and each cuff link has channels with cut and polished turquoise stones inlaid.

Francis Leekya's niece confirmed that he made the turquoise and coral bolo at right. The age estimation is based on the handmade bolo clasp, which consists of two silver wire loops and one W-shaped silver wire. The central channel, where the coral twig is set, is unusually large, considering the size of the bolo, and the remaining area is divided into small channels in the way his sister, Alice, usually made jewelry.

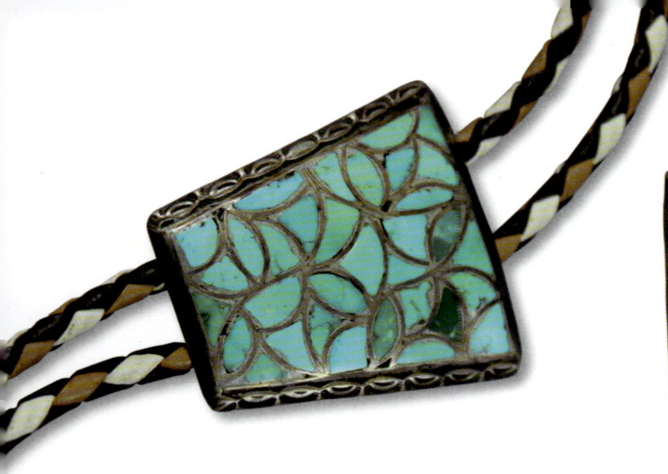

Turquoise bolo, channel inlay, Francis Leekya, no hallmark, 1940s–1950s, 1.62" × 1.68", $400–600.

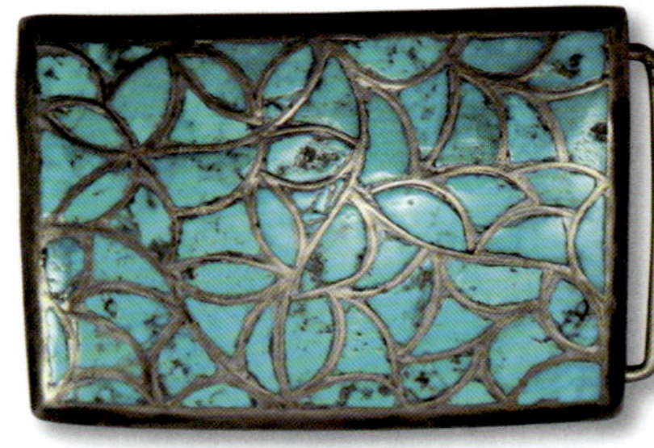

Sleeping Beauty turquoise buckle, channel inlay, Bessie Vacit, no hallmark, 1970s, 2.97" × 2.11", $300–450.

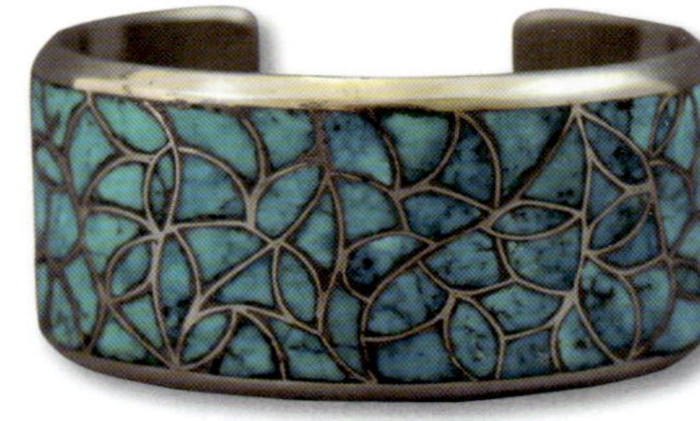

Sleeping Beauty turquoise bracelet, channel inlay, Bessie Vacit, no hallmark, 1972, 1.24" wide, $300–450.

Francis probably made the next bolo as well. It has two W-shaped silver wires as a bolo clasp, and a reverse-S line runs from mid-left to the lower right corner. Except for the stamping on both sides, this channel arrangement is very similar to Alice's,

Bessie Vacit made this Sleeping Beauty turquoise buckle. A reverse-S line runs from the middle of the upper side down to the middle of the bottom, and the remaining area is divided into small channels in the forms of petals and leaves. She confirmed herself that this is one of her early, larger pieces.

Bessie also confirmed that she made this Sleeping Beauty turquoise bracelet, which has a reverse-S line running from the middle of the upper side to the middle of the bottom and small flower and ginkgo channels. Both sides of the silver cuff are filed, but not stamped—the defining characteristic by which Bessie's bracelet can be differentiated from Alice's.

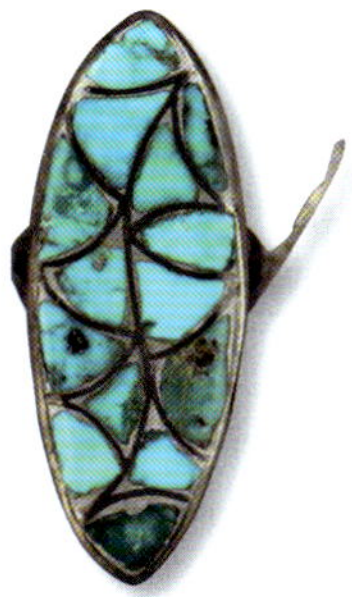

Sleeping Beauty turquoise ring, channel inlay, Bessie Vacit, no hallmark, 1970s, 0.67" × 1.76", $120–180.

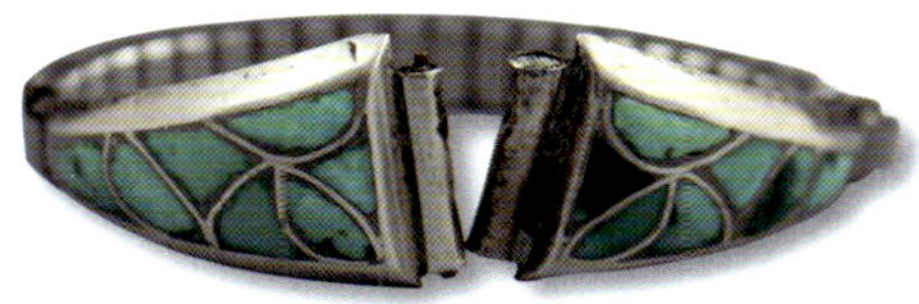

Sleeping Beauty turquoise watch band, channel inlay, Bessie Vacit, no hallmark, 1970s, 1.17" × 0.62", $120–180.

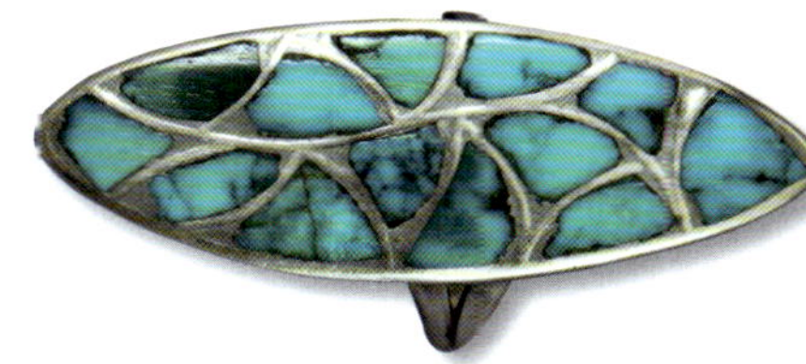

Sleeping Beauty turquoise ring, channel inlay, Jovanna Vacit, no hallmark, 1980s, 0.62" × 1.80", $120–180.

In this Sleeping Beauty turquoise ring by Bessie Vacit, an S-line runs from the upper right down to the lower left, creating fourteen channels.

Sleeping Beauty turquoise watch tips follow. Each tip has only seven channels set with cut and polished turquoise.

Jovanna Vacit, Bessie's sister, made this Sleeping Beauty turquoise ring. An S-line runs from the upper right down to the lower left, creating thirteen channels. It is almost identical to the one made by her elder sister, but its narrower and longer ring face is the defining characteristic of Jovanna's silver work.

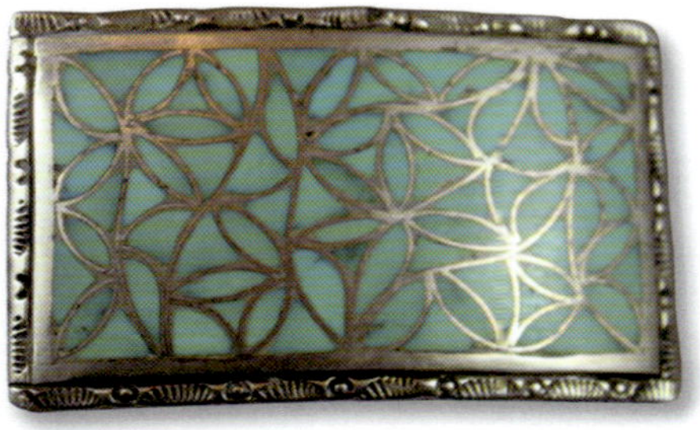

Turquoise buckle, channel inlay, Joe and Lola Hechilay, J. H. L. H., 1970s–1980s, 2.95" × 1.78", $300–450.

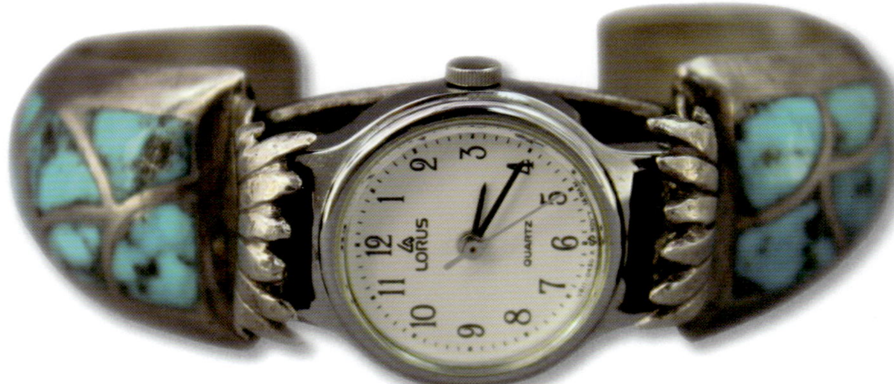

Turquoise watch bracelet, channel inlay, Robert Leekya, no hallmark, late 1960s, 0.78" wide, $200–300.

Joe and Lola Hechilay made this turquoise buckle, which is similar to Alice Leekya Homer's pieces. The difference lies in the whole surface being ground flush in the Hechilays' piece after stones are cut and set. Furthermore, stamped edges are added outside the edges of the inlaid body. These are key features that we do not see in Alice's pieces.

Robert Leekya's niece told me he made this heavy, thick Morenci turquoise watch bracelet in 1968 or '69, before he married Bernice Ondelacy. He made it in the cast channel style, and its inlaid parts are domed.

2. Geometric and Foliate Patterns

This is an introduction to two types of patterns Zuni artists have used to create pieces in a wide variety of styles. Because I've already featured Dishta-style jewelry in this volume, I am excluding it in this section.

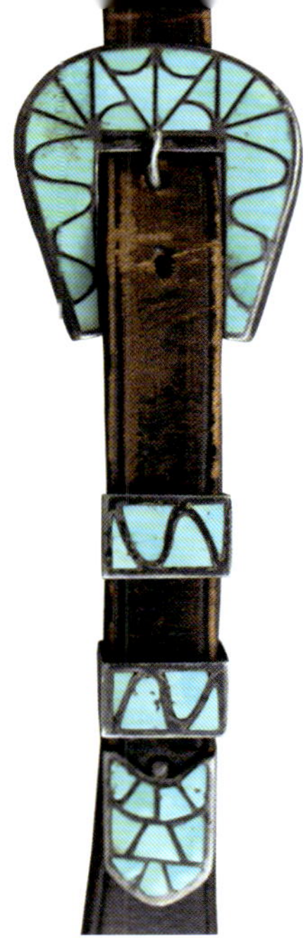

Turquoise ranger buckle set, channel inlay, Frank Vacit, ear of corn, 1940s–1950s, 1.99" × 1.65" for the buckle, $1,000–1,500.

The channel walls in Frank Vacit's ranger buckle above consist of straight, wavy, and arched lines, and the channels are inlaid with Blue Gem turquoise. Although Frank, his wife, Elizabeth, and his daughters used a common hallmark on their jewelry, his daughter Bessie Vacit confirmed this was his.

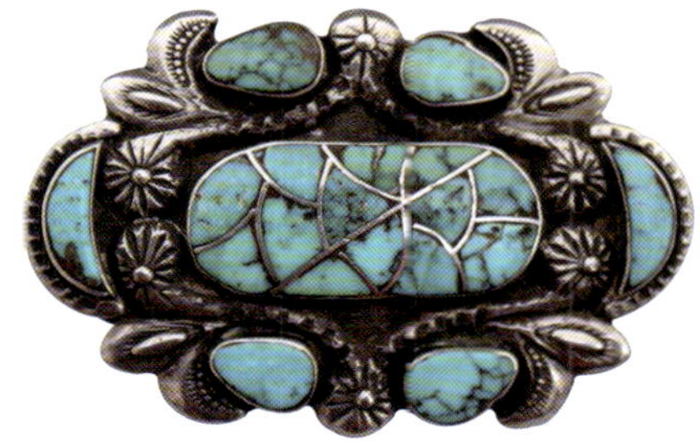

Turquoise buckle, channel inlay, Dan Simplicio, no hallmark, 1940s–1950s, 3.26" × 2.15", $2,000–3,000.

When I bought this large turquoise buckle, the seller attributed it to Juan de Dios, but Dan Jr. confirmed as Dan Simplicio Sr.'s. The stamped silver foliate adornments are also a clue that this is the work of Dan Sr., even if the flower head has no dimple in its center.

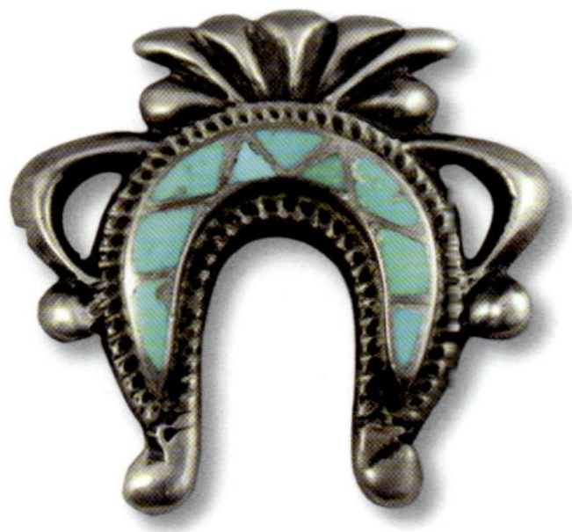

Turquoise pin, cast and channel inlay, Horace Iule, no hallmark, 1950s–1960s, 1.44" × 1.40", $200–300.

The channel walls of Horace Iule's pin above consist of straight lines, and the inlaid surface is ground flush.

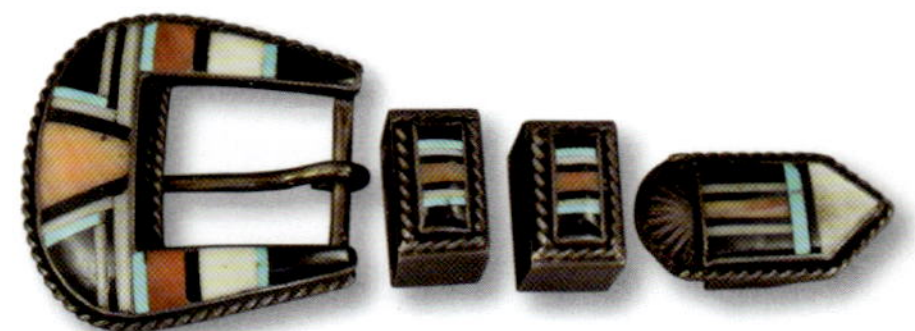

Multiple stone ranger buckle set, mosaic inlay, Lambert Homer Jr.(?), no hallmark, 1950s–1960s, 1.62" × 1.70" for the buckle, $400–600.

It's likely that Lambert Homer Jr. made this ranger belt set. Although it looks like mosaic overlay, the vertical silver line runs between the right and left parts of the buckle, making it inlay. The silver backing was made first, and then, the lapidary laid in the stones and shells in what became an extremely complicated inlay pattern.

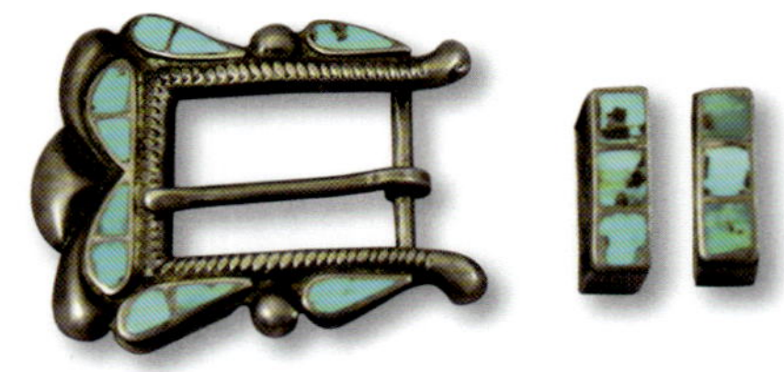

Turquoise ranger buckle set, cast and channel inlay, Jack Weekoty, no hallmark, 1950s–1960s, 1.99" × 1.65" for the buckle, $300–450.

I bought this ranger belt set by Jack Weekoty without its end from my collector friend, who attributed it to Horace Iule. His daughter, Lupe Iule Leekity, confirmed it as Jack's, however. As Jack's mentor was his uncle Horace Iule, it is no surprise that their pieces bear close similarities. This piece's inlay pattern is very simple, considering the size of its inlaid parts.

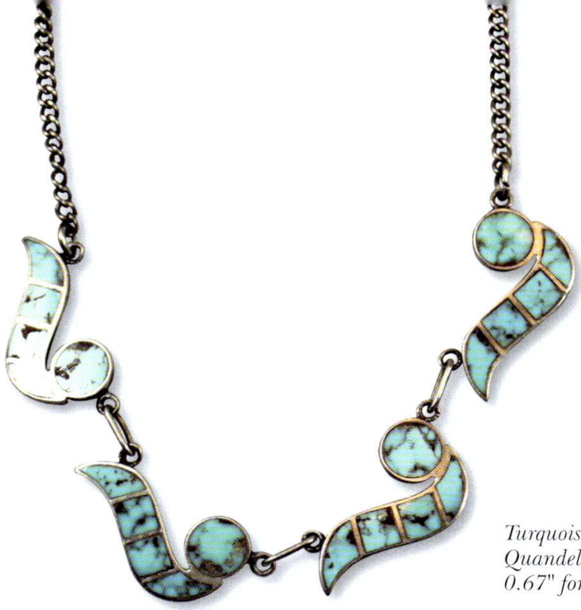

Turquoise necklace, channel inlay, Ellen Quandelacy, no hallmark, 1950s–1960s, 1.08" × 0.67" for one piece, $300–450.

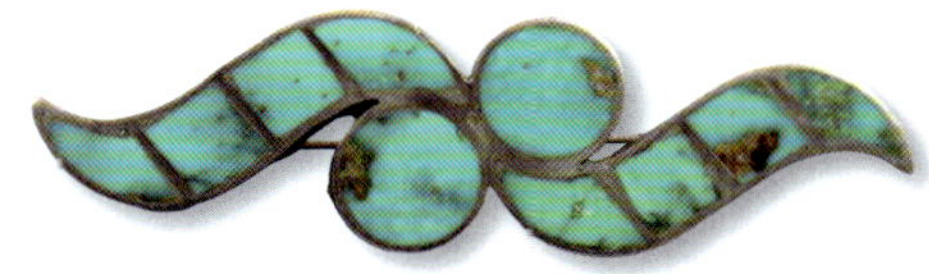

Turquoise pin, channel inlay, Ellen Quandelacy, no hallmark, 1950s–1960s, 2.16" × 0.61", $200–300.

Turquoise Jewelry of the Indians of the Southwest includes a necklace and earrings set with the exact same design as the Ellen Quam Quandelacy necklace above (Bennett, 1973, p. 63). Bennett's necklace consists of two side panels (mirror images of each other) and a center piece with the same design concept, while my necklace consists of four identical pieces connected with handmade chains. Both necklaces have commercial chains in both ends.

Here is another piece by Ellen Quam Quandelacy in the channel work style. This Blue Gem turquoise pin's arrangement is different, but the basic design is identical to that of the previous necklace.

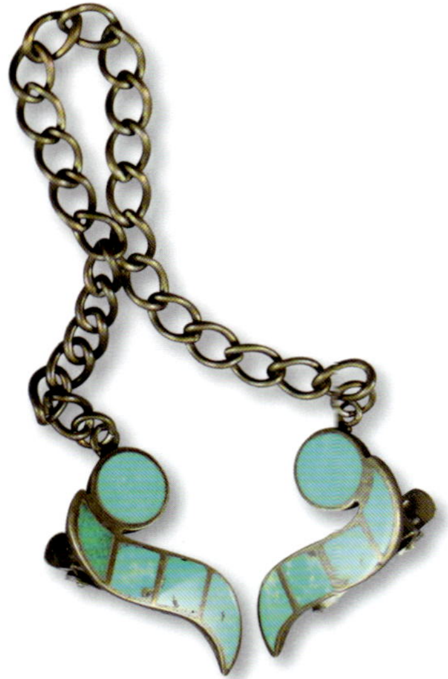

Turquoise sweater guard, channel inlay, Ellen Quandelacy, no hallmark, 1950s–1960s, 0.80" × 1.03" for one piece, $200–300.

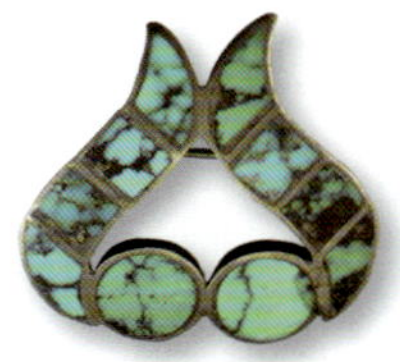

Turquoise pin, channel inlay, Ellen Quandelacy, no hallmark, 1950s–1960s, 1.21" × 1.19", $200–300.

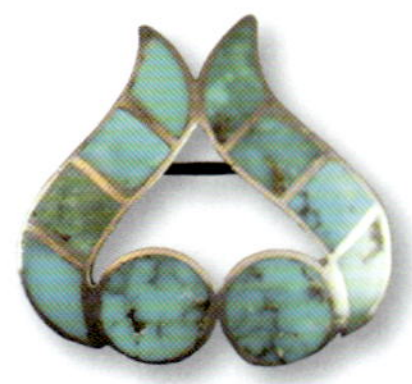

Turquoise pin, channel inlay, Ellen Quandelacy, no hallmark, 1950s–1960s, 1.19" × 1.18", $200–300.

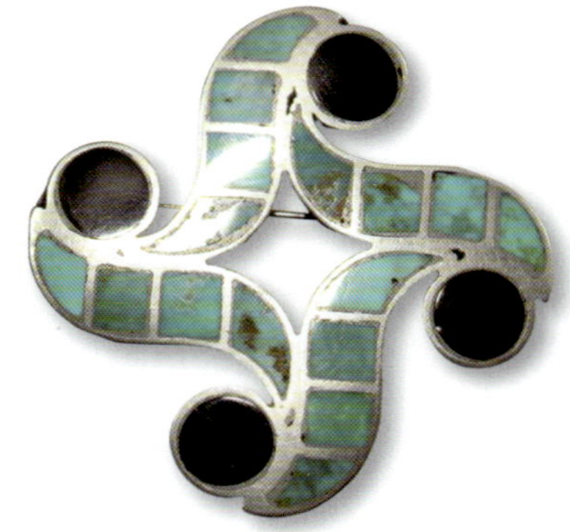

Turquoise and jet pin, channel inlay, Ellen Quandelacy, no hallmark, 1950s–1960s, 1.87" × 1.88", $300–400.

Generally speaking, Zuni sweater guards, like the turquoise one above, are relatively difficult to find in the market. I have seen fewer than ten Zuni-made sweater guards in the last ten years.

The two pins above are identical to the center piece of the necklace in *Turquoise Jewelry of the Indians of the Southwest.* Two pieces that mirror each other are welded together.

Last on this page is a Blue Gem turquoise and jet pin. Four identical pieces are welded together and constitute a pin. Each of these four pieces is similar to the other pieces in this section, but when they are combined together into one piece, the end product looks completely different.

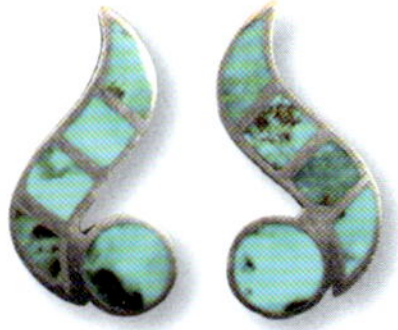

Turquoise earrings, channel inlay, Ellen Quandelacy, no hallmark, 1950s–1960s, 0.71" × 1.18", $120–180.

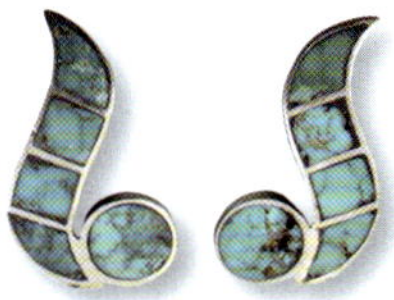

Turquoise earrings, channel inlay, Ellen Quandelacy, no hallmark, 1950s–1960s, 0.84" × 1.15", $120–180.

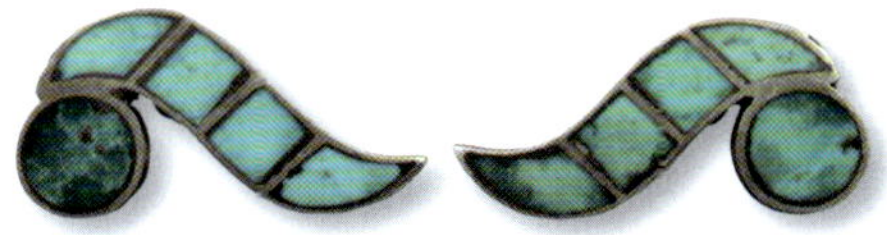

Turquoise earrings, channel inlay, Ellen Quandelacy, no hallmark, 1950s–1960s, 0.60" × 1.12", $120–180.

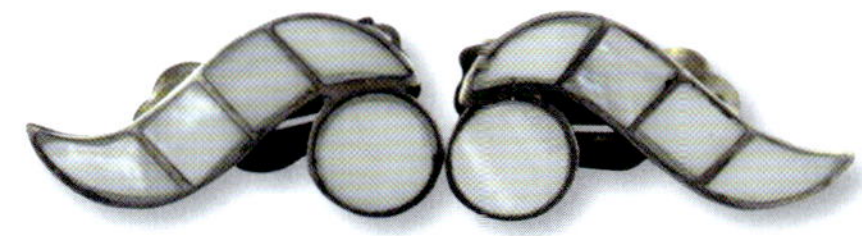

Mother-of-pearl earrings, channel inlay, Ellen Quandelacy, no hallmark, 1950s–1960s, 0.66" × 1.13", $120–180.

Each of the Blue Gem turquoise earrings above, top, measures 1.18 inches long and has a screw-back. The pair of earrings on the bottom once had screw-backs, but they were later replaced with pin backs.

The third pair by Ellen has screw-backs, and each of them measures 1.12 inches long.

Ellen's mother-of-pearl earrings on the right, above, are identical to the other three sets. They have screw-backs, and each of them measures 1.13 inches long.

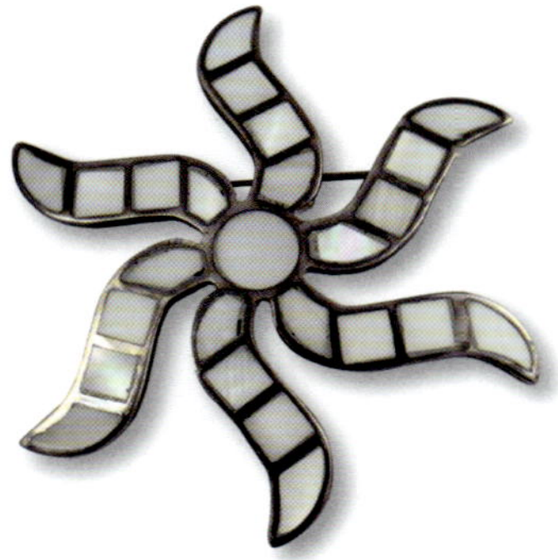

Mother-of-pearl pin, channel inlay, Ellen Quandelacy, no hallmark, 1950s–1960s, 2.16" × 2.28", $200–300.

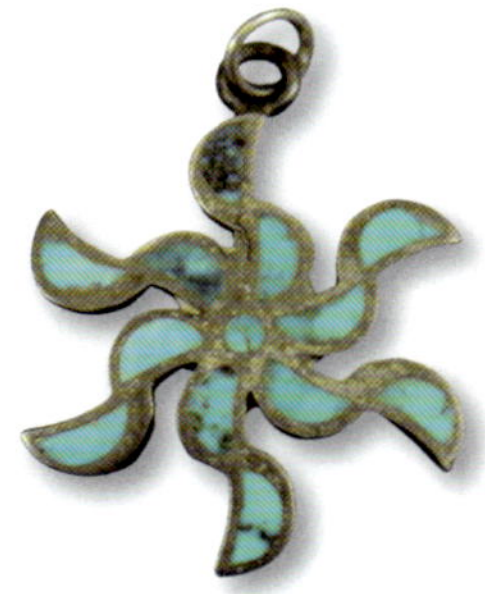

Turquoise pendant, channel inlay, Annie Quam Gasper (?), no hallmark, 1950s–1960s, 1.16" × 1.43", $120–180.

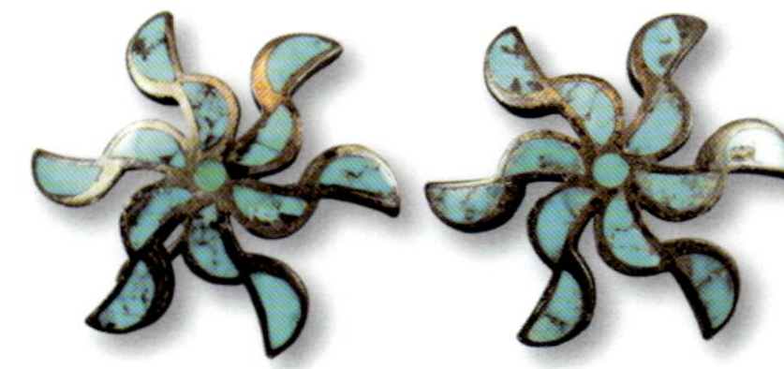

Turquoise earrings, channel inlay, Annie Quam Gasper (?), no hallmark, 1950s–1960s, 1.18" × 1.20", $160–240.

The mother-of-pearl pin above looks like a starfish and may be a variation of the same basic design seen in Ellen's earrings. It is different from her other pins described earlier, as it is slightly domed.

Above is a Blue Gem turquoise pendant. It looks like a pinwheel with a more complicated design, in which two crescents are combined together to constitute each wing. The pin is slightly domed and measures 1.43 inches long, including its bail. The Blue Gem turquoise earrings above are identical to the pendant in design.

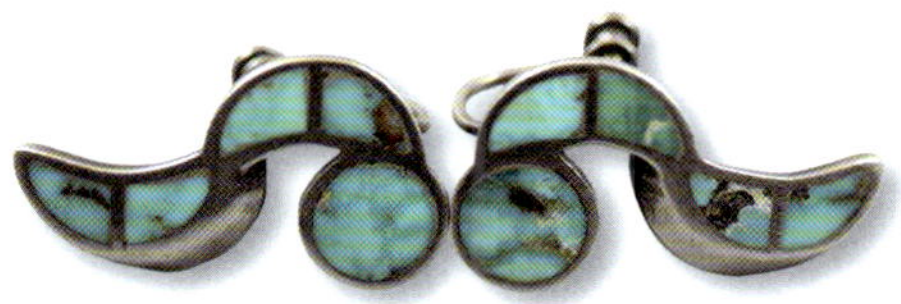

Turquoise earrings, channel inlay, Annie Quam Gasper, no hallmark, 1950s–1960s, 1.09" × 1.62", $160–240.

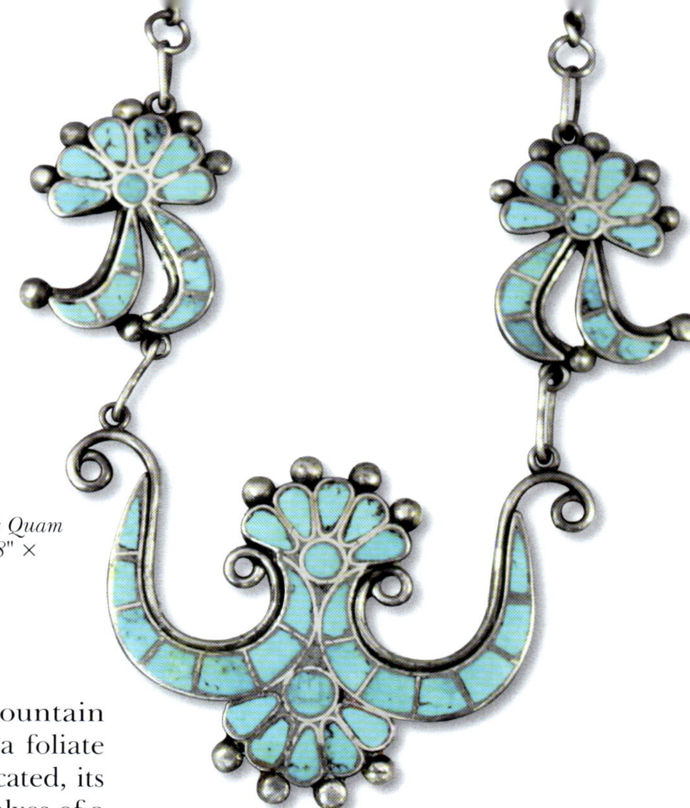

Turquoise Necklace, channel inlay, Annie Quam Gasper, no hallmark, 1950s–1960s, 2.38" × 1.90" central medallion, $1,200–1,860.

Annie also probably made the Blue Gem screw-back turquoise earrings above, which are similar to Ellen's four sets of earrings, have a feature identical to two of Annie's own pieces described previously in that two crescents are combined together to constitute one long, wing-like implement.

The motif in this Lone Mountain turquoise necklace could be a foliate pattern. Elegant and sophisticated, its center piece consists of two halves of a flower head and two leaves, while the two side panels are mirror-image variations of the center piece design. The two long chains in both ends are commercially made.

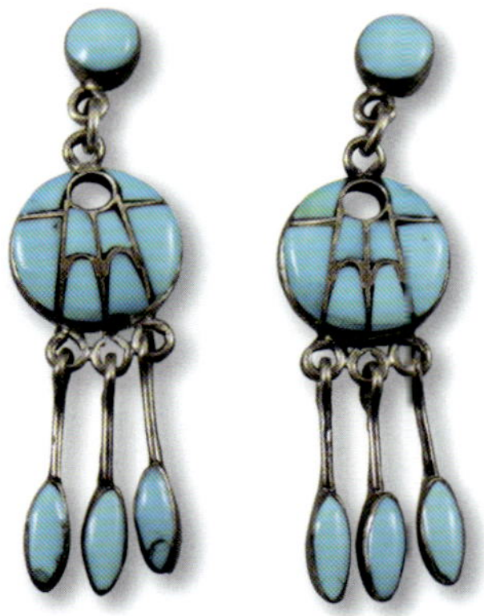

Turquoise earrings, channel inlay, Annie Quam Gasper, AQG, 1996, 0.58" × 2.08" central medallion, $200–300.

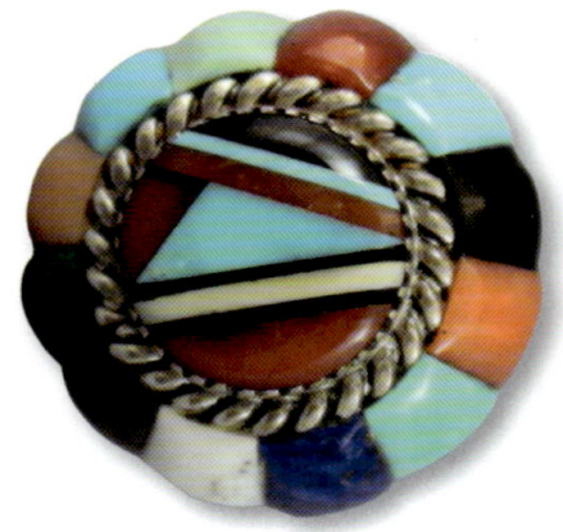

Turquoise ring, mosaic inlay, Lee and Mary Weebothee, Lee & Mary, 1980s–1990s, 0.74" in diameter, $300–450.

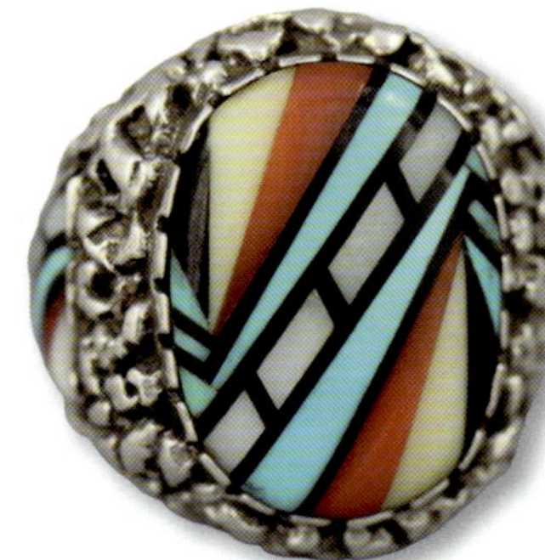

Turquoise ring, mosaic inlay, Lee and Mary Weebothee, Lee & Mary, 1980s–1990s, 0.68" × 0.91", $600–900.

I bought the Sleeping Beauty turquoise earrings above, with two fetish necklaces, from Annie. These earrings are made in her famous spider web design. One of Annie's other famous designs, the hummingbird, can be found in my fourth book.

Above, in the middle, is a multi-colored ring made by Lee and Mary Weebothee. The central piece, made in the mosaic overlay snake-eye style and set with saw-tooth bezel, consists of turquoise, coral, fossilized ivory, and jet. The rim of the ring, which consists of turquoise, coral, lapis lazuli, malachite, purple lip mother-of-pearl, fossilized ivory, and black jet is set in the mosaic inlay style.

The center and side pieces on the ring above are made with several colorful materials: turquoise, coral, jet, and yellow shell. This colorful ring's arrangement is identical in design to the Weebothee's all-turquoise, nugget-work ring.

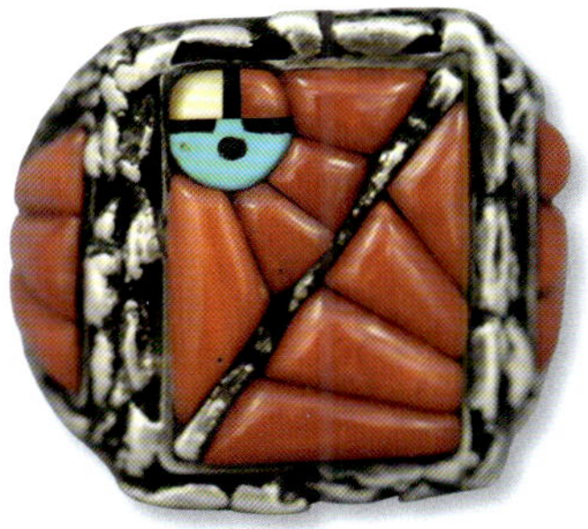

Sun Face in coral ring, mosaic inlay, Lee and Mary Weebothee, Lee & Mary, 1990s–2000s, 0.77" × 0.90" central medallion, $600–900.

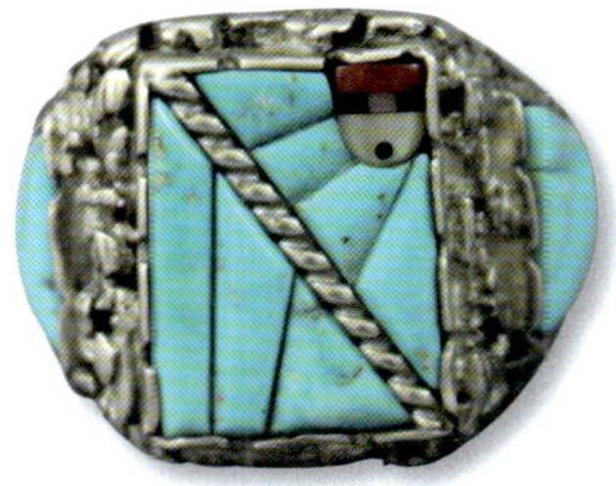

Sun Face in turquoise ring, mosaic inlay, Lee and Mary Weebothee, Lee & Mary, 2000s, 0.55" × 0.81" central medallion, $600–900.

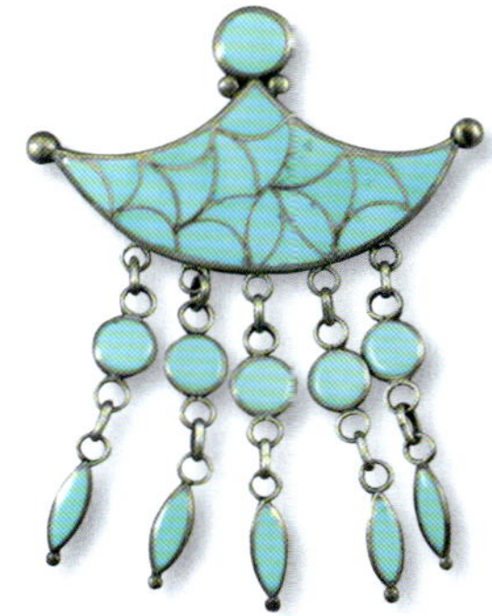

Turquoise pin/pendant, channel inlay, Bessie Vacit, her father's ear of corn stamp, 1980s–1990s, 3.16" × 4.28", $500–750.

The same couple made this coral-dominant Sun Face ring. As opposed to the previous ring with only one side panel, this ring has two, in addition to the center, which consists of one Sun Face in the upper left corner and a coral background. From the upper right corner down, diagonally, to the bottom left runs a silver line.

I bought the ring above from Lee when I visited him on September 11, 2003. The face in this ring is not a Sun Face but a Knifewing or Rainbow Man, while the face of the previous ring is a typical, round Sun face. A silver twisted wire runs diagonally from the upper left corner down to the bottom right.

When I saw Bessie Vacit's turquoise pin/pendant above, I thought it was made by her father, Frank Vacit. We notice almost no filler among the silver walls and cut turquoise stones. The many ginkgo leaves and flower petals are typical of the random-pattern channel inlay pieces created by Bessie and Alice Leekya Homer. When I showed it to Bessie, she smiled and said it was hers.

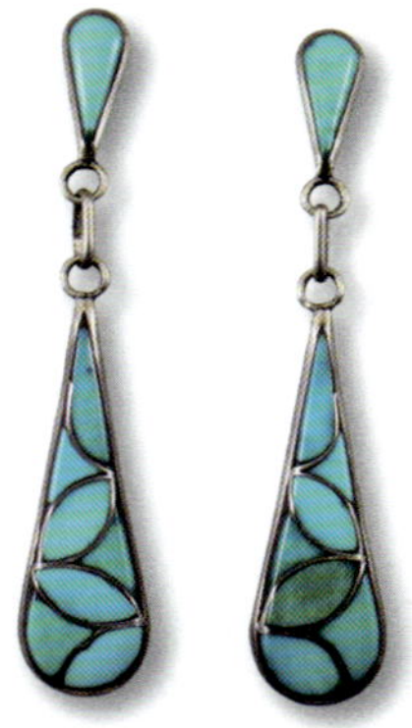

Turquoise earrings, channel inlay, Bessie Vacit, her father's ear of corn stamp, 1980s–1990s, 0.52" × 2.83" central medallion, $120–180.

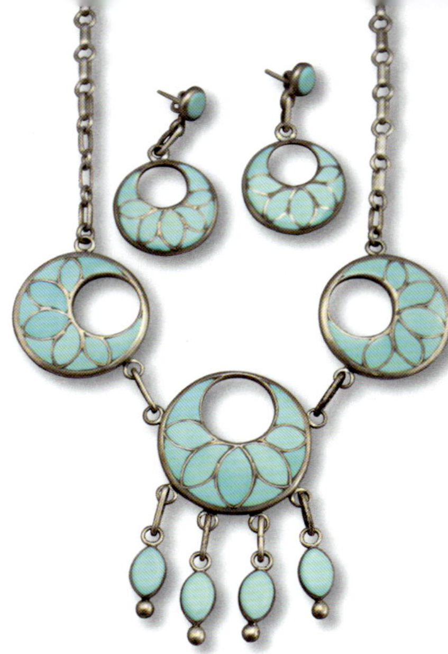

Turquoise necklace and earrings set, channel inlay, Bessie Vacit, her father's ear of corn stamp, 1980s–1990s, 1.34" × 2.58" central medallion, $300–450.

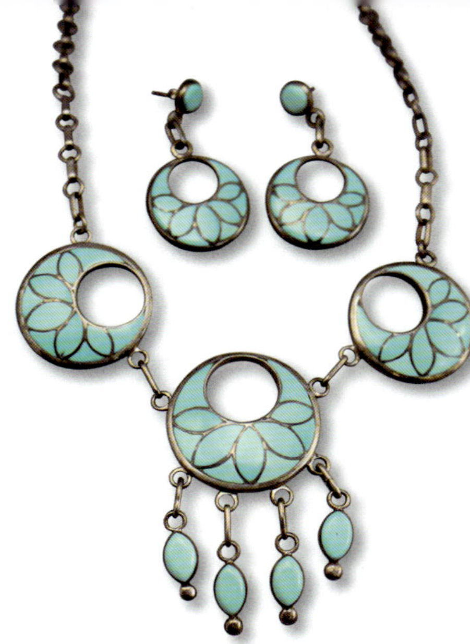

Turquoise necklace and earrings set, channel inlay, Bessie Vacit, her father's ear of corn stamp, 1980s–1990s, 1.35" × 2.62" central medallion, $300–450.

Flower petals and ginkgo leaves adorn her matching earrings as well. All of her pins/pendants and earrings have the same "ear of corn" hallmark as her father's. Because of this hallmark, her pieces have been frequently misattributed to Frank Vacit. If pieces with this hallmark look newer (i.e., from the 1980s or '90s) they are most likely Bessie's. If the pieces are hallmarked "F. Vacit" with the ear of corn stamp, they were probably made by Frank after 1975.

Although we see flower petals and ginkgo leaves in this Sleeping Beauty turquoise choker-necklace-and-earrings-set, it does not look like a random pattern, but a regularly successive one. These pieces used to be misattributed to her father, Frank, as well. Next is another set, which is reminiscent of Bessie's drawings.

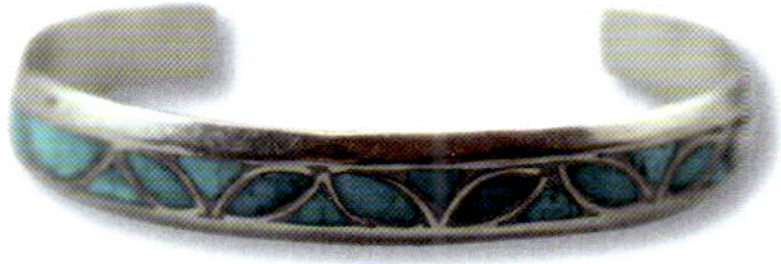

Turquoise bracelet, channel inlay, Bessie Vacit, no hallmark, 1970s–1980s, 0.41" wide, $100–150.

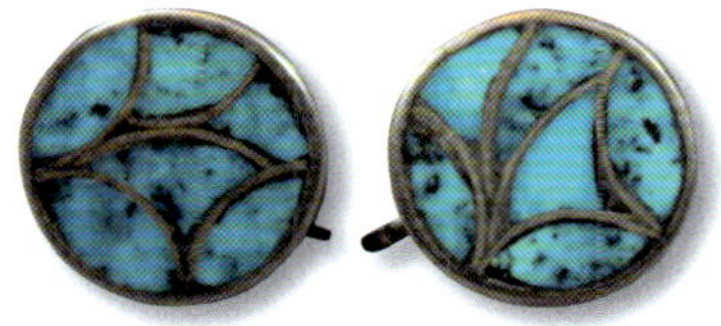

Turquoise earrings, channel inlay, Bessie Vacit, no hallmark, early 1970s, 1.27" in diameter, $100–150.

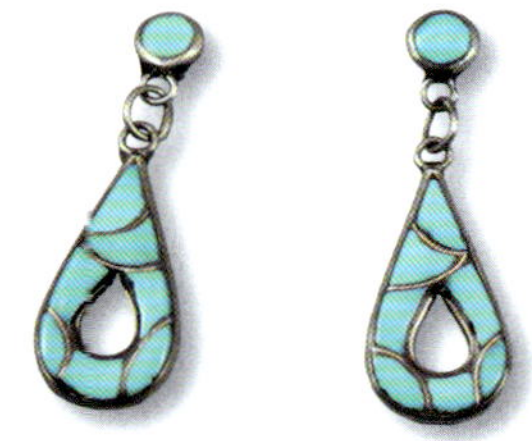

Turquoise earrings, channel inlay, Bessie Vacit, no hallmark, late 1970s, 0.54" × 1.59", $100–150.

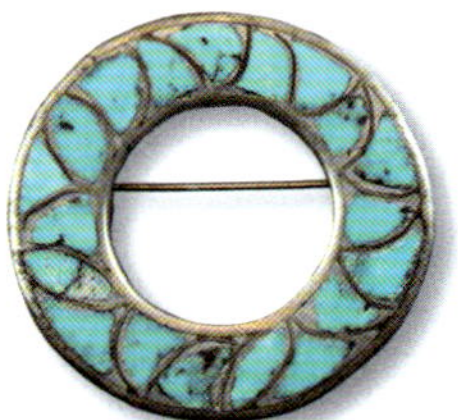

Turquoise pin, channel inlay, Bessie Vacit, no hallmark, early 1970s, 1.27" in diameter, $100–150.

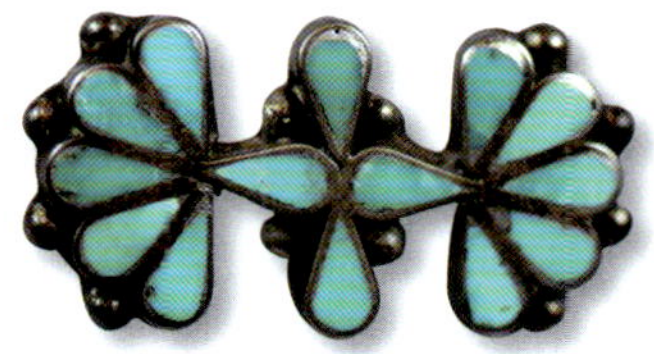

Turquoise pin, channel inlay, Bessie Vacit, no hallmark, early 1970s, 1.17" × 0.62", $100–150.

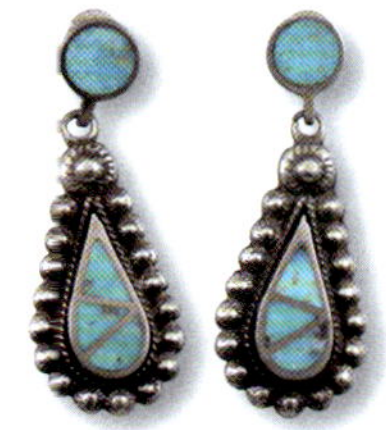

Turquoise earrings, channel inlay, Bessie Vacit, no hallmark, 1970s, 0.64" × 1.69", $100–150.

Bessie Vacit's turquoise bracelet above, top, is made in the successive flower petal pattern. A narrow bracelet, it measures only 0.41 inches wide. Below it is a turquoise pin from the early 1970s that is not in the successive flower pattern seen in her later pieces, but that more closely resembles the random pattern.

Bessie Vacit made the Kingman turquoise earrings above, center, top, in which we see flower petals and a ginkgo leaf. She told me it was her first pair. The small Lone Mountain turquoise pin under is made in a variation of the flower-head pattern, which her aunt, Sarah Leekya, taught her.

Flower petals and a ginkgo leaf adorn the small, but cute, Sleeping Beauty turquoise earrings above, top. The Blue Gem turquoise earrings underneath are made in the geometric pattern, which is not frequently seen in her work. Bessie has personally confirmed them as her own.

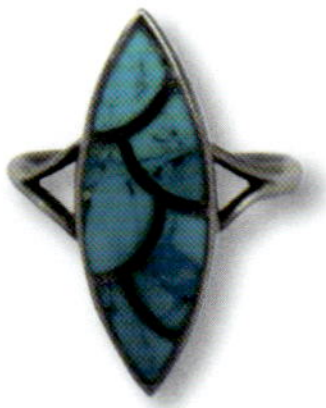

Turquoise earrings, channel inlay, Jovanna Vacit, no hallmark, late 1970s, 0.34" × 0.97", $80–120.

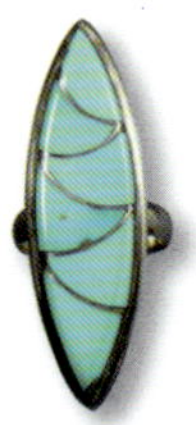

Turquoise earrings, channel inlay, Jovanna Vacit, her father's ear of corn stamp, late 1980s–1990s, 0.56" × 1.88", $100–150.

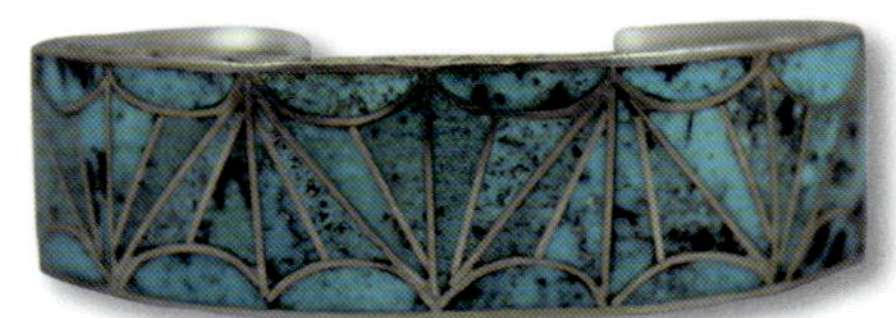

Kingman turquoise bracelet, channel inlay, artist unknown, no hallmark, late 1950s–1960s, 0.83" wide, $500–750.

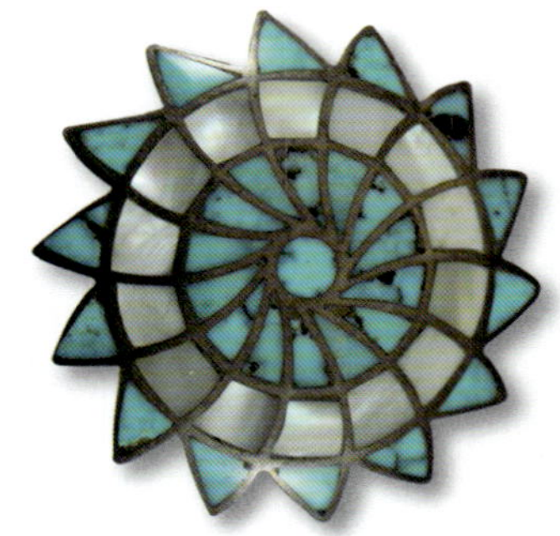

Sleeping Beauty turquoise and mother-of-pearl pin, channel inlay, artist unknown, no hallmark, late 1950s–1960s, 1.87" in diameter, $200–300.

Jovanna Vacit made the small turquoise ring above, top, which has a ring face that is highly domed. It is made in the channel-inlay style, in a pattern close to Bessie's successive one. Above, bottom, is a long Sleeping Beauty turquoise ring made in a successive pattern of Jovanna's own design, which is based on Bessie's drawing. It has her fathers "ear of corn" hallmark.

One of my informants attributed the Kingman bracelet above to Annie Quam Gasper. All the turquoise pieces are cut cleanly and fit into each channel quite well in this geometric design.

An unconfirmed artist made this Blue Gem turquoise and mother-of-pearl pin in a pinwheel design. One of my informants has attributed it to Marietta Soseeah.

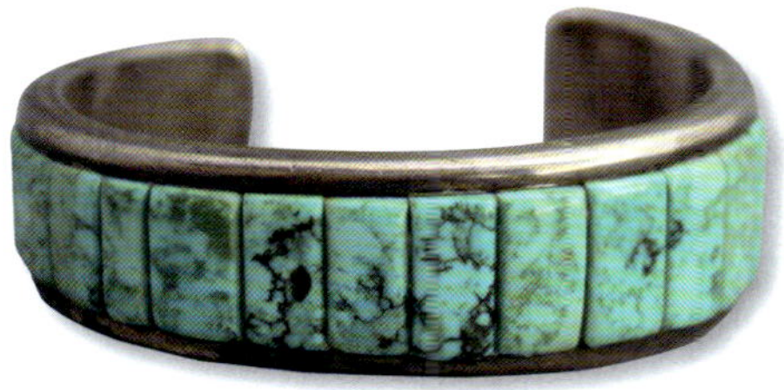

Turquoise bracelet, channel inlay, Jake Livingston, J-I Livingston, 1980s–1990s, 0.83" wide, $500–750.

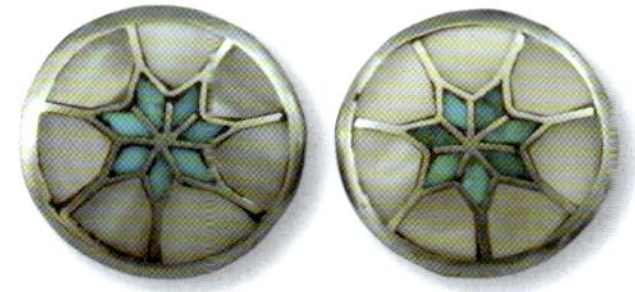

Turquoise and mother-of-pearl earrings, channel inlay, Jim Paywa (?), no hallmark, late 1950s–1960s, 0.91" in diameter, $80–120.

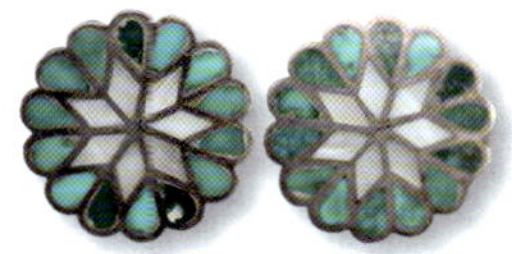

Turquoise and mother-of-pearl earrings, channel inlay, Jim Paywa (?), no hallmark, late 1950s–1960s, 0.92" in diameter, $80–120.

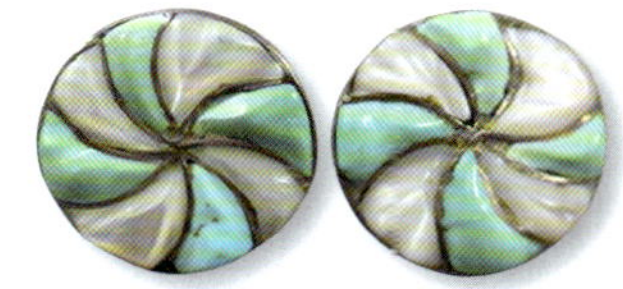

Turquoise and mother-of-pearl earrings, channel inlay, Lambert Homer Jr. (?), no hallmark, late 1950s–1960s, 0.85" in diameter, $100–150.

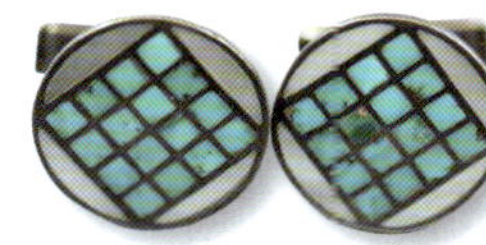

Turquoise cuff links, channel inlay, Lambert Homer Jr. (?), no hallmark, late 1950s–1960s, 0.79" in diameter, $200–300.

Jake Livingston made this turquoise inlay bracelet, which is technically similar to designs seen on the sides of rings made by Lee and Mary Weebothee.

Jim Paywa probably made the turquoise and mother-of-pearl earrings above, top, which feature the flower-head, or pinwheel, design and have clip backs. The same artist most likely made the pair below them as well, which were made in the flower-head design and also have clip backs.

The artist most likely responsible for the pinwheel-shaped turquoise and mother-of-pearl earrings above, top, is Lambert Homer Jr. Next are a pair of well-designed turquoise and mother-of-pearl cuff links, made in the flush channel-inlay style and probably by Lambert. Inside the round background a square is placed, which is divided into sixteen squares.

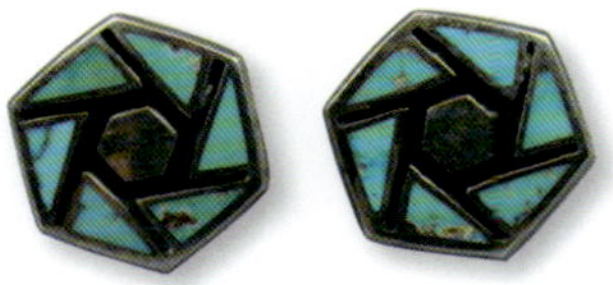

Turquoise cuff links, channel inlay, Lambert Homer Jr. (?), no hallmark, late 1950s–1960s, 0.87" × 0.95", $100–150.

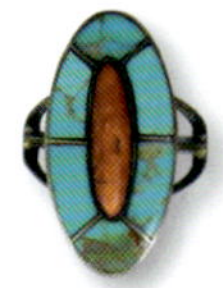

Blue Gem turquoise and spiny oyster ring, channel inlay, Bowman Paywa (?), no hallmark, late 1950s–1960s, 0.63" × 1.30", $120–180.

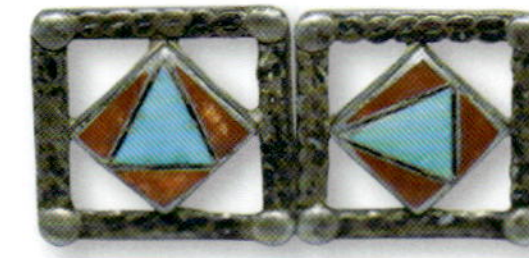

Turquoise and coral cuff links, channel inlay, Chauncy Simplicio (?), no hallmark, late 1950s–1960s, 0.87" × 0.85", $100–150.

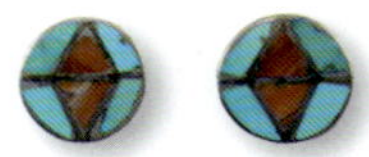

Sleeping Beauty turquoise and spiny oyster earrings, channel inlay, Sarah Leekya, no hallmark, late 1950s–1960s, 0.59" in diameter, $80–120.

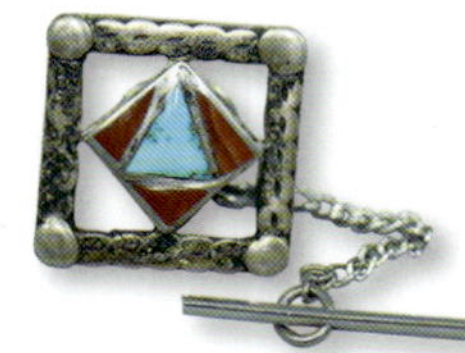

Turquoise and coral tie tack, channel inlay, Chauncy Simplicio (?), no hallmark, late 1950s–1960s, 0.78" × 0.77", $80–120.

Inside the unique background of the turquoise cuff links above (most likely Lambert Homer Jr.'s), a silver hexagon is arranged and surrounded by six right triangles. The silver work may have been done by a Navajo silversmith.

The Blue Gem turquoise and spiny oyster ring above, top, was probably made by Bowman Paywa. The center cabochon is set higher from the surface, and the surrounding turquoise pieces are set flush. Next are Blue Gem turquoise and spiny oyster earrings with screw-backs by Sarah Leekya.

Chauncy Simplicio probably made the turquoise and coral cuff links above, top. The square frame is composed of four flattened, twisted silver wires and silver drops, and the inner square is set so its four corners touch the mid-points of the frame's sides. The inner square is divided into four triangles. Underneath is a matching tie tack, that Chauncy Simplicio probably made.

3. Dishta-Style Channel Inlay

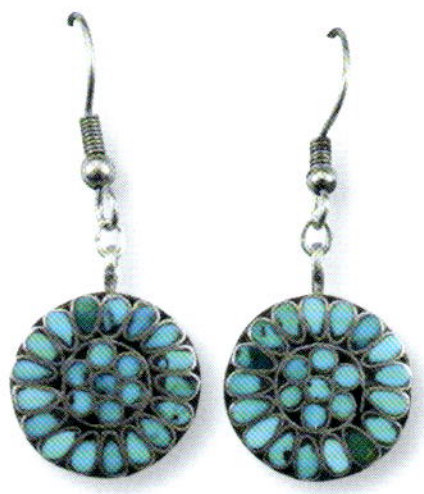

Turquoise earrings, channel inlay, Pauline and Frank Dishta, no hallmark, 1940s–1950s, 0.67" in diameter, $200–300.

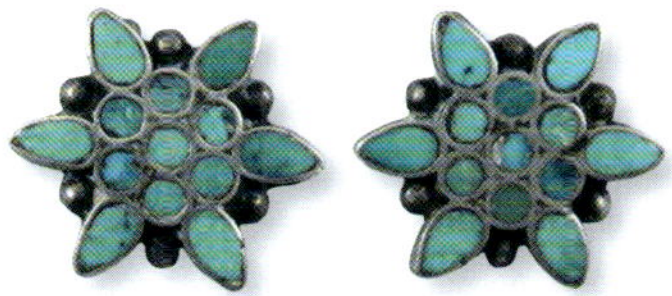

Turquoise earrings, channel inlay, Pauline and Frank Dishta, no hallmark, 1940s–1950s, 0.62" × 0.71", $200–300.

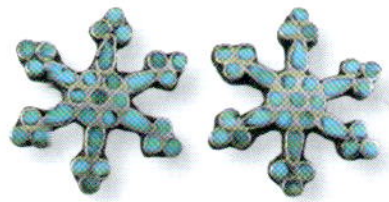

Turquoise earrings, channel inlay, Pauline and Frank Dishta, no hallmark, 1940s–1950s, 0.78" × 0.88", $200–300.

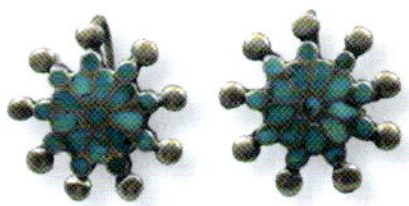

Turquoise earrings, channel inlay, Pauline and Frank Dishta, no hallmark, 1940s–1950s, 0.76" × 0.76", $200–300.

Frank Dishta and his son Virgil Dishta Sr. created a distinctive channel-inlay style. Their silver channels are made of extremely tiny round and teardrop compartments, which are combined to form clusters. Into these tiny channels, minutely cut stones are set first, ground flush, and then polished.

Pauline and Frank Dishta's great granddaughter confirmed that they made the tiny turquoise earrings above left. They originally had screw-backs, but they were replaced by french hooks. The following pair were also made by the Dishtas and also have screw-backs.

The tiny pair of turquoise earrings above, too, are made in a snow flake design with screw-backs. The earrings underneath are even smaller and are made in a flower-head design.

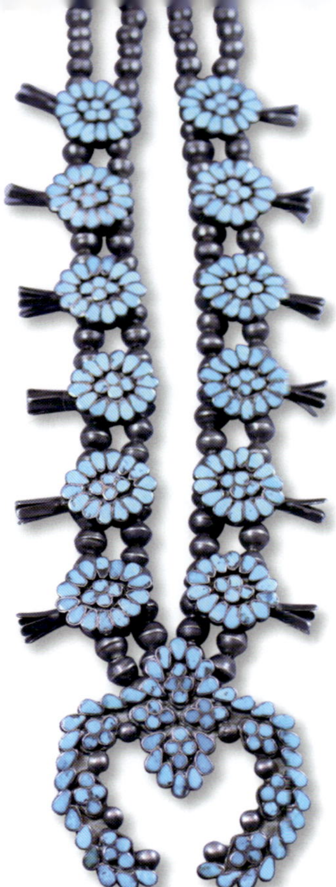

Turquoise squash blossom necklace, channel inlay, Virgil Dishta Sr., no hallmark, 1940s–1950s, 2.01" × 2.03" naja, $2,000–3,000.

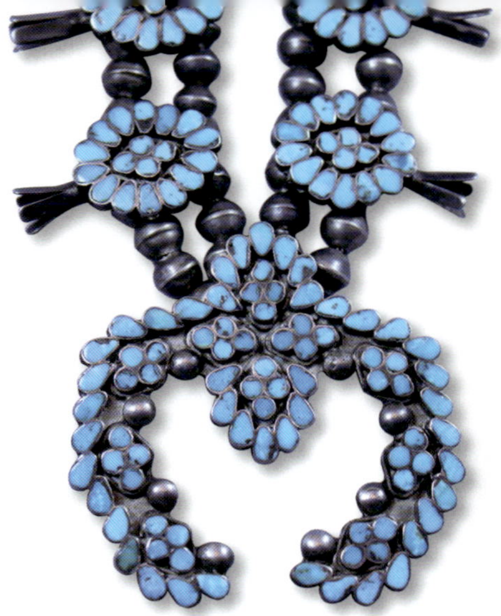

Close-up of the naja.

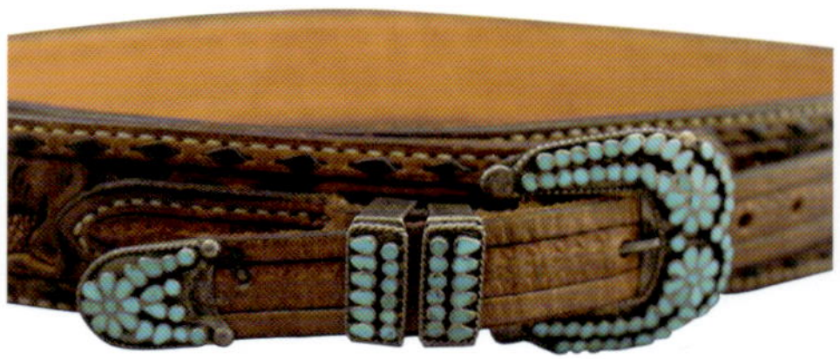

Turquoise ranger buckle set, channel inlay, Virgil Dishta Sr., VDISHTA, 1980s–1990s, 1.70" × 1.53" for the buckle, $800–1,200.

Virgil Dishta Sr. made this small turquoise squash blossom necklace. It consists of a central naja and six squash blossoms, with turquoise panels, on both sides. Four round channels encircled by a silver wire are set in each panel, which are surrounded by fourteen pear-shaped cabochons. The handmade silver beads are very tiny, measuring only 0.25 inches in diameter.

The Ranger belt buckle set above is singed "VDISHTA." The double-flower-head buckle and all the inlaid areas are surrounded by silver wires. A flower with a wire adorns the tip of the belt.

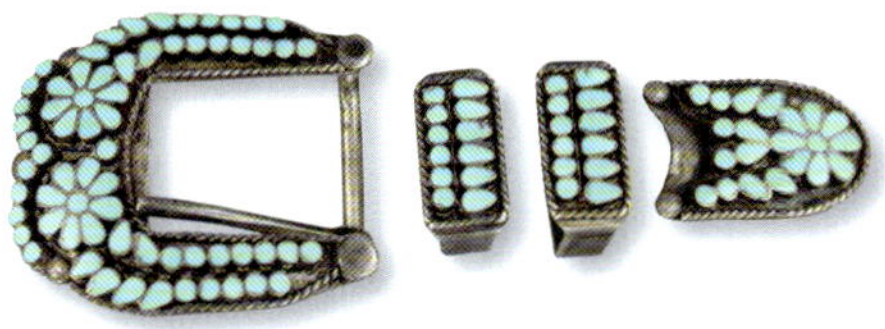

Turquoise ranger belt and buckle set, channel inlay, Virgil Dishta Sr., VDISHTA SR, 1980s–1990s, 1.91" × 1.66" for the buckle, $1,000–1,500

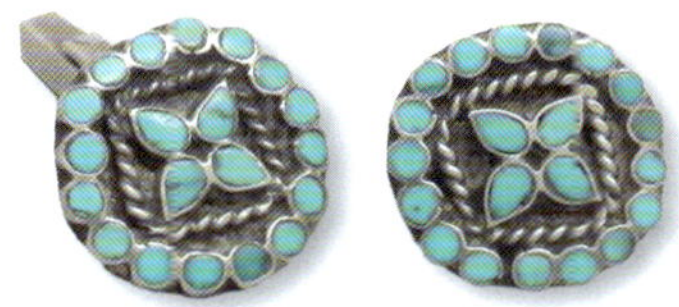

Turquoise cuff links, channel inlay, Virgil and Nancy Dishta, no hallmark, 1940s–1950s, 0.61" × 0.59", $200–300.

The Ranger belt buckle set above is singed "VDISHTA SR" and is made in the same design as the previous one, but this set is a little larger.

Four petite point turquoise cabochons are set in the center of Frank and Pauline and Dishta's turquoise cuff links, above, which are encircled by a twisted silver wire and seventeen round turquoise cabochons.

This turquoise squash blossom necklace consists of a central naja and six squash blossoms with turquoise panels on both sides. Roosevelt and Bernice Tekala made this small necklace, with handmade, 0.25-inch beads, for children. The lozenges on the side panels could be considered characteristic to their work.

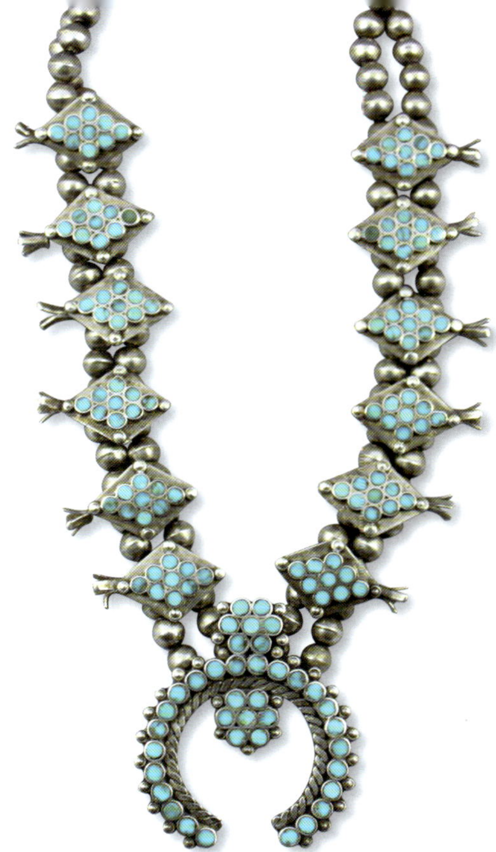

Turquoise squash blossom necklace, channel inlay, Roosevelt and Bernice Tekala, no hallmark, 1940s–1960s, 1.55" × 1.77" naja, $600–900.

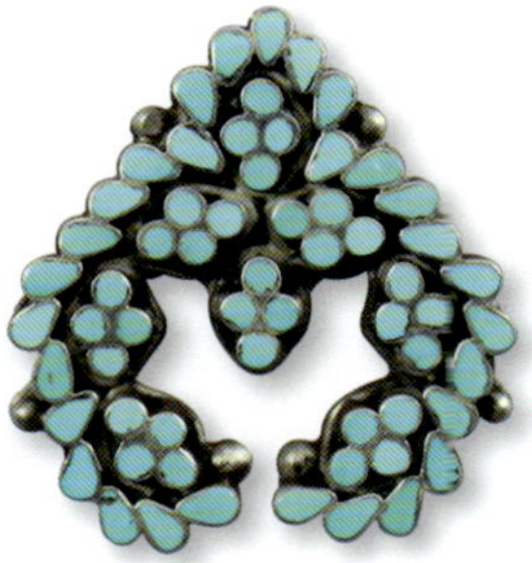

Turquoise pin/pendant, channel inlay, Roosevelt and Bernice Tekala, no hallmark, 1950s–1960s, 1.43" × 1.57", $200–300.

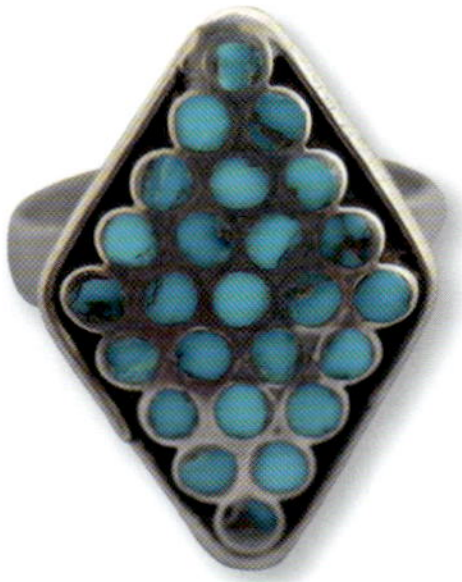

Turquoise ring, channel inlay, Roosevelt and Bernice Tekala, no hallmark, 1940s–1960s, 0.69" × 1.05", $100–150.

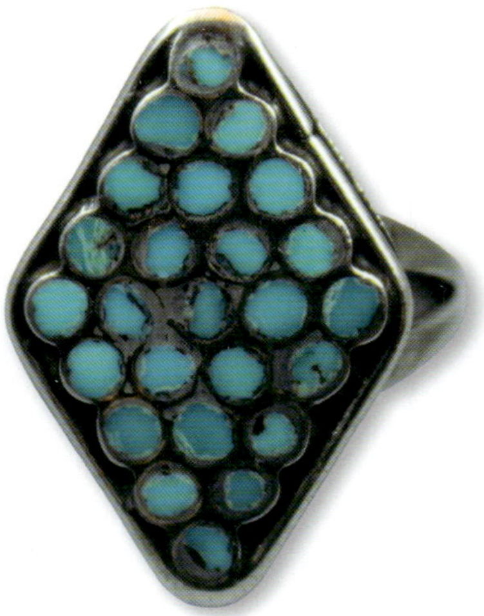

Turquoise ring, channel inlay, Roosevelt and Bernice Tekala, no hallmark, 1940s–1960s, 0.68" × 1.02", $100–150.

Roosevelt and Bernice also probably made this turquoise pin/pendant, which is extremely similar to the central naja of the squash blossom necklace made by Virgil Dishta Sr., but their silver works are visibly different from Virgil's. Silver tone filler is observable in the Tekalas' design, however, while none can be seen in Virgil's necklace.

The next two turquoise rings above are made in a lozenge shape, similar to the side panels of the Tekalas' squash blossom necklace. We can clearly see silver tone filler amidst the silver walls in each.

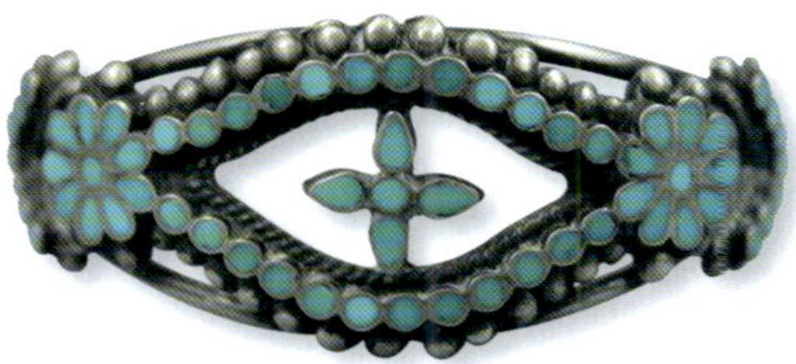

Turquoise bracelet, channel inlay, Matthew and Rosemary Lidase, M & R, 1970s–1980s, 1.02" wide, $200–300.

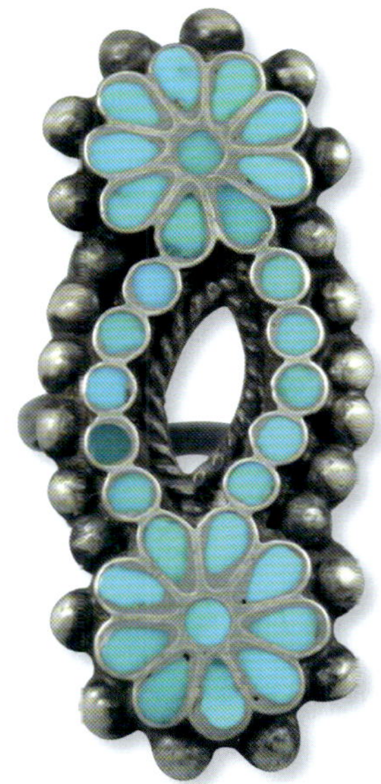

Turquoise ring, channel inlay, Matthew and Rosemary Lidase, M & R, 1940s–1960s, 0.67" × 1.60", $100–150.

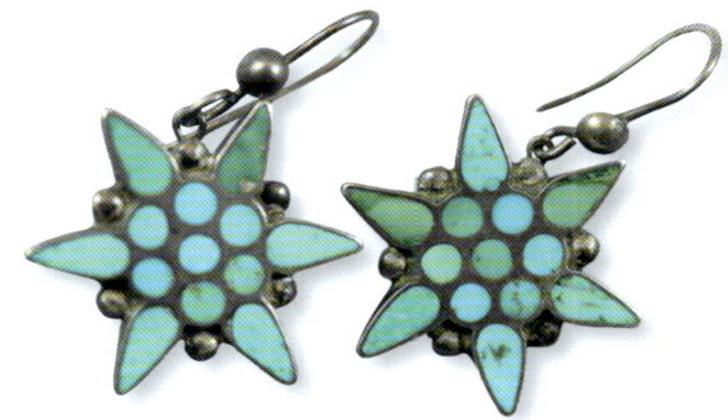

Turquoise earrings, channel inlay, artist unknown, no hallmark, 1950s–1960s, 0.88" × 1.02", $100–150.

Matthew and Rosemary Lidase's bracelet, above, is signed "M & R" in cursive with an electric pen. Its design is similar to pieces made by Virgil Dishta Sr. The matching ring, like the bracelet, is signed in the same way.

These turquoise earrings are identical in design to the second set of earrings made by Pauline and Frank Dishta (p. 149), but are larger and less intricate. One of my informants attributed them to Bowman Paywa's wife, Louise Paywa.

4. Row Work in Channel Inlay

Channel-inlay row work is just like ordinary row work, in which rectangular, square, needle-point, and snake-eye cabochons are set, and channels are created in one or more rows, in which turquoise stones are set. Wonderful examples pieces made in this style can be found in the *C. G. Wallace Collection of American Indian Art* (Sotheby Parke Bernet, 1975, pp. 77, 118) and *Indian Silver*, Vol. 2 (King, 1976, pp. 112–113). The latter features two bracelets made by Bowman Paywa in 1951 and 1952.

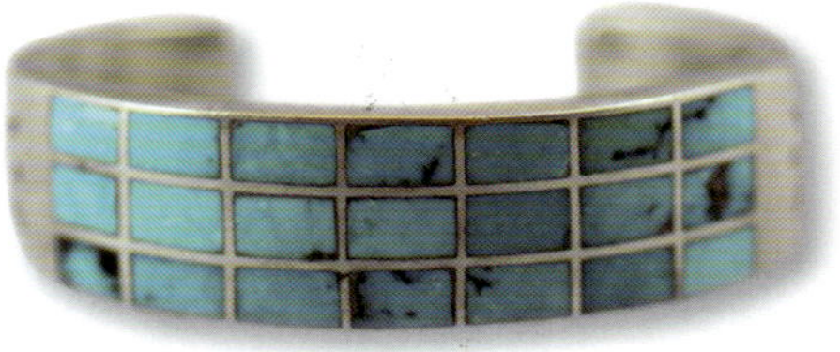

Blue Gem turquoise bracelet, channel inlay, artist unknown, no hallmark, 1950s–1960s, 0.71" wide, $500–750.

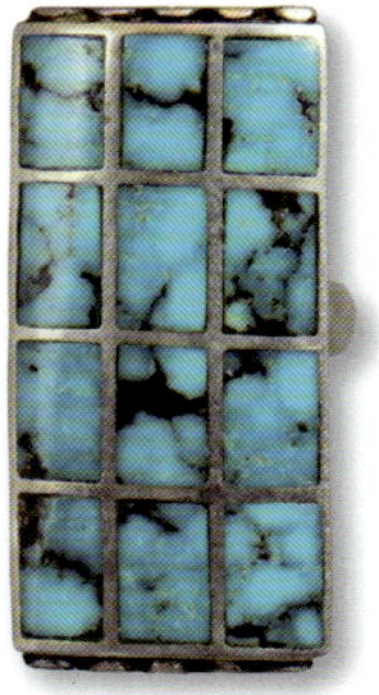

Kingman turquoise ring, channel inlay, artist unknown, no hallmark, 1940s–1960s, 0.72" × 1.53", $200–300.

Twenty-one pieces cut like rectangles and arranged in three rows by seven columns are inlaid flush in this thick, heavy bracelet, which an informant has attributed to Lambert Homer Jr.

An informant attributed the Kingman turquoise ring, above, to Della Appa, but I haven't been able to confirm this theory. Twelve pieces, arranged in three rows by four columns, are inlaid flush, and its surface is concave, for fitting a finger.

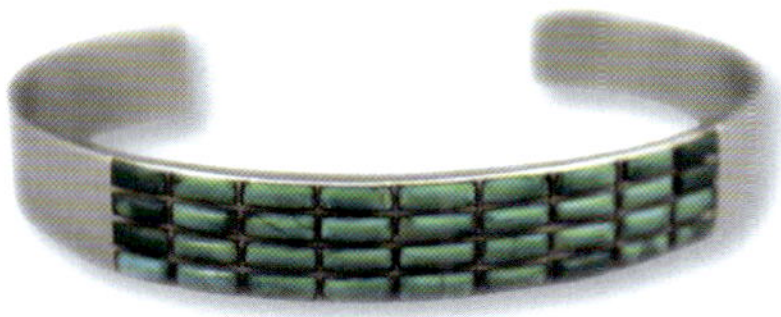

Blue Gem turquoise bracelet, channel inlay, artist unknown, no hallmark, 1940s–1960s, 0.40" wide, $500–750.

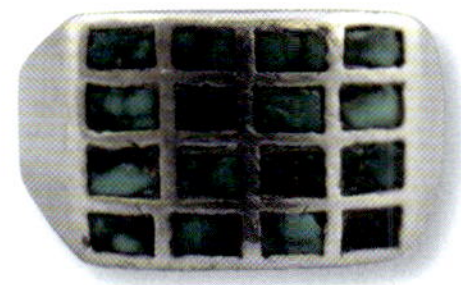

Blue Gem turquoise ring, channel inlay, Alice Leekya Homer, no hallmark, 1940s–1960s, 0.52" wide, $100–150.

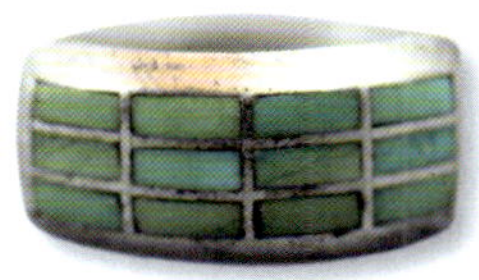

Turquoise ring, channel inlay, Alice Leekya Homer, no hallmark, 1940s–1960s, 0.34" wide, $100–150.

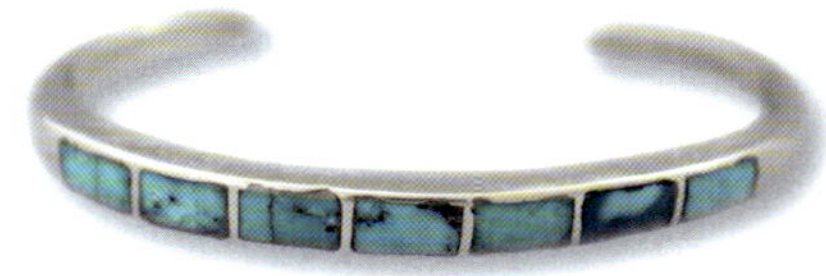

Kingman turquoise bracelet, channel inlay, Annie Quam Gasper (?), no hallmark, 1940s–1960s, 0.24" wide, $150–225.

The lapidary work in the 0.40-inch wide Blue Gem turquoise bracelet above exhibits extreme intricacy. Thirty-six tiny pieces, arranged in four rows by nine columns, are cut and polished, then set in channels a slightly above the cuff surface.

Alice Leekya Homer made the Blue Gem turquoise ring above, in which sixteen pieces, arranged in four rows by four columns, are set at the same level of the ring surface, even though the surface does not feel flush. Twelve pieces, arranged in three rows by four columns, are set flush in the ring underneath, which we can probably attribute to Alice.

Seven rectangular turquoise pieces are set flush in the Kingman turquoise bracelet, above.

CONCLUSION

We cannot help but be amazed by all of the non-figural Zuni jewelrystyles , including nugget work, cluster work, petite point, needle point, snake eye, row work, random-pattern channel inlay, Dishta-style channel inlay, and other channel-inlay styles.

In nugget work, it is important to correctly distinguish Dan Simplicio's pieces from those made by Mike Simplicio, Dixon Shebola, and others by carefully examining stamped silver drops and stamped silver leaves.

In cluster work, the extended Ondelacy family, the Weebothee family, and the Tsabetsaye family are the most prominent. It is important to distinguish Doris and Warren Ondelacy's work from pieces by other lapidaries, as they are undoubtedly this style's central figures.

Lee and Mary Weebothee, Andy and Fannie (Weebothee) Ondelacy, Leonard and Lela Weebothee, and Julie Ondelacy Lahi are all members of the Weebothee family by blood or marriage. Fannie and her husband, Andy, should be regarded highly as traditional cluster-work lapidaries, while Lee, Mary, and Julie should also be noted for their innovative lapidary works.

The Tsabetsaye family is made up of Joe and Susan, Edith, and Roger Sr. Although their cluster-work jewelry is similar to that made by Doris and Warren Ondelacy, their relationship to the Ondelacys remains a mystery. I regret that this book features only one ring made by Joe and Susan, but you can find fine examples of Edith Tsabetsaye's work in *Zuni Jewelry* (Bassman, 1992, p. 62), and a selection of Roger Tsabetsaye's innovative cluster work designs in *Roger Tsabetsaye: Daring to be Different* (Bulow, 2013, p. 27). Their cluster-work jewelry can only be found on the market.

Bryant Waatsa Sr. is credited as the creator of the needle-point style, while Edith Tsabetsaye is the creator of three-dimensional needle point (a.k.a. "Queen of Needle Point"). Since she created her half moon–shaped needle point, lapidaries such as Hugh and Agnes Boweekaty and Octavius and Irma Seowtewa have made superb jewelry. Hugh and Agnes Boweekaty are among the least evaluated—but I believe they deserve much more attention.

In the snake-eye style, I prefer pieces with relatively larger cabochons, represented most notably in this book by Duane Quam and Fannie Weebothee Ondelacy.

In the random-pattern channel-inlay style, Alice Leekya Homer, Sarah Leekya, Bessie Vacit, Francis Leekya, and Roger Leekya are noted lapidaries. It is important to distinguish Alice's pieces from those made by other lapidaries—and it is especially difficult to tell Alice's from Bessie's. If a piece was made before 1970, it is likely Alice's; if it was made in the 1970s and has an "ALH" hallmark, it is most definitely hers. If there are many flower petals along the reverse-S line, it could very well be Bessie's.

Frank and Pauline Dishta, Virgil Dishta Sr., Roosevelt and Bernice Tekala, Vincent Dishta, Virgil Dishta Jr., and Matthew and Rosemary Lidase are featured workers in Dishta-style channel inlay. We should try to prevent ourselves from attributing all pieces to Frank Dishta or Virgil Dishta Sr.

Annie Quam Gasper, Ellen Quam Quandelacy, Lambert Homer Sr., Lee and Mary Weebothee, Bessie Vacit, Jovanna Vacit, and others represent channel work, excluding random pattern and Dishta style. It is difficult to distinguish Annie's from her sister Ellen's. His daughters Bessie and Jovanna have used the same hallmark, the "ear of corn," as their father Frank Vacit, since 1975. Frank used it together with the "F Vacit" stamp afterwards.

The channel and row-work style is one of the most attractive styles in Zuni jewelry. Although it is known that the greatest Zuni lapidaries, including Lambert Homer Sr. and Bowman Paywa, have made wonderful pieces in this style, I could not feature their pieces in this book. I am very fortunate, however, to present pieces made by Alice Leekya Homer.

REFERENCES

Adair, John. *The Navajo and Pueblo Silversmiths*. Norman, Oklahoma: University of Oklahoma Press. 1944.

"The Allure of Turquoise". *New Mexico Magazine*. Second Edition. Santa Fe, New Mexico: New Mexico Magazine. 2005.

Arizona Highways. January 1945. Phoenix, Arizona: The Arizona Highway Department. 1945.

———. August 1952. Phoenix, Arizona: The Arizona Department of Transportation. 1952.

———. August 1959. Phoenix, Arizona: The Arizona Department of Transportation. 1959.

———. August 1974. Phoenix, Arizona: Arizona Department of Transportation. 1974.

Bahti, Tom. *Southwestern Indian Tribes*. Las Vegas, Nevada: KC Publications. 1968.

Bassman, Theda and Michael. *Zuni Jewelry*. Atglen, Pennsylvania: Schiffer Publishing, Ltd. 1992.

Bauver, Robert. *Masterworks and Eccentricities: The Druckman Collection*. Pittsburg, Pennsylvania: Four Winds Publishing. 2002.

Baxter, Paula A. *Southwest Silver Jewelry*. Atglen, Pennsylvania: Schiffer Publishing, Ltd. 2001.

Beddinger, Margery. *Indian Silver: Navajo and Pueblo Jewelers*. Albuquerque, New Mexico: University of New Mexico Press. 1973.

Bell, Ed, and Barbara Bell. *Zuni: The Art and the People*, Vol. 1. Grants, New Mexico: Squaw Bell Traders. 1975.

Bell, Ed, Barbara Bell, Steve Bell, Ralph McQueary, and Jerry McQueary. *Zuni: The Art and the People*, Vol. 2. Grants, New Mexico: Squaw Bell Traders. 1976.

Bell, Ed, Barbara Bell, Steve Bell, Ralph McQueary, and Jerry McQueary. *Zuni: The Art and the People*, Vol. 3. Grants, New Mexico: Squaw Bell Traders. 1976.

Bennett, Edna Mae and John F. *Turquoise Jewelry of the Indians of the Southwest*. Turquoise Books, Colorado Springs, Colorado 1973.

Bulow, Ernie. *Mysteries of Zuni Silver: And Who Was Mingos House Anyway?* Gallup Journey February 2012. 20-21, Gallup, New Mexico: Gallup Journey Magazine. 2012.

Bulow, Ernie. *Mysteries of Zuni Silver: Part Two*. Gallup Journey March 2012. 20-21, Gallup, New Mexico: Gallup Journey Magazine. 2012.

Bulow, Ernie. *Roger Tsabetsaye: Daring to be Different*. Gallup Journey March 2013. 26-29, Gallup, New Mexico: Gallup Journey Magazine. 2013.

Chalker, Kari (Ed.). *Totems and Turquoise: Native American Jewelry Arts of the Northwest and Southwest*. New York, New York: Harry N. Abrams Inc. 2004.

Frank, Larry. *Indian Silver Jewelry of the Southwest 1868–1930*. Atglen, Pennsylvania: Schiffer Publishing, Ltd. 1990.

Harmsen, Bill (Ed.). *Patterns and Sources of Zuni Kachinas*. The Harmsen Publishing Company. 1988.

King, Dale Stuart. *Indian Silver*, Vol. II. Tucson, Arizona: Dale Stuart King. 1976.

Levy, Gordon. *Who's Who in Zuni Jewelry*. Denver, Colorado: Western Arts Publishing Co. 1980.

McManis, Kent. *A Guide to Zuni Fetishes and Carvings*. Tucson, Arizona: Treasure Chest Books. 1995.

McManis, Kent. *Zuni Fetish Carvers: The Mid-Century Masters*. Santa Fe, New Mexico: The Wheelright Museum of the American Indians. 2003.

Nahohai, Milford and Elisa Phelps. *Dialogues with Zuni Potters*. Zuni, New Mexico: Zuni Ashiwi Publishing. 1995.

Ostler, James; Rodee Marian; and Milford Nahohai. *Zuni: a Village of Silversmiths*. Zuni, New Mexico: Zuni Ashiwi Publishing. 1996.

Ray Manley Photography. *Ray Manley's Southwestern Indian Arts & Crafts*. Tucson, Arizona: Ray Manley Photography, Inc. 1975.

Rosnek, Carl and Joseph Stacey. *Skystone and Silver: The Collector's Book of Southwest Indian Jewelry*. Englewood Cliffs, New Jersey: Prentice-Hall, Inc. 1977

Schaaf, Gregory. *American Indian Jewelry*, I. Santa Fe, New Mexico: CIAC Press. 2003.

Schiffer, Nancy N. *Jewelry by Southwest American Indians: Evolving Designs*. Atglen, Pennsylvania: Schiffer Publishing, Ltd. 1990.

———. *Turquoise Jewelry*. Atglen, Pennsylvania: Schiffer Publishing, Ltd. 1990.

Sei, Toshio. *Hopi Bird and Sun Face in Zuni Jewelry*. Atglen, Pennsylvania: Schiffer Publishing, Ltd. 2012.

———. *Knifewing and Rainbow Man in Zuni Jewelry*. Atglen, Pennsylvania: Schiffer Publishing, Ltd. 2010.

Slaney, Deborah C. *Blue Gem, White Metal: Carvings and Jewelry from the C. G. Wallace Collection*. Phoenix, Arizona: Heard Museum. 1998.

Wallace, C. G. *The C. G. Wallace Collection of American Indian Art*. New York, New York: Sotheby Park Bernet. 1975.

Wright, Barton. *Hallmarks of the Southwest*. Atglen, Pennsylvania: Schiffer Publishing, Ltd. 2000.

INDEX

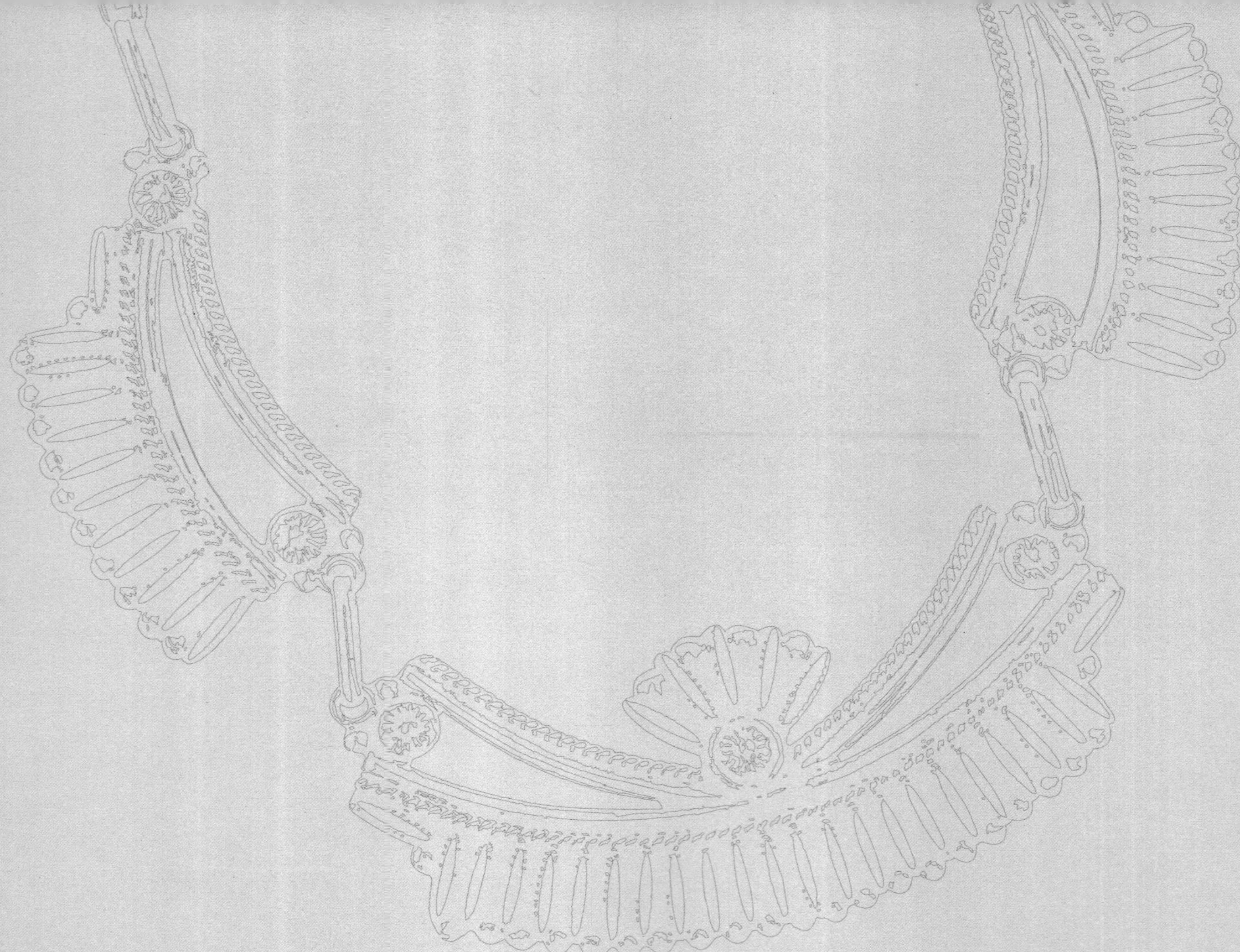